Relying on the Kindness of Strangers

A MEMOIR BY LYLA ILLING

To S and D, thank you for giving me a space to write and be creative in.

ISBN 9781077913172

Cover design by Lyla Illing

Photographs from personal collection and by Justine Hery, Nomadixx & Thabang Radebe

Maps sourced from Google Maps

FOR MY MANY MOTHERS AND FATHERS AROUND
THE GLOBE

(The Dalai Lama continued, "whoever gives you love, that's your parent."
The Book of Joy)

CONTENTS

PART 1
whatever helps you sleep at night 2
one year before 3

PART 2
special circumstances kid 11
rainbow baby 14
pineapple trucks 18
elsie 1958 – 2003 23
when you've lost your mother 26

PART 3
operation bin laden 29
ambush 36
backfire 42
stockholm syndrome 45
torture 51
sos 55
childline 60
surrender 61
you never know your luck in a big city
68
no man's land 69

PART 4
the war is over 75
lurking 77
hey dad, i won't be there 86
terrie the lion 87
stories about terrie 88
lonely soldier cry 89
drunk texting 90

PART 5
adopted at eighteen 95
eyes on the prize 100
a sinner's prayer 103
5fm mornings 104
no one 105
connor-valerie 110

PART 6
one good year 115
born to die 118
we were fire 123
sometimes i picture you 123

PART 7
carpet burns 127
lines 130
so not sexy 131
meet me in india 133
fourteen orgasms 135

PART 8
abstinence app 139
no-no nomad's mating call 145
my wedding night 149
for as long as I'm sad 150
sala kahle (goodbye) 151
lyla before new york 154

PART 9
liminal individual 161
not a drive-thru 165
why I choose to date assholes 166
identity crisis, zululand-girl goes
uptown-girl 168
piss or get off the pot 170
in the news 172

PART 10
i am not okay 177
have a little faith, kid 178
i'm not coming home 186
do you know where you are? 187
three-hundred-and-thirty-nine sunrises
189
does she look you in the eye? 191
gin & tonics at someone else's blackjack
table 191
sixty seconds 194
breaking someone's heart – got the t-
shirt 195

PART 11

you want me to do what on international tv? 199
new yorker 201
the new york minute 203
easy 207
dominant 207
manhattan man 208
i think you know you
love someone 210
calls from uganda 213
"lyla; the voice of a nation" – people magazine south africa 217
singing for nelson mandela in pt shorts 221
wall street serendipity, ubuntu pathways charity show 221
twenty-five – dead or alive 223
i have been loved 224

PART 12

my solo twenty-sixth 227
the chosen people 232
i'm going to call 911 but don't worry about me 244
out of place, on purpose 247
below the surface 251

PART 13

welcome to the...family 255
can you keep a secret? 257
common ground 257
unintended revenge 261
amor fati 262
lyla who belongs to everybody (but has no one) 269
english 272
a sore throat and depression 272
tyrone's wedding song 274
apricot 276
i love you and you
are my best friend 278
full moon on figure eight island 279
don't rock stars die at twenty-seven? 281
things I want to do before i die 289

FOREWORD

Lyla (or "Sibongile" as her peers lovingly nicknamed her) caught my attention when I was in New York to do a show at Carolines on Broadway. When I learned of her music ventures, I invited her to be a guest on my vlog "South Africans living in… New York." We ended up talking less about her music and more about what it means to be a member of The Rainbow Nation. I was taken back with her dedication to break down racial and cultural barriers in her day-to-day life, even if that meant having to cut family ties in the pursuit of standing up for freedom and equality. Lyla's story entices the reader to reconsider racial stereotypes and serves as a reminder that you can't judge a book by its cover. – **David Kau, Comedian, Blacks Only Comedy Show**

I met Lyla in the hallways of the 5FM studio when I was doing my Hollywood Report on Gareth Cliff Mornings. Lyla was an intern for us back in 2013. We had a lot of interns then, but there was something very special about her from the first time we met. She was always very specific about where she was heading with her career, and had the drive and enthusiasm to match. I selected Lyla out of a long list of people who applied to assist me at events, and invited her to some A-List and red carpet events to get her foot in the door back then. It was certainly no surprise to me when in 2018, I bumped into her as I exited a NYC taxi – she had taken the leap to further her career in the Big Apple. We caught up in the back of a yellow cab on our way to an event I was covering for New York Fashion Week, and it became apparent that Lyla had come into her own and already achieved some of the goals she set out for herself. I knew my job was done!. **– Jen Su, TV and Radio Presenter**

Wide eyed and wet behind the ears, I met Lyla – broken dreams in hand - at her lowest low when the Concrete Jungle knocked the wind out of her for the very first time – New York's rite of passage not many newcomers have the grit to stand tall and stay through. Instead of buying a one-way ticket home, she rolled with the punches and continued the fist-fight with the things that stood between her and her wildest dreams. Rooting for Lyla has been a nail-biting, "yes! – cheering" experience, watching her grow into the real New Yorker that she is today. **– Jen Glantz, CEO of Bridesmaid for Hire, author of "All My Friends are Engaged" and "When You Least Expect It"**

Lyla stole the hearts of Springbok fans across the globe when she seized the opportunity to serenade me with an impromptu performance, aptly singing the theme song from "Beauty and the Beast" when we met by chance in a New York restaurant. I am excited to see which other doors Lyla's sincerity and wit will open for her in her music ventures. – **Beast, Springbok Prop and Author**

I met Lyla when she was working the Breakfast Show at a leading Johannesburg radio station, Hot 91.9FM. She mentioned that she was a singer-songwriter and could she swing by and play me her demo, I said sure. The songs were pretty angsty but lacked a clear focus stylistically. However they filled with an honesty that I haven't come across too many times in my long career as a label head. I said to her that she needed to find the balance between telling the story and at the same time crafting a definable musical hook. I played her Alanis Morrisette`s debut album as an example (she had not heard it before). Listening to her more recent songs that she has penned in the US, I am amazed at the extent of her growth, both as a writer and performer. You'll be hearing a lot from Lyla Illing in the years ahead, I suspect that her best is yet to come.– **Benjy Mudie, Music Guru & Radio Host**

Back in 2013, Lyla took me by surprise when she was the first person to upload a cover of one of my songs onto YouTube. This was long before cover videos became a trend – at least in South Africa. Lyla was always looking for loopholes and clever ways to catch the attention of the people she was aspiring to be like or wanted to learn from. I wasn't surprised when she ventured into radio and made use of her new connections to advance in music. – **Mark Haze, Musician, Idols South Africa Season 7 Runner-up**

A NOTE FROM THE AUTHOR

To the ones close to me, reading some parts of this book might not be easy. In some ways, might even make you question everything you thought you knew about me. To leave the regrettable parts of my story out of the book would have been easier, less torturous to write, but if I were not brave enough to tell my whole truth – what good would telling my story be at all.

Despite its sensitive contents, this book is written out of gratitude only.

PART ONE

WHATEVER HELPS YOU SLEEP AT NIGHT

(I have a theory. It goes something like this.)

It was my turn that day. I opened the doors into the white, bright room and walked in, to find them waiting for me. Only - they weren't sitting at the boardroom table, waiting. They were standing around in groups of four to five, deeply engaged in conversation and laughter. I liked that about them.

As the door shut behind me, I just stood there for a second, watching them. Taking it all in.

I heard myself breathe in, I felt the smile of contentment forming on my face - I experienced consciousness, as I felt myself realize that I knew and understood exactly where I was.

"I'm ready!" I exclaimed joyfully, with their attention shifting towards my presence.

I sat down at the head of the table, and they joined me.

"Thank you all for being here. With my journey on earth as a human being starting soon, I wanted to go over my life purpose with you before we start. I am going to be needed in different parts of the world, I'm going to be needed in many different families' lives, and I am going to need a lot of time alone. We are not going to be able to stay in each other's lives for a long time - I am going to need you to let me go when the time comes, so that I may move forward in my journey without any ties holding me back.

The path I have chosen for my life on earth, is unconventional, it is messy, and I am excited to have you all on board! We will go around the table introducing ourselves. Let's start with you." I nodded at the person on my left.

She reached for my hand, and held it firmly in hers.

"I am going to be your mom, I will be with you for the first ten years of your life, and then I will have to go. I will teach you about joy and love in these ten years, and I will make sure you know who you are before I blow out my last breath of air." She masked the tear in her eye with the most comforting smile I've ever experienced. "And I'm going to put the music in you."

She gently let go of my hand and nodded at the person on her left.

"I am going to be your dad. I will be absent for the first ten years of your life but I will take over when your mom goes away. I will teach you everything I learned from my thirty years serving Special Forces in the Army. I will teach you how to survive. I don't have anything else to offer. I can only stay for five years before they need me in Iraq again. So you will be free to go your own way then."

He nodded at the three people to his left.

"We're your older siblings. We will all be separated when you're ten, but we will come back into your life for good in your late twenties, when you're ready."

We went further and further down the table, with each one of them introducing themselves to me. The boyfriends and the mentors, until we came full circle to Nelson Mandela, on my right. "You're going to sing our National

2

Anthem for me on my 100th birthday," he nodded with a smile, his eyes squinting half closed as he saw the surprised look on my face. "People will be watching from across the globe, and your mom and I will watch, hand in hand, from above. She is going to be so proud."

"It's an honor, Tata Madiba." I smiled back.

I knew it was inevitable that I would forget these declarations and reasons for people coming and going in my life, as soon as my time on earth started - but I was hopeful that I would recall it all again when I was ready to. Recall the reasons, recall the meanings, and recall that it was what I chose.

And then I did. On my twenty-sixth birthday in New York City, I remembered it all, clearly. I remembered what I chose around that boardroom table in that big white, bright room before my journey on earth started.

Up until that moment on my twenty-sixth birthday, I did not understand the fearless force that drove me to continue moving forward, despite the losses, despite the abuse I suffered, despite the loneliness, despite the unfair hand of cards life dealt me. But when I suddenly remembered that I chose for it all to be this way - I celebrated the freedom I created for myself, I celebrated the freedom I found. I celebrated coming back into consciousness, as I felt myself realize that I knew and understood exactly where I was.

From that moment on, I understood why it was always easy to be delusionally, and disproportionately grateful for everything that has gone right, as well as "wrong" in my life. Some part of me always understood that I needed to go through it, to be where I am today. That is, at my desk, in my room, on the twelfth floor of an apartment building in lower Manhattan. It's 1pm on a Wednesday, and I am having the freedom to tell the story of how I found the way back to my conscious-self.

At least, that's my theory.

What I'd like to believe.

The only thing that helps me sleep at night.

ONE YEAR BEFORE

"Jen, I don't know if I can do what you're asking me to. I can't stay in New York, working this demanding job for another year in the state I'm in. I just can't. I'm a wreck."

I was sitting with Jen Glantz who I had met just months before – a CEO, an author, a strong woman whose opinion I valued, but what she was asking of me was inhumane. I had already made up my mind about going back to South Africa. I had already handed in my resignation, and cut my contract short by 6 months.

No. I was going home. I was going to donate my guitar to a children's home in Harlem so that I didn't have to pay airfare for it, and I was going to ask my brother for a hand me down once I was home. There was no way I could stay in New York, working a forty-five hour a week job in childcare, for six days each week. I had to be emotionally available and had very little time left to work on my emotional healing, never mind the energy I needed to chase a career in music and media in my "free time." I felt exploited by the agency I was working for (they lost a class action lawsuit a few months later.) I was still dealing with culture shock, losing my identity, my "career change," or rather the frustration of putting my radio and music career on hold. In addition, I had just opened a case of rape against someone I once trusted. Having to start over in a new country - this was no longer fun. I thought I could handle it until the assault happened. I don't think anyone understands how much it takes of me to say the words "I am not okay." I would much rather accept the panic attacks as my new reality, I'd rather cry myself to sleep night after night, I'd rather make sure everyone has everything they need from me even when I am busy falling apart inside. So when I said those words "I am not okay" – I was really, not okay.

"Is there any way you can ask for your job back?" Jen asked.

I couldn't fight back the tears anymore, so I blinked and let a tear roll down my cheek, breaking eye contact with her momentarily to try and mask my vulnerability. I tried to smile and crack a joke, but she didn't smile back. She looked me square in the eye and fought back the tears herself. The expression on her face let me know that there was no bullshitting her. So I stopped trying to.

I stared out of the big windows of the coffee house on 8th avenue as she pleaded her case, as if her life depended on me staying, depended on me picking myself up, and trying one more time, staying one more year.

I was dissecting the failures of the past year with someone I had met only once before. She was putting together my game plan.

The type of parent-daughter talk I was never given.

My stepmother's idea of parenting was holding my Avril Lavigne albums over the blazing fire pit, threatening to burn what was bible to me, my guide book on how to be. My idol. Threats.

Asking me questions like, "who are you?" Over and over again, as if she was trying to drive some demon from my body. Telling me to go and play with my Barbie dolls like a normal little girl should be doing. This was at the age of 14.

She was threatening to burn my albums if I didn't tell her why I wrote about my feelings in my diary, which she bought for me. The diary she bought for me and encouraged me to write in, only to read it when I went off to school and interrogate me about it after.

My father beating my thighs black and blue with a clothes brush, and my stepmom hitting me in my face with belts - that was their idea of parenting.

Jen spoke to me, woman to woman, parent to daughter, creative to creative, and I ended up staying in New York to pursue the case I opened.

I went to therapy. A lot of it.

I started listening to my old Avril Lavigne albums again. I made her my desktop wallpaper so I could have something to smile about at least once a day. A grin every time I flip my laptop open. A reminder that I made it through to the other side, and that I can play my Avril albums as loud as I please, without ever being victim to my parent's threats and abuse again. A reminder that I can get through anything, including what was lying ahead of me.

When Jen and I parted ways after the two large coffees I gulped down to keep functioning, I walked away with a spark of hope in my pocket, and I could not have asked for anything more than that on that icy New York winter's night. Maybe it was the comfort of speaking with someone who had just recently come out alive on the other side of her own messy twenties. Someone with a degree in poetry, someone who speaks my language, in more ways than one. Someone who has been chewed up and spat out by New York herself.

As the florescent lights blinded me in the hospital room I was lying alone in, a couple of weeks earlier when the assault took place, it came as no surprise to me when I realized the mess I was in. It's like it's been following me my whole life. "Just let it happen, let them take care of you now that they know."

"I can't! I don't know how to be vulnerable! I HATE when other people have to step in, I don't want them to know what I'm going through!" I shout to Yvette in tears on a 3am phone call to South Africa, when she tried to calm me down after I had to tell my agency and the host family I lived with, what was going on.

I had driven myself to the hospital earlier that night, in the family's car. I drove myself home 7 hours later, souvenirs in hand - a pair of yellow hospital socks, a blue bag – in case of vomit – on my lap, which the nurse gave to me, and what was left of the little bit of trust I used to have in human beings.

When you go through something like this, it is like you go through it twice. Once when it is happening, and a second time when you have to talk about it. Which is why I don't. Which is why most of us probably don't.

Having been in New York for a mere 8 months at that point, I did not exactly have a support system in place, so when a representative from a rape survivors' organization showed up next to my hospital bed, I made her my best friend, my mom, my entire support system right there and then. She sat with me through the multiple injections I was given, the heaped hand of pills I was given to swallow, and while the rape kit was being put together she was there to make sure I was coping, whilst somebody had their hand up my vagina, swiping for evidence. I was immediately started on antiretroviral treatment in case I was exposed to HIV. The medication I had to take for a month, felt like a second attack on my body.

I talk about not having a support system in New York, but I look back on my life and realize I never really had a support system anywhere, ever. Mostly because I don't let people "that" close to me, even when they want to be there for me. I think it has a lot to do with being shoved into boarding schools after my mom's passing, and being forced to be independent, being forced to have no other option but to be okay, even in the worst situations, because there was no time to cry, no time to feel sorry for myself, and no one around who gave a shit, if I sat in a corner and moped. Even after all the people who have shown me kindness in my life, who have given me a place to sleep, who have fed me - nothing has been able to replace the security, stability and trust that was ripped from me at such a tender age, and I don't think I have ever really dealt with that. I don't think I have ever looked it straight in the eye and seen it for what it was. It was just who I became, and I did not know anything else, it was my normal.

And I think, that's why it was easy for me to leave people behind when I had an opportunity to move forward in life. I think that's why, at age eighteen, it was easy for me to leave my boyfriend of two years when I saved enough money for a one-way ticket out of Vanderbijlpark to Durban. I had my grudges against his wandering eyes when I thought I gave him everything he wanted. But I stayed, and we made a home together, we had our cat and we did love each other, but when I had that ticket in my hand, I packed my bags while he was sleeping and I walked out the door at four am without saying goodbye. I honestly can't say that I even thought twice. I changed my number and I left him behind like damaged goods.

The same way I, at age twenty-three, left my scooter on the side of the road when it stopped working after the accident that I had with it. I remember looking at it as I stood on the side of the road, opposite the Ticket-pro Dome in Joburg. I looked at it as if I was saying, well it's been real…bye Felicia, and then I hitched a ride with a stranger who dropped me off at home, and I went straight to sleep. That was my idea of dealing with a problem. Leaving it on the side of the road to be stolen, instead of calling up a friend to help me tow it to a motor garage to be fixed. I had a sense of community where I lived in Johannesburg, but I can't quite explain how I still felt alone. It wasn't like having your brother living around the corner whom you felt comfortable enough with to just call up for help. I knew people cared about me, but I wasn't sure they cared about me enough for me to bother them on a Saturday night, asking for help. Yvette picked me up from my place the next morning, rather annoyed that I hadn't called her when the scooter gave up the ghost. We went for coffee at Doppio Zero after first driving past the area I left the scooter at, and having my suspicions confirmed - it was indeed gone.

Yvette and I had been working together at the radio station for nearly a year, but until then, hadn't really developed much of a friendship. As she sat across from me at that table at Doppio, trying to make sense of how I simply climbed off the scooter and just walked away from it, like it was nothing - I think that was the moment I realized that we were about to become homies for life. She did not understand anything that was going on in my head or world, but she seemed super interested in understanding, which was new to me.

I use to think that she kept me around for the amusement and insanity I brought into her world. But she made a bigger effort than anyone I ever had in my life, to become a part of, and stay in it. This was a new experience for me. For the most part of the early days of our friendship, it annoyed the shit out of me that I now had a best friend, who wouldn't let me walk out her door whenever I decided the visit was over.

Before I knew it, we were taking impromptu road trips down to Durban, spending Saturdays walking around her huge garden in nothing but our PJ tops and panties. One Christmas, she was shyly confronted by her sweet mother, hesitantly asking if she and I were "intimate". We laughed, and still do, about that. You know what they say, the friendship isn't real until there's gay rumors about you! I of course thought it was the funniest thing, and entertained anyone who asked the same question, continuing to explain how we were all over each until they weren't sure if I was telling the truth or not.

In an interview I did with my dear friend Boo Prince, before I left South Africa, I spoke about how this friendship with Yvette changed my views on relationships. For the first time I felt comfortable with not ending a relationship abruptly, when I felt it had run its course, or when I felt someone was wronging me. I started looking for healthier ways to say goodbye, and more honest ways to connect with those around me, although it's a daily challenge still.

People see me speak openly at events or on social media about my dating life, and about my abusive childhood, and they think I am showing 100% of myself - they assume I am not a "private" person, that I have no discretion. But, what I show to even the closest people around me, is not even half of what is going on in my head and life. They don't realize that the things I am open about hardly cover the surface of my story, hardly expose the tornado of feelings and thoughts constantly storming through my mind.

I am still not sure how therapists look me in the eye after a session and tell me, "Lyla, you are fine". You are so positive and so good at rising out of bad situations." My insides are screaming out "help" but they see a girl who is coping. I understand that, to the untrained eye (the trained ones too), I come across as "she has her shit together" but, I really don't. It's all coping mechanisms.

Therapists continue to compare me to other people who are self-harming and praises me, by saying I am okay, because I don't have scars on my wrists. People think depression looks a certain way, like there are visible warning signs, drug abuse or alcoholism. Part of me looks the other way and carries on although I hurt so badly inside. I look away because I am afraid to take medication that will change me, that will change what I feel and how I feel. I am addicted to the intensity of my feelings and I can't imagine that being taken away from me. As inviting as an ounce of peace and sanity sounds, I am not convinced that all cases of depression should be treated with medicine. I'd rather look the other way and leave the depression unaddressed for as long as possible.

So, there I was, in another massive mess, pretty much alone in New York - alone because I failed again to rely on the people who could have been a support system to me. Eventually I said it out loud, I told them I was not okay. Still, I refused to take time off work because I didn't want to be alone with my thoughts. But more so, I did not want to let my employers down by taking time off after the assault.

I think I get this from my workaholic dad, who has a history of 30 years in Special Forces and is an expert (according to the internet) on handling unstable security situations. I can't help but see the irony in that…where was his expertise in handling unstable security situations when his unstable wife was compromising my security and safety as a child in their house…? Anyway, he's a fucking robot, and I am like him, but not as cold. Maybe sometimes.

I have left so many people behind, the same way he left me, standing alone at my mother's open grave when I was 10. He left me standing alone with only two suitcases to start my own life with, at 15. I watched him drive away after I admitted I would rather live on the street than be abused by his wife any further. So he left me. And although we are so alike, the fundamental difference is, I genuinely care about the relationships in my life, and that it is excruciatingly painful for me to end any of them. Even the ones in which I am the victim.

I think my biggest disappointment in the whole New York City rape-saga, was when my sister called me to let me know that there was in fact an option for me to return home, to end the program or even just to visit, if that was what I wanted. In the multiple phone calls and in-person conversations I had with my employer and agency during this time, they all failed to tell me this. Being the damaged-kid workaholic that I am, going through a crisis, in my messed-up state of mind, I had just assumed that there was no option of taking time off, or ending the program. It was pretty disappointing that my sister had to call and drag it out of my agency that there was an option for me to get on a plane back home, if I wanted that. When I confronted them about this information that they failed to communicate to me, I was told: "We didn't tell you because we didn't want you to feel confused about staying or leaving." But all I heard was that they didn't tell me they could put me on a plane back home, because that would have been inconvenient for them, if I ended my contract early. I decided not to hold it against them.

No matter how hard I try to work on trusting people, there is a reason I am the way I am. I think we all have our reasons. And I know how shut down I am - completely capable of having groups of friends and acquaintances, but feeling alone. Not in a lonely way, but just feeling that I can't rely on anyone but myself. But I am so okay with that. As good as it is to aspire to have healthy relationships and support, it is pretty fulfilling to look back and see that I have always had myself.

I always laughed when therapists and ex-boyfriends told me in the past, "you need to learn to be alone with yourself, you need to get to know yourself and you need to love yourself, before you can love someone else." I am not sure which part people miss when they look at me. I have been alone most of my life, I have had to hold my own hand when no one else was around to. I have had to love myself fiercely, when the people who were supposed to protect me, abused me. I have already been through the phase they all tell me I still need to go through. But I believe people project, and I believe they are the ones who have yet to experience the type of relationship that I already have with myself. Their opinions never changed the way I saw myself.

I know myself so well, to the point that if I give you an hour of my time, you better know it is because I value you. It is not because I am needy or don't want to be alone.

The problem with being so picky about who I let into my space, is that when I do allow someone in, I latch on. I don't exactly show it. It's something that happens without me thinking about it, without choosing to, without realizing it until it's over.

And most of the time I blame lovers for leaving when I never even asked them to stay.

And when I was brave enough to try and date again, he said he would call me, and he spoke about "the next time we see each other." But I knew it. I knew it when he looked at me for a second longer than he wanted himself to, looked at me as if it was the last time, kissed me like it was the last time. I know what "the last time" looks like.

Because I have stood at my mother's open grave as she was lowered into the ground, and I remember with every ounce of my body and soul exactly what "the last time" feels like, and what the last time looks like.

And when they leave me, I remember how many times I have been left by those who were not supposed to leave me. And all the hurt comes back, all the mistrust comes back, the feeling of abandonment comes back, but I've had to realize that none of that is on them.

Those feelings are on me.

PART TWO

FROM KWAZULU-NATAL TO PRETORIA

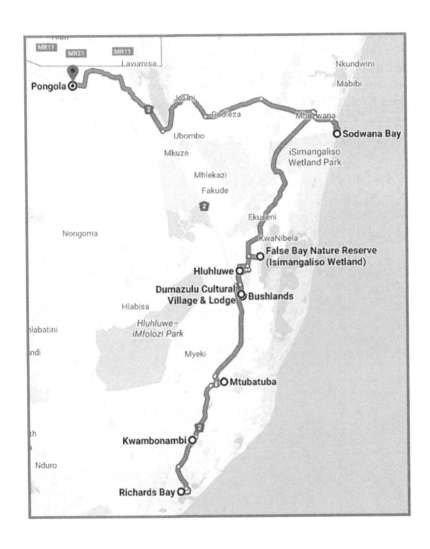

SPECIAL CIRCUMSTANCES KID

I like to think of my mother's death as the day I had my first spiritual awakening.

I had never given much thought to how that day fundamentally changed me, until recently. Life without a mom was my new normal. I didn't know any better.

The day she died, the sun set and the moon rose, like any other day.

I still looked like the same person, when I looked at myself in the mirror.

I didn't change. The way people looked at me -did.

And that changed me.

At least, that's how I saw it. And I was mad at people for changing everything I ever knew about myself. I was mad at them for changing me into the helpless ten-year-old version of myself whose future was a big question mark all of a sudden. Because according to the way they looked at me, and their whispers in the hallways - kids who lose their moms at the age of ten, turn into problem kids who fall into drugs and get themselves pregnant before their sweet sixteen. Kids who lose their moms at the age of ten, need everyone to go easy on them, as if they are disabled in their own special way. Kids who lose their moms at the age of ten, have the right to always feel sorry for themselves, because everyone else does. Kids who lose their moms at ten, will never be normal again.

A part of me feels like every adult in my life failed me the day my mom died, failed me because of how they taught me to see myself from that point on. Another part of me knows that every one of them did the best they possibly could to take care of me the only way they knew how.

On the afternoon, moments before my mom lost the battle with cancer – despite me putting up a fight, her best friend managed to get me out of the house to "run an errand" with her. They told me afterwards, that they believed my mom (who was in a coma at that stage) was fighting to keep breathing because I was there, and that she didn't want me to see her blow out her last breath of air. They say I was barely out of the house when they told her that I am not around, and that was apparently when she "decided" to die. Having to accept their version of her last moments, not knowing or seeing for myself – that will haunt me forever.

During the last moments of my mom's life, I was out with her best friend - who was a teacher like my mom - we stopped at the headmaster's house because their kids were having a play date. We walked into his house just as he was putting the phone down. "Talia! I am so sorry to hear about your mom!" He said it with a smile. I remember his teeth showing. I'm sure he didn't mean to, and that it was just the shock taking over.

I didn't believe him, and in my head I was like "yeah whatever." He left it at

"I'm so sorry to hear about your mother." He didn't say anything about her dying. So I wasn't about to make assumptions. All I knew was that I hated him. Even though he tried very hard not to, he was the first person to look at me like I was damaged goods. He was essentially the person who brought me face to face with the reality that my mom had died, not that it was his choice.

We made our way back to my uncle's farm where my mom was. There must have been about twenty cars lined up outside the house as we approached.

My mom's friend I was with, Miss Helia, pulled off to the side of the road before we arrived at the house. She was preparing herself to break the news to me. I turned to her and said: "Tannie Helia, ek weet my mammie is dood." (Aunt Heila, I know my mom has died.)

As an adult, I've gone through different phases about how I felt about Miss Heila taking me away from the house that day. Sometimes I was mad at her for taking me away, only to return to my mom having died. I felt angry towards her even though I was told it was my mom's wish, to not have me around to witness her very last moments.

It was in writing about these moments that I made peace with the situation.

I cried whilst writing to her in 2019.

"Miss Heila, thank you for being brave enough to take care of me that day. You had a very difficult job to do."

Our minds will do what they have to, in order to protect us, but I felt at peace when I rewrote the story of that day. She was not the bad guy, she was the hero.

When we arrived at the scene, people couldn't look at me without breaking down. They all looked at me the way the headmaster did – like I was damaged goods.

After a few moments, we made our way to the room my mom was in, and we held hands forming a circle around her bed. Her brother said a prayer, and I kissed her cold, stiff lips to say goodbye.

I have had to listen to everyone telling me that ten is too young to come face to face with the reality of mortality. That ten is too young to see your own mother die. That ten is too young to become a grown-up overnight. But nothing they could say or do could stop me from being changed, forever.

The hard part was that everyone assumed I was changed for worse.

And I can understand that they wouldn't have known any better, but I sure wish they had tried harder to help me instill a little bit of faith in myself.

That part, I had to do all on my own.

The moment they looked at me that way, as if this was the beginning of the end for me, I knew it was up to me to choose who I was going to become.

The moment they labeled me as "special circumstances," I knew it was up to me to turn myself into something more than the contents of the box they placed me in.

The moment I saw my own mom lifeless, I knew I had to fight hard, everyday, to fulfill the dreams I had for myself, because I knew that one day, I would breathe out my last breath of air, too. The first clear thought I remember having of myself, was that I refuse to live a mediocre life. It is a clear thought I have had over and over again since that day.

When I imagined not living a mediocre life, I wasn't dreaming of money, I wasn't dreaming of bright lights, I wasn't dreaming about being idolized or being better than anyone else. I was just dreaming about becoming the best version of myself.

This meant speaking up when everyone else kept quiet.

It was to ask "why?" when everyone else just did as they were told. Like asking my dad why he forced me to take business economics over music, when I am so clearly wired for creativity and not numbers.

It was using my common sense when everyone else would rather practice ignorance. Like when I chose to decide what God meant to me when everyone else forced Christianity down my throat.

It was making up my own mind. Like when the elders in the family raised me to hate other humans based on their race, and I decided not to. And I went on to being the first person in my family to date interracially. No one spoke to me for a year.

It was to pursue a life where I could turn my creativity into a career – or die trying.

These are the things that got me into trouble, got me shouted at, got me kicked out of the family.

Standing up for what I believed in, always came with a hefty price to pay, but one I was always willing to pay. And now that I am older, I don't regret being this way as a child.

I will never know how my dad or stepmom remember me, maybe they truly remember me as a menace, a kid who caused problems wherever she went. But between the memories of the abuse I suffered by their hands, I remember myself as a quiet girl who only spoke when she was spoken to. Who said "please" and "thank you." Who was a pleasure to have around until they told me who to be, until they decided my values for me, until they messed with my plan for my life. I quietly took the abuse for five years until I started realizing that even when I tried to alter myself to fit into their idea of who I was supposed to be – it was still not good enough for them. They would use any excuse to hit me, punish me, abuse me. That's when I started challenging them, and started saying "no," and admitted that I would rather live on the street than be their victim of abuse any longer. At the age of fifteen – that was my reality.

The first psychologist that worked with me after my mom's death - told my dad and stepmom that even though I was ten, I had the mentality of an eighteen or twenty-year-old in certain situations, because of what I had gone through losing my mom. My stepmom hated me for my "grownup mentality", punished me for it, shamed me for it, as if I had any control over it.

The second psychologist - that tried to get me through a failing relationship when I was twenty-two - told me I was more mature than my forty-year-old partner, as a result of me having gone through life experiences most people twice my age have never gone through.

Once again leaving me feeling as though "my maturity" was the reason for a relationship of mine, falling apart.

Growing up too fast has caused its own problems in my life, but is still something I embrace wholeheartedly - even when it doesn't work in my favor at times.

The things that happened to me, forced me, in the most beautiful way, to appreciate life in a different kind of way.

To feel – everything.

To know – what I want.

To understand – who I am.

To be brave enough to forget everything I know, get lost on purpose, fall in love with dead-end-roads, in any way.

I have walked hand in hand with people who have never experienced my type of reality. People who don't know much about loss, people who don't question anything. And they are as they should be. And it is as good a way of life as any other.

In my eyes - they are having the ultimate human experience. Perhaps, knowing only joy, knowing nothing but inner-peace, never having had any reason to question it. It seems peaceful. And I hope I have lived a life like that in one of my previous lives.

I think some people are meant to never question life, as much as some people are meant to do nothing but question it.

And one day they will be eighty years old and come face to face with their own mortality and think that they are having their first spiritual experience.

But if I learned anything from seeing my mom lifeless, at the age of ten, it is that I am a spiritual being, having a human experience. That is how I choose to see my life.

I have been awake to that idea, since the day she passed away. And have – for the most part, subconsciously - lived my life in a certain way ever since, as a result of it.

So, even though I have had to listen to everyone telling me that ten is too young to come face to face with the reality of mortality - I like to argue that ten was the right age, for me.

RAINBOW BABY

My mom used to tell me I was her little miracle. That's what moms do, I know. But I believed her. I still do, even at times when it doesn't make any sense to me.

When I was born, she gave me a Hebrew name and explained to me when I was old enough that it means "Gift from God." Given the circumstances – I understand the backlash I received from people close to me when I decided to

14

change my name to Lyla when I was eighteen. But I like to believe my mom would have cheered me on all the way, to do what I felt I needed to do.

My two older siblings are seven and eight years older than me.

When I was little, my mom used to tell me - in the most PG way possible – that she lost twins, and two more babies before having my sister. Then after the birth of my brother, my dad had a vasectomy.

She was done having babies. Having a third baby was not an option.

The story goes that, sometime after my dad had the snip, he was ambushed and shot multiple times whilst driving through Mahamba, Swaziland, around the Komatiepoort/Lebombo Border. Serving in the military at that time, the incident was believed to have been an accident where his own men opened fire on him. I remember different variations of the story, but my sister told me that my dad pulled his car off to the side of the road to sleep whilst making his way to Mtubatuba to visit them, and the men fired at him because of the suspicious activity of his car pulled off the side of the road at that specific area.

My mom seemed to believe that the vasectomy was reversed by mistake during his surgery following the shooting, and to her surprise, she fell pregnant with me after that. I haven't watched enough Grey's Anatomy to know if things like that happen, if something like that is even possible – but that was the story I was told.

Wait, what?!

I have been a little busy trying to survive the last sixteen years - that I haven't exactly had the time to question that story until now. It's hard not being able to ask my parents about it now that I am older. Is it possible that the story isn't true? Is it possible that the vasectomy was never reversed? Is it possible that I am not his child? Am I the reason they got a divorce? Is that the reason he doesn't want me? I think I look like him. I think he is my dad. Long ago, I ran my fingers over the bullet scars on his tummy and arms. She also said he wasn't present when she gave birth to my two older siblings, but I've seen photos of him in the delivery room with her when she held me for the first time, he was there for my birth. I feel like there was a time he celebrated my existence – although I don't know it for sure.

After a failed attempt of trying to talk myself down from doing it - I texted my brother. It has only been in the last year that he has been able to talk about our mom. The other day he sent me a voice note of a song she used to sing to me every morning when she woke me up – "Op Blouberg Se Strand" (a song about the sunrise over the beach in Cape Town) – by Laurika Rauch. Each time my brother manages to speak about her to me, it feels like a miracle, a party in my heart, but a sense of incredible sadness too.

"Hey. Sorry, I know this is random and deep at the same time. Mom used to tell me dad had the snip and it was reversed by mistake when he had surgery after being ambushed and then they had me. Do you know anything about that? Lot of things coming up as I'm writing."

"That is how I remember it as well, sis." – I was as relieved, as I was surprised when I read his reply. I wasn't losing my mind – after all.

The modern-day term used for the firstborn after a miscarriage is "rainbow baby." My sister is our rainbow baby in the family. My mom always used to say that was the reason for my sister turning out to be a brat – she hardly ever put my sister down and loved her so much after losing four babies.

I feel the loss of our four siblings although I am not the rainbow baby in our family. It is an unspoken feeling we all share.

Being aware – at the age of twenty-six - of the fact that I am getting to live a life that four of my siblings did not get to experience, comes with its own treasure chest of feelings. Feelings of guilt, feelings of hope, feelings of responsibility, feelings of loss, and feelings of purpose.

My mom also made sure I understood the fact that I was conceived and born was a miracle to her. Even if my dad's vasectomy wasn't reversed during the surgery – research shows that the chances of conceiving a baby after the snip, is 1/1000.

On some level, I feel like her choice to tell me about the circumstances of my conception – has been a heavy burden for me to carry. Heavy for a ten-year-old – in any way. On some level, I can't even fathom that she told me all of this when I was little. There's a lot of pressure that comes with being told that you are a walking miracle, and an even bigger chance of developing a chip on your shoulder.

Telling me about the intimate details surrounding my conception, couldn't have been a decision she made lightly – which is why it is something I can't take lightly either.

I like to believe that she made the decision to tell me every detail - however age-inappropriate for me to hear, and despite her pain - tell me every detail as honestly as possible, so that I would be able to see myself clearly when I was older. To see myself clearly when she wasn't around to remind me who I am, or to remind me that I have a place in this world when I feel like I don't. Remind me that by some drastic turn of events, I exist. And that I ought to live my life accordingly.

My mom was diagnosed with breast cancer when I was two years old and the divorce followed soon after that.

My elder siblings were away at boarding school for most of their schooling careers. They were only home over the weekends and holidays.

From as far back as I remember, it was mostly just my mom and I at home. Before the divorce, I don't remember my dad being present much either. The youngest memory I have that involves my dad, is when my mom's brother brought a moving truck to our house and took us away while my dad wasn't there. When he found us, they tried to work it out. We moved into a massive brick house in Hluhluwe. I remember the feeling of hope hanging in the air - a new beginning. I must have been three or four years old at that stage. I can see him sitting with us in the dining room unpacking boxes, laughing and being playful whilst hanging the cutlery on the hooks of the set's rack, I remember that.

The swimming pool was groggy-green and covered in toad eggs - white foam lining the edges. But we were going to fix it up, along with the broken treehouse in the backyard.

There was a room with a built-in bar and alcohol cabinets – that room was his pride and joy. The white walls throughout the house had arches connecting different rooms – making it all feel open.

But there were things I heard behind closed doors, things I saw through keyholes, they couldn't hide from us kids, no matter how they tried. It was clear that my dad was hitting my mom.

At some stage they hosted a big party at our house. One thing led to another and he allegedly hit her in front of their friends. One of my mom's friends woke me up and held me in her arms, pressed tightly to her chest as if my dad was trying to take me away and she was saying no. The music stopped, the police arrived. The hope of a new beginning that we were all holding on to, was gone. Like a rug ripped out from under our feet.

In the last two years when I started having flashbacks about their fights, my sister confirmed it and told me that one night, my dad allegedly tried to strangle my mom over my crib I was sleeping in, and blamed it on his PTSD from going to war.

We moved out of the big brick house. My mom and us three kids lived with one of our neighbors for a while – aunt Nonnie. We stayed in her one-bedroom hut-like-apartment until we moved into my uncle's extra apartment on his farm.

I saw my dad twice during that period. Once where he completely ignored my mom when he came to see us kids, and another time where he showed up out of nowhere trying to fix things with her, but it turned into shouting and that was the last I saw of him before he moved across the country to Pretoria. I just remember him screaming at her in front of me, as if I wasn't there. And then he left without saying goodbye. I don't think I was even five years old. That's the first time I consciously felt traumatized.

I think the hardest thing about my parent's divorce was the fact that I did not know how to hate my dad for what he had done. I loved him as much as I loved my mom. I wanted him in my life as much as I wanted my mom.

I will always admire the character she showed in never trying to paint my dad as a bad guy to me – ever. If I wanted to call him, she let me call him. If I wanted to talk about him, she let me talk about him.

And even though I only saw him once a year, and some years not at all, even though he missed my birthdays and hardly ever kept in touch – her love for me was so hardcore, man. She made sure I was more than okay. It was always hard for me not to have my dad around for concerts and sports matches, but because of her, my life was good. Even when we were down and out, she made sure I was happy and loved, to the point that I didn't feel like I was missing out on anything everyone else had.

I had her.

Looking back – I was so attached to her. Oh my god. She could hardly get me to go to play dates and parties unless she went with me. The fact that she was a teacher at the school I attended, was everything to me. I got to spend two years as her student as she taught the grade 2 and grade 3 classes, as well as choir and music classes.

The best part was - I think she might have been as attached to me as I was to her.

It was when we went through the hardest times, that she reminded me – hard – that I was her little miracle. She really made me feel like I was.

I had never given much thought to the mysterious circumstances surrounding my conception. People have sex, they have babies. I don't feel like me coming into the world really was different from anyone else. Regardless of the medical questions that remain unanswered. But looking back, I believe more than ever that my mom needed me as much as I needed her for those ten years of our lives.

With my older siblings off to boarding school and my dad no longer around – we had each other.

I was there to put a cold washcloth on her forehead, migraine after migraine. Make her a cup of tea. Sing her a song in the car on the way to her chemotherapy and doctor's appointments. Try on wigs with her! And I wouldn't leave her side every time she needed to vomit. When she got sick at school, I skipped class and sat with her in the bathroom until it was over. And when she had her chemical stroke from all the chemo – which permanently paralyzed one half of her body – I was alone with her, trying to wake her up, realizing that something was wrong and that she had lost her speech. I had to call for help and tried to take care of her for hours before someone showed up.

So, I don't know if it's true - if my dad is my dad. I don't know how the hell they reversed his vasectomy "by mistake" – if they actually did. I don't know how she gave birth to me with a history of three miscarriages.

But I know she needed me as much as I needed her.

Because sometimes she took care of me, and sometimes I took care of her.

PINEAPPLE TRUCK TO PRETORIA

When you Google the name of the town I grew up in - "Hluhluwe" – some words that show up in the search engine are
- Underdeveloped
- Malaria area?
- Pineapples
- The Big 5
- 3500 population
...and a LOT of pictures of elephants walking freely across dirt roads. This is the elephant coast of South Africa, after all.

When you Google - Lyla Illing, Hluhluwe – some words that show up in the

18

search engine are
- Identity crisis
- Zululand-girl goes uptown-girl
- Down and out
- Rural

I didn't think he would have read the People Magazine article – "Hluhluwe-born songstress to sing anthem for the Springboks" – but he did. And he chose to open our interview with a sentence that threw me off in ways I was never prepared for.

I was sitting in a hotel room on Seventh Avenue, talking to David Kau on camera for his series "South Africans living in… New York City." We initially got in touch because I wanted to interview him for my podcast, but he had other plans.

"You used to sing to your mom on the way to school because you guys were too poor to afford a car radio" – he started the interview with this sentence and it was like I saw a light flash before my eyes. He had done his research, and he was right.

My world stopped.

Everything went quiet.

I felt my heart – beat.

I felt my eyes - blink – in slow motion.

Then I breathed out and smiled with my whole heart as I felt myself coming back into the moment. It was time for me to tell my story.

"Yes, that's true. She was so much fun, that I never realized we were down and out to be honest.

The forty minutes spent in the car on the way to school in the mornings were the highlight of my day. I got to belt out Celine Dion to my biggest fan cheering me on in the driver's seat next to me, telling me what a big star I was going to be one day. What could be more awesome than starting your morning like that?"

Speaking to him about my childhood is one of my most treasured experiences. Not because he is a famous comedian. Not because it was going out to thousands of viewers. But because he gave me the opportunity to see myself clearly in the midst of my "Zululand-girl goes uptown-girl, identity crisis" that I was reliving over and over, with each bigger gig I added to my resume.

I have typed vague answers about my past over email to journalists, but there was something about sitting in a hotel, on Seventh Avenue in New York City, with a fellow South African creative, and saying it out loud for what it was.

Hearing myself talk about where I come from helped me to remember the good things about my childhood. There is more to the first ten years of my life than "her parents got divorced" or "her mom died."

As tragic as that all is - those first ten years were the good part of my young life. It was the ten years that came after my mom's death that nearly ruined me.

When I changed my name at eighteen, I tried to put everything that hurt me, everything that shaped me, everything that I was forced to be as a teenager – into a box I never had to unpack again. In trying to escape the trauma I experienced living with my abusive dad and step-mom as a teenager, in trying to erase that part of my life, I ended up erasing the whole eighteen years from my memory without meaning to. Without realizing it.

I had to get away from it all, now. That's all I remember thinking. I picked a new name and a new direction and I ran as fast as possible into a new life and identity for myself. There were monsters I couldn't face. There were stereotypes I had to disassociate myself from. There were ways in which I didn't want people to see me. There was baggage breaking my back that I had to cut loose. So I decided to be Lyla Illing who is pursuing a radio and music career – there was nothing more to that story. No one had to know I was an Afrikaans-girl – and no one had to know about the trauma that came with being her.

Changing my name and deciding not to introduce myself as her, the special circumstances girl, was the only way I knew how to give myself a fair chance at a future. I used to think I was trying to change who I was perceived as – so I could change how other people saw me, but in retrospect, it was because I needed to change how I saw myself.

I needed to peel off the labels stuck to my forehead. Because I felt like it was written in big red letters on my face for everyone to see. Like sharpie I couldn't scrub off every time I looked at myself in the bathroom mirror.

"Abused."

"Abandoned."

"Afrikaner."

"Boer."

"Broken."

"Lost case."

All the things my dad and step mom told me I was and had to be.

After the interview with David, I found myself in a world where I allowed my mind to wander back to the better memories of the first ten years of my life, and in doing so, I remembered why I am a certain way. Why I like certain things. Why I see the world in the way I do. As if my mom wired me a certain way in those ten years. Something she did, some sort of strength she instilled in me, sense of identity – it helped me to get through the war my dad and stepmom ambushed me with.

So, there is more to the first ten years of my life than "her parents got divorced" or "her mom died."

In retrospect, those are the two least important things about my childhood. The two - really boring things - about my childhood.

If I really had to give you a glimpse into the crazy parts of my childhood, let's talk about the dung beetles I watched for hours, rolling their balls of cow dung across the dirt road. That was TV to me. The monkeys I shouted at across from me in the mango trees I climbed barefoot, to get the ripest one first, and peel the skin off with my teeth before eating it to the pip – like they do.

The leeches we pulled off our legs after swimming in the dam on my uncle's farm, the buck and buffalo that came to drink from the water there in the afternoons.

I can't help but feel that these are the bigger events of my childhood.

Spending every weekend fishing at False Bay, part of the iSimangaliso Wetland Park – just down the road from us - the R22 – my 5th avenue.

Saved from dune mining, the 358 534 hectare iSimangaliso Wetland Park was listed as South Africa's first World Heritage Site in 1999, recognized by the Convention for its outstanding examples of ecological processes, superlative natural phenomena and scenic beauty, and exceptional biodiversity and threatened species.

But it's more than a World Heritage Site to me. It's the place I learned to assemble a fishing rod, learned to tie earthworms onto the hook before throwing the line and sinker over my shoulder into the water whilst bonding with my brother. It's also the place I learned to run from hippos, quietly emerging from the water onto dry land quicker than you would imagine an animal that size could move!

Koorsbome (fever trees) next to the water there – their trunks, branches, twigs and thorns - yellow. Not bright, but not dull yellow, either. Sick looking trees, as if they are about to throw up. The shade they provided under the scorching African sun always made me feel a certain way. There was one I loved in particular. It was a lone tree, by the mouth of the river. It was on the left of where we used to park our car, and on the horizon behind it, lay two long, green islands. Close to each other. In the distance, the tiny space between them, like a gate or passage. Most times we could hear the echo of drums and ululating coming from them, it always sounded like a party. It was hard for me to imagine a society existed that I could never get to and see with my own eyes.

Unlike the New York Waterway ferries speeding past my Manhattan room window every five minutes, at False Bay there was no ferry to hop on, to go see what's on the other side of the river.

Those days, I was in love with not knowing. Those days it was easy to accept that, some things, you just don't know, and I learnt how to find some sort of joy in that.

I feel like I forgot that part of my childhood until I sat down and spoke to David.

And now I know that there's a reason I can't relate to my New York friends, telling me they sometimes wish that they could just stop the rat race and all chill at home together in front of the TV with their families – but they can never find the time to not be busy. I can empathize but I can't relate.

I sat in my mother's lap seven nights a week around the fire pit outside, watching the stars and wrapping sourdough around twigs I pulled off trees, roasting the dough on the side of the fire and covering my treat with syrup before eating myself almost-sick. We could never find the time to be too busy. We were too busy being happy. We were too busy – just, being.

Now I know why when vacationing, I find myself with sand between my cold toes, alone on Vero Beach at night, lying on my back, contently watching the stars, instead of running around town, partying with the cute boy I met from London earlier that day.

I was just completely intrigued by how different the stars look in Florida compared to in South Africa. The way I can't spot the Southern Cross in the same place I am used to seeing it when I look up at the black sky – it's a reminder of where I am, a reminder that I am on the opposite side of the world, and that I am aware of it. Those moments of clarity, and consciousness, mean everything to me.

Thinking about all these good things I was lucky to experience with my mom – suddenly, my troubled childhood seemed not so troubled after all.

When we weren't fishing at False Bay, we were on the beach in Sodwana, a scuba diving destination known for its vibrant coral reefs and snorkeling pools. Being friends with the locals, we used to stay at one of the hotels for free. The hotel was owned by a family who also ran a diving school there. Spending so much time in the company of diving instructors, I could tell you everything about the Ragged-toothed sharks congregating at Quarter Mile Reef every January and February. And when the sun started to set, you could find me running toward the boats as they beached - to see the Marlin and Sailfish that the deep-sea anglers pulled out of the water that day.

We never had money for anything, but we had Mother Nature – and it was free.

Getting stuck behind a troop of elephants in the middle of the day – free.

Being unable to cross the road because a python swallowed a baby buck and couldn't move – free.

Having the driveway flooded for a week and rowing around on the water in a cut-in-half water drum – free.

Watching feeding time for the snakes and crocodiles at DumaZulu Lodge – free.

Seeing my mom freak out as a newborn baby crocodile latched onto her finger and seeing her pull it out of its half-hatched egg into the air – priceless!

Clapping along to the Zulu dancers only dressed in beads, putting on a show for the tourists – free.

Fighting my mom's boyfriends' hunting dogs off a family of Meerkat, and taking in the babies who survived – free.

Watching guys smear the blood from their first buck-kill, all over their face – gross, but free.

Eating pineapples for breakfast, lunch and dinner – free. 95% of South Africa's pineapples are produced in Hluhluwe.

We might have been down and out, but I learned that you didn't need to own something in order to enjoy it – from a young age. My friend's parents all owned guest lodges, game lodges, sugarcane farms and pineapple fields.

Which would explain how my mother managed to put us three kids in a pineapple truck transporting produce to Pretoria, for free, so that we could go and visit our dad. It was the only option we could afford. A ten-hour-trip each way - just us three kids, the driver, and a ton of pineapples.

I might not have grown up with fancy trips to Disney World, but I grew up hardcore. This was our idea of fun. And I wouldn't have wanted it to be any other way.

ELSIE 1958 - 2003

Lyla Illing is at Battery Park by the Water.
Facebook Post 4 April 2019 · New York ·

[Update: TY for keeping the memory of my mom alive by sharing these stories about her with me]

Hey. I'm homesick AF … and it's making for a beautiful chapter in my forthcoming memoir - "Relying on the Kindness of Strangers."

Today's writing session included pulling up aerial views of False Bay, Hluhluwe, St Lucia, Sodwana Bay. The R22. And I might or might not have been listening to Johnny Clegg on repeat because that album was playing on repeat at Dumazulu Lodge.

Writing about the Koorsboom (fever trees), dodging hippos, and remembering my mom.

I have reached out to people from my past at the weirdest times about the weirdest things, trying to piece certain things together. If there's anyone willing to share some memories they have of my childhood or mom with me, I'd love to connect.

Nonnie You know where to find me.

Gillian Your mom was an amazing example of love. I learnt so many valuable lessons from her …. all my best Dumazulu memories are singing with your mom and you guys. She loved the three of you fiercely!! I remember her smile. I can only imagine how proud she must be looking down on you, Lenteli and Hanrè. Big hugs and lots of love xxxx

Bianca Grade seven punk rock dress up at school. You singing an Avril Lavigne tune, like it's no one's business! And of course... playing Mini Cricket together!

Linda Lyla - please my darling – don't get homesick - you are in a better place than we will ever be - stick it out my darl - Well your Mom and I - cannot begin to tell you our stories - we need a lifetime - we were definitely joined at the hip - we loved each other like nobody ever loved before - I can write a book about our lives together - I wish I had the time to tell you what we did - darl she was a legend - believe you me - I can start with the cotton bales in Magudu and end in Hluhluwe - I Miss your Mom every day of my life - she was my cuz and my best friend - I love her - and when you were baba - you sang Carina for us - and we loved you - and I still do - Mom went away far to early my darl - be brave - one day we will talk - when you come home for a visit I will tell you everything - you going to laugh till you cry - Love you lots.

Johan The day you are no longer homesick will be the day that we lose you. It would be really sad.

Jennifer Su Me too, I'm homesick.

Andre My sister would have lots of stories for you about your mom xx I know the feeling of being homesick. Have a boerie roll.

Juney Yes my mom always tells me about her fun times with Tannie Elsie.

Deirdre I remember one Sunday afternoon being bored - me, your mom an auntie Linda drove around collecting stuff from vendors and driving away (without paying) until one vendor hit your mom on the leg with a wooden spoon! And smoking banana leaves by Dukuduku sawmills until we were sick. So many awesome memories. I still blow the hooter every time we pass Bushlands where you used to live. Chin up my koekie.

Heila I think of you in the days when I used to teach at Hluhluwe Private School.

Your mom and I were great friends and best SMOKING PARTNERS!!

But I had to do the saddest thing in my life..... I had to tell you that DAY..... That your mom passed away. Can you remember I stopped the car next to the gravel road after I spoke to someone, then you gave me one look and said: tannie Heila, ek weet my mammie is dood. (Aunty Heila, I know my mom has passed away.)

My heart broke into thousand pieces!!! The only words I could get out was, ja Talie... (yes.)

Still love you lots, little girl from HOELIE HOELIE!!! (Hluhluwe)

Antoinette Hey my love. When I think back to the days Elsie had us laughing, you've got me missing her too. I remember a concert we had at the school where your mom played the character of the mischievous widow. She had us bursting out with laughter and the audience even more so. She was so loved by us all. You will always be part of the Hluhluwe Private School family. Love and greetings from us all at the school.

Rina Your mom was a fantastic person. With my son Jason's death, she visited me, she was so sick but didn't complain about her own situation once. She was a strong woman. We always loved having you for sleepovers.

Brother ♥

Sister As a little girl, probably seven years old, I remember how mom sang "Op Blouberg Se Strand" to you at your crib. She was so shocked when Doctor Stokkies told her she was expecting. I remember how she leaned on the wall with the phone in her ear, crying. And I remember the smile when she met you and got to know you. She loved you so deeply and still does. You were truly her gift from God. Not planned. And ours too. You were her absolute pride and joy. When she used to drive us to school in the morning she would often forget her cup of tea on the roof of the car! She always had a flask of tea with her and loved having a smoke with miss Helia. When I completed standard five, she took us all to the hotel with miss Heila and miss Sanet, and she threw back shots of Flaming Lamborghinis – burning her hand, of course. She parked herself under the tree outside, throwing up. The next day she wore sunglasses to school.

On the farm with our cousins, mom took so much pleasure in giving us frights when we least expected it. And also jokingly cursing at us in Zulu. She was always ready to have fun. She always saw the best in others and always wanted peace.

On the farm there was a bathroom in the spare room with a gas geyser. Mom always came to light it for us if we wanted to bathe. One day the flame shot out and our hair was scorched. We laughed so much. I can still close my eyes and hear how mom plays the piano. How privileged we were. Her time on earth was too short. My heart will never be whole again.

Cousin The good old days! Will never forget the evening that we waited for my sister at the gate to give her a fright. And your mom hitting the frogs with hockey sticks! The towel we lost in the dam ... your mother wanted to annihilate us! Do you still remember Hortoetsie? That meerkat bit the crap out of us. I remember the gas geyser - it was Lyla's hair ... it was very funny, shame she got such a fright. On the farm we rode on our bikes one night with just our panties on in the rain. Do you remember that old wreck of a car that always backfired and then all the pedestrians dove into the grass? There are so many beautiful memories. Your mom will always live on in our hearts.

We used to put the leeches from the dam into the bath. Oh no! There are so many things I can write a book! I went with our grandmother's false teeth and wig into Wimpy with your mom, you all wanted to run away !!! You broke your arm at aunty Nonnie's house, then you said "Mom I have a headache in my arm."

Deirdre I think back to our days in Umfolozi when your mother smoked at the table one night after dinner, she didn't like pumpkin but it was served up, she never smoked in front of your grandfather AB. That night he walked into the dining room unexpectedly to ask your grandmother Betty something. Your mother was so caught off guard that she killed her cigarette in the pumpkin. It was so funny - the heap of pumpkin and the cigarette that was on top. Your grandfather told her he knew she was smoking, she didn't need to waste food to kill her cigarette in it. Love u

Andre Bliksem (South African curse word) I took you and your mom out to the Quarterdeck (restaurant in St. Lucia) one night, never seen a kid eat spareribs like you!

Sanet Your mother and you three children will always be on my mind. She always laughed and played the most beautiful music. She had the kids at school singing songs I couldn't imagine in my wildest dreams. When I think of your mother I see her with a white dress, singing and dancing in heaven. She once prayed with me and said she was asking the Heavenly Father to always look after you three and keep His hand on you. And it gave her peace. And yes ... that evening with her and Miss Heila .... What an evening. And I can see so much of your mother in your children.

WHEN YOU'VE LOST YOUR MOTHER
Poetry & Prose

"You're still young and breathing is easy, suck it in." – The words of an aKING song I imagine my mom would whisper in my ear, every time I don't appreciate the gift that is time.

But mom,
Loving casually, is hard when you've lost your mother.
Being easy going, is hard when you've lost your mother.
Laughing along to be polite, is hard when you've lost your mother.
Trusting, is hard when you've lost your mother.
Commitment (and equally, the lack thereof) is hard when you've lost your mother.
The thought of ever being a mother, is hard when you've lost your mother.
Talking about the weather is hard, when you've lost your mother.
Being patient with love, is hard when you've lost your mother.
Playing hard to get, is hard when you've lost your mother.
Letting anyone take care of you, is hard when you've lost your mother.

So lover,
I speak my mind, because it's easy to, when you've lost your mother.
When you have felt the absence of a soul.
When you have seen someone's time run out.
When you have heard a heart stop.
So don't tell me that time will tell.
Don't make me wait. I am not here to participate in a game played by those who do not grasp the gift that is time.
A game played by those who have never lost someone, to the lack of it.

PART THREE

FROM GAUTENG TO BOTSWANA

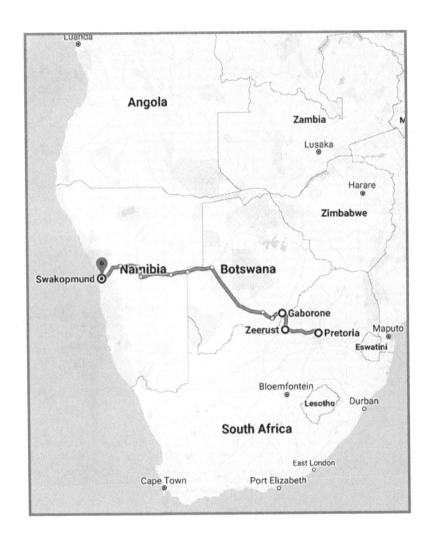

OPERATION OSAMA BIN LADEN

(**Operation, noun:** *a piece of organized and concerted activity involving a number of people, especially members of the armed forces or the police / preceding a code name for an organized military or police activity.*)

In the corner of my brother's room, stood the army green military trunk my dad left behind after the divorce, which only meant one thing – all the boys in my class wanted a play date with me - at my house, specifically.

My mom was cool enough to let my friend Reghardt and I take the washed-out-red cushions off the couch for our fort we were building in the dusty backyard. We took turns wearing my dad's heavy, and heavily dented helmet, pretend-playing war into the late afternoon.

It's like I shut my eyes for a moment, and when I opened them – somehow, I was in a real warzone, standing at her grave, saying goodbye, not only to her, but also to life, as I knew it.

The school's outdoor amphitheater where my mom once was given standing ovations for her musical talents, saw her audience come together one last time – only, she was there in a white coffin this time, and her limousine – a hearse.

I remember nothing about the funeral service other than the people who were there and the way it was set up - the chairs on the lawn. All my friends in school uniform and me in a two-piece cream-color outfit from the local PEP-stores my aunt bought me the day before. Oh, and the fact that my dad was not there to hold my hand. I remember that.

My mom did an amazing job at making sure I never saw my dad in a bad light despite their problems. My mom was a class clown though and took any opportunity to make light of tense situations. On the odd occasion when we were expecting a call from my dad, she'd joke "ah, daar is Bin Laden nou" (ah, there's Bin Laden calling now.) Around the year 2000 Osama Bin Laden's name trended into the ears of people in even our small little town where nothing ever happened, and I guess because of my dad's involvement in the military and the divorce that felt almost war-like – she thought it was funny to call my dad Bin Laden.

My uncles did not get on with my mom's boyfriend - uncle Steve - who I grew very close to during their relationship. I didn't understand their hate towards him. My brother later explained to me that my uncles gave my mom a very hard time after her decision to divorce my father. Because of their religious views, they were against her decision, regardless of the fact that my dad was allegedly hitting her and not present to take care of us, especially when she was diagnosed with cancer and needed him more than ever.

When she found love after the divorce, her brothers made a point of digging up any dirt they could find on her new boyfriend. They would have done the same to any man my mom was seeing at that stage – they were just pissed off at anyone trying to take my dad's place. Unfortunately - it didn't help that uncle Steve was English. They wanted nothing to do with him if he wouldn't conform to their religious and Afrikaner views. They also insisted that if he wanted to see my mom, he had to marry her, regardless if my mom even wanted to get married again or not. They threatened him often, telling him to stay away from my mom and did ridiculously childish things, such as breaking into his house, and dusting the clothes in his cupboard with itching powder.

Because my uncles did not approve of my mom's decisions regarding my dad and uncle Steve, it left her, and us kids, feeling as though we were always looked down on by the rest of the family. They felt like we were not living "in the truth" of what our religion stood for in terms of marriage & divorce. They labeled my mom as a woman living in sin. As children, we loved our cousins and spent a lot of time with them – but there was a clear distinction between the ways in which we were raised. My cousins were homeschooled because my uncles did not want the outside world to influence them in any way. My mom gave us kids more room to explore and make up our own minds - but provided guidance when we needed. There is a very real chance that her brothers would have cut us off from the family completely had it not been for the fact that she had fallen ill. Although they were insisting that her divorce was the type of thing that would deny her "eternal life," not one ounce of me believes that her brother thought his sister was about to enter the gates of hell when he stood next to her as she breathed out her last breath of air.

I think my mom was very enlightened in the last ten years of her life because of her near-death experiences - and being aware of the fact that she was going to die soon. When she was diagnosed with cancer, I imagine that her black and white world she was forced to live in, changed a lot. Like a colorblind person putting on a pair of colorblindness glasses and experiencing the world in red and yellow and blue and green for the first time. It's very hard to accept that my mom's death did not have any impact on her family's beliefs and the way they treated people around them. Her death was a moment of impact in all of our lives, and it could have been an opportunity for them to do away with the beliefs and systems that caused so much hurt in our lives, the unnecessary shit they put her through when she just needed her brothers. The fact that nothing changed, the fact that they still live their lives as if they are holier than thou - it makes me feel as though she died in vain.

Before my mom and uncle Steve decided to move in together, we used to visit him where he lived just off a dirt road not far from False Bay. He was obsessed with collecting frog ornaments, big and small. My mom could spend hours visiting him, sitting around a table just talking and laughing with him. Then one night I got sick at his house from eating too many marshmallow and chocolate Easter eggs. I have never managed to enjoy Easter treats after that! He was a building contractor, working on various big projects for game lodges in the area, and also built the assembly hall, ablution blocks and accommodations at the school my mom was teaching at. Sometimes we would accompany him to Phinda Game Reserve where he and his workers were building new accommodations for the lodge. He used to call his workers his "guys" and I fondly remember him full on talking away in Zulu, conversing and laughing with them.

He used to transport them to the building sites himself. My mom and I would sit with him in the tiny front of the truck, and the workers, piled out on the open-back of the truck. I tried my luck over and over again – "Oom Steve, kan ek asseblief ook agter op die bakkie sit?" (Uncle Steve, please can I sit on the back of the truck too?)

Sometimes I got away with it, he let me, until one day I fell off the back of the truck when he pulled away after being stationary at a gate. I was fine, but that was the end of my fun.

My mom didn't own a car for a long time. My dad kept the Camry after the divorce. Sometimes uncle Steve let my mom borrow his Dutson "skedonk" to run errands. It was an old wreck of a car that backfired at least a couple of times each time we drove it. We often had to push start the Dutson, and every other car we owned after that.

I have to say, that I grew up with a strong sense of community. Whenever we got stuck on the side of the road (which happened very, very often) no car would ever pass without stopping to lend a helping hand, or if there were pedestrians walking on the side of the road, they helped us too. It took three or four people to push start the car when it broke down. It took one person behind the wheel of the car, and two or three people pushing the car from behind. Almost all cars in South Africa were manual transmission back then. I'd stay in the car with my mom and watch her switch the engine on, push the clutch to the floor, and put the car into first or second gear. The people in the back would start pushing the car until we reached a speed of approximately 20km p/h. "Okay!!!" She would shout to let the people know to let go and get out of the way as the car would jolt when she popped the clutch. "Gee hom gas!" (Give it gas!) the rest of the people would shout back – that saying they shouted back was all part of the fun. Whoever was pushing and needed to be back in the car, would run after it and I would swing open the door so they could jump back in. This was nothing strange to us, we did it on a regular basis.

My mom and uncle Steve moved us into a big wooden house in Bushlands, a twenty-minute dirt-road-drive from the town of Hluhluwe. In the mornings he fed his dogs and left to go and pick up his guys - and spent the day building. When he was home, he could almost always be found under the car, working on it, listening to panpipe music.

Uncle Steve lived with us for years, at some point I started calling him daddy. I loved and trusted him. He trained me for cross-country races, and took me to horse riding lessons. He showed up. And he was an important adult to me in my life. Like anyone else, he had his flaws. At times it was clear that he was mostly interested in being my mom's boyfriend and not so much a father to us three kids. There was a lot of pressure on my brother who was fourteen at the time, to act as the head of the house when he really was supposed to be out having fun with his friends or studying for a math test. My brother took on the responsibility of making sure that our gate was locked at the end of the night, that our curtains were drawn. Countless little things that wouldn't seem like a big job to anyone looking in from the outside – but it is unfair that that type of pressure was thrust onto him. Both him and my sister worked as waiters at the local Wimpy restaurant from a young age. Every weekend and holiday. It was their only chance of having some money for things they needed, like a few coins to use the public phones at their boarding school, buying toiletries, or being able to afford going out with their friends. There was no such thing as pocket money for fun things. To us, getting new clothes meant being given someone else's old bag of clothes to sift through for a size that fit. We were disproportionately excited to sift through those bags – each time. We didn't know any better.

We have many beautiful memories with uncle Steve, and we loved him because we knew he made our mom happy, but it is hard for us kids to look back and feel like he failed us as much as our own dad did, when he couldn't step up to be the head of the house, a full on father to us when we really needed one. And my mom needed more than just a boyfriend too, she deserved someone who would have stepped up to the plate and take care of things. Instead, we had many people stepping in, taking care of us.

My friend Reghardt's parents bought my mom a car, so that we could have reliable transportation to school and her doctor's appointments. My mom's cousins, Andre and Hennie, put my mom on their medical aid and helped with clothes and money for us kids where they could. We used to visit them where they lived in St. Lucia and they would take us out to the Quarter Deck restaurant. The walls of the restaurant were covered with fish trophies – and one massive marlin trophy I could never stop staring at. Hennie and Andre would let us order whatever we wanted to eat or drink and gave us kids some money to go spend at the curio and surf shops next door to the restaurant whilst they hung out with my mom. We didn't know what it felt like to be able to walk into a store and just buy a toy or shirt we wanted. They allowed us to do that and feel normal, like we were just kids for a day.

They never made a big deal out of it, they were just there for us.

When uncle Steve started seeing my mom, he knew she had cancer. Whenever they argued, said goodbye, or shared a special moment, he would say to her "give me five" and hold her hand in his. He was asking her to give him just five years with her – no matter the backlash they received from her brothers, no matter her poor state of health.

My brother had to learn to drive at the age of twelve because of the migraines my mom often experienced. "It's like a pressure cooker, and my head wants to explode" she used to tell my brother. The migraines were so bad, she wasn't able to move or speak. They would almost always cause her to vomit. So many times, my mom pulled off to the side of the road so that my brother could take over and drive us home from wherever we were – sometimes he had to drive for distances

32

of over an hour.

My mom battled three rounds of cancer over the years. We were hopeful that she won the fight when she beat the second round of breast cancer, but the disease returned in the form of three cancerous tumors – one on a rib, another on her pelvic floor and the other on her adrenal glands.

She received aggressive chemotherapy after the tumors were found – the chemo caused the ischemic stroke my mom had.

My siblings were away at boarding school when the stroke happened in my mom's sleep one night. For the first time, my mom didn't wake me up with the song "Op Blouberg Se Strand" like she did every day before that. I woke up on my own and walked to her bed. Uncle Steve was about to leave for the day. He noticed something was drastically wrong with my mom, she had trouble moving and speaking, but he was more worried about picking up his guys and getting them to the building site. He left us there, when she was in dire need of medical attention.

With all the migraines she was having, it could just as well have been an honest mistake that he didn't think the situation demanded more attention, but a mistake that has been hard for us to forgive nonetheless.

Living on a farm, we had no close neighbor next door. Walking from our driveway to the nearest dirt road would have taken me a good thirty minutes alone. We were a twenty-minute drive away from town and a forty-minute drive away from the school my mom was supposed to be teaching at that day. I have no recollection of who found us hours later, but I believe it was my uncle. I can't remember if I managed to get a hold of anyone over the phone, or if the school called my uncle when my mom didn't show up for work. I just remember trying to take care of her and being absolutely horrified for hours, feeling so helpless. When her brother found us, it was another hour and a half drive to the nearest hospital – The Bay Hospital in Richards Bay – the same hospital I was born in.

Because my mom did not receive medical attention for hours after the stroke, there was excessive, irreversible damage to her brain. Damage that could possibly have been reversed or prevented had she received the necessary medical attention in time.

The stroke caused total loss of speech, and half of her body was permanently paralyzed. My uncles took us in for the months leading up to her last days. They wouldn't allow uncle Steve onto their property. I will never know if my mom had any anger towards him for leaving her that morning when he should have been there for her, but now that we were living with my uncles, my mom couldn't see him whether or not she wanted to. My guess is that – she still wanted to. To make peace with it all, if anything.

I carry resentment around in my heart toward my uncles for denying her that opportunity - and I don't want it to be this way, but I don't know how to forgive them for denying him the opportunity to attend her funeral. For her sake, his sake, and us kids. He was family to us, and he lost her that day as much as we did.

When things quieted down after the funeral that day, my uncle sat me down to talk about the first big decision I ever had to make in my life. At ten years old I had to decide if I wanted to continue living with my uncle and his family, carry on going to my same school, continue living in the only place I ever knew as home, or leave it all behind to go and live with my dad in Pretoria. My uncle promised to take care of me as if I was his own if I stayed, but I wanted to be with my dad even though I basically did not know him.

My dad told my uncle to put me on a ten-hour bus to Pretoria, alone. My uncle had his flaws, but he fought like hell for me. "No! If you want her, you can come and get her yourself" I heard him shout before throwing down the landline. That's the thing about growing up in a cult, its members will fight over you, and will try very hard to protect you from anything they consider harm, and that can be very comforting in its own way. Sadly though, just as much harm takes place within a cult and there's very little you can do about it when you're cut off from the outside world.

The week after my mom died, I spent a lot of time with my seventeen-year-old brother who was basically living with his girlfriend and her family at that point. I don't know who was more attached to his girlfriend Nicole - him or me. Funny enough – my uncle did not approve of her either, based on the fact that she was English.

My mom's family was very set in their views when it came to culture and religion. "Praat Afrikaans of hou jou bek." (Speak Afrikaans or shut the hell up.) A phrase I heard often, along with "Jesus Christ!"

In our family, you were allowed to use Jesus' name as a curse word no matter your age. We weren't Christian. To be honest, I still don't know what the hell we were. We identified as "Die Uitverkore Volk" (The Chosen People.) We used the names Yaweh and Yashua in the place of Jesus. We didn't celebrate Christmas, and the elders used to go on about how they believed that people of color did not go to heaven.

One time, my mom threatened to resign as a teacher if the school allowed children of color to attend. Despite my mom sharing the family's racial views, I still had a feeling that she was flexible about what I wanted to grow up to believe and stand for. She was religious but sort of spiritual towards the end, not openly, though. Sometimes after school we visited an old lady in a trailer on a farm – I have no idea who she was. From what I remember my mom explaining to me, she was a psychic seer. I guess my mom had some questions about the future when she realized her time was running out. My mom did not always see eye to eye with her brothers when it came to their inflexible views on race and religion, but she wanted to be in their lives, so I think she just gave in at some point.

Despite the elders' attempts at instilling animosity towards people of color, in me – it didn't stick. I absolutely adored our domestic worker, Unice. She was family to me. She taught me how to speak isiZulu – I spoke Zulu more fluently than English. At the end of her working day, I walked her down to the shed on our farm where she had a room she stayed in. Sometimes she let me watch her prepare Umqombothi - a beer made from maize (corn), maize malt, sorghum malt, yeast and water. Prepared over the fire and then poured into a big plastic vat once cooled. If she really wanted to spoil me, she'd come back from town with Madumbi - an indigenous starchy vegetable commonly found all along the eastern regions of South Africa. I like to believe my mom found beauty in the relationship Unice and I shared. I think my mom loved her too. There was never any hate speech or disrespect towards Unice. Back in the elders' company (who have since passed on) it was a whole 'nother story though. The "k-word" was thrown around loosely and workers were also addressed as such. I feel sad when I remember the hate and gross unfairness I had to witness growing up.

There was always something awful my mom's brothers were upset about. If my brother wore too much black clothes – he was worshipping the devil. If we listened to American music – we were worshipping the devil.

God, maybe that's why it was so easy for me to choose my dad over my uncle. I hardly knew my dad but opting for the unknown must have seemed like a more sane option to me. Even at the tender age of ten when you don't know your ass from your face, I think I had a pretty good head on my shoulders.

I went to school one last day to say goodbye to all my friends. I walked up and down the rugby field with my friends during recess. My twin friends, Phillicia & Varuscjka stared at me like deer in headlights. "So, what happens now?" they asked in a panic, very concerned for me. I was calm and collected. Laughingly telling them not to worry. "I'm going to be fine. I am probably going to become a famous singer once I get out of this small town. This is a good thing. I'm going to miss you so much but I want to leave. I have a feeling that I must."

I really was excited to see my dad and live this new life ahead of me. I felt like I knew exactly who I was - I don't remember feeling worried about any of it.

When school was out, I was almost sure that I spotted uncle Steve's pale yellow Volkswagen-Jetta between all the other parents' cars. I couldn't help but run up the hill to the parking lot, hopeful to see him, and I did. It was him – my "daddy." He showed up at the right place at the right time and by some miracle we managed to say goodbye to each other.

God, I can't even recall his last name. But I remember he had something like eight ridgeback hunting dogs, all of whose names started with the letter "P." Porkus, Plutus… and so on.

He used to take the dogs bush pig hunting on pineapple farms for fun. We'd load the dogs onto the back of the truck after the sun had set and head out – it was a very exciting outing for us, one of our only forms of entertainment. The only other thing as cool as this was spending time outside around the fire pit, or going to the town's rugby club every other night, kicking around the ball with our friends whilst our parents got tipsy at the bar.

Upon arriving at the pineapple fields, my brother and uncle Steve would take the dogs out to sniff out and track the bush pigs, shotgun in hand. My mom and I would stay in the truck, windows rolled down, watching the stars while she drank her tea from a flask and smoked her Peter Stuyvesant cigarettes. We couldn't speak very loudly because it would scare off the bush pigs. "I can close my eyes and still remember the smell of the pineapple fields, the deafening silence ringing in my ear, the feeling of suspense hanging in the air, and the clear, clear sky" my brother told me over the phone. I remember it too. The absolute quiet - for hours on end sometimes - and then the chaotic commotion. Hearing the dogs bark and attack, the bush pigs squeal and the gunshots go off. And then it goes quiet, my mom and I would look around trying to spot uncle Steve flashing the torches at us, so we could flash the truck lights back at them, so that they could find their way back to us, dead bush pig in hand. I don't know if he fed it to the dogs or if it ended up in my plate. Maybe a bit of both.

He once chained the dogs to the washing-line-pole and beat the crap out of them for killing one of my cats. I didn't like that he did that to them. But that's the only bad memory I have of him. He tried to call me a month after I moved in with my dad, but my dad wouldn't allow it. I tried finding him when I got older, but rumor has it he passed away – although, I don't know for sure.

My dad showed up to take me away to Pretoria. My sister was there with me, and we visited my mom's grave together one last time. I took off the necklace I was wearing and left it on the soil still freshly heaped high on her grave. My dad waited in the car for us.

We drove from my uncle's farm to my brother's girlfriend's house in town, but when we got there, she kept saying my brother wasn't home. We stuck around for quite a while – I begged my dad to wait for my brother to show up. I couldn't leave without saying goodbye to my brother. I was devastated when my dad told me to get in the car and that we were leaving.

It wasn't until I was twenty-two that my brother told me the story of what really happened that day. We were together in Durban for the weekend, the first time us three siblings were together in years. Everyone else had already gone to bed, but him and I sat on the balcony outside, trying to get to know each other again.

"The day dad came to take you away, I hid under the bed at my girlfriend's house. I was devastated. We had just lost mom and I couldn't cope with losing you too. I couldn't deal with him taking you away. I was under the bed when you guys came in looking for me. I'm so sorry. I was broken."

We both cried, but he needed to say it, and I needed to hear it.

AMBUSH

(**Ambush, noun**: *a surprise attack by people lying in wait in a concealed position.*)

Seeing my dad park his big blue Mercedes Benz outside my uncle's house to pick me up a week after my mom was buried, brought back that same feeling I had when we moved into the big brick house years before. It was that same feeling of hope that hung in the air when they tried to make it work between them, one last time. Where the swimming pool was groggy-grass-green and the edges were lined with toad eggs, but we had a home and we were going to fix it up and be a happy family.

I had that same feeling of hope, desperate hope, hanging around me like a cloud of smoke with every step he took toward my uncle's front door to meet me. I was delusionally happy to start this new life that included my dad for the first time. The fact that he hadn't been present in my life up until that point – didn't count for me. Every birthday he missed, every phone call he ignored – forgiven without any explanation or apology asked for from me. The fairytale of finally having my dad around was coming true – the past was irrelevant.

When we hit the road from Hluhluwe to Pretoria, all I kept thinking with every hour passing by was – my hell, this car hasn't backfired or broken down yet! Of course my dad found it in bad taste that I thought push-starting cars were cool. He tried explaining to me that things are a bit different in his house and life, and that I needed to stop saying things like that out loud.

I had a very outgoing personality at the time and tried to buddy-up with him. I didn't understand child-adult relationships. I didn't see a difference between him and I. But he grew up in the era of "kids are to be seen and not to be heard" – so it wasn't a good combination.

I asked him anything I could think of, for the sake of trying to get to know him and bond. I felt a sense of responsibility to bring us back into conversation after every long and awkward moment of silence. The more I spoke to him about things I remembered about him, the less he spoke to me.

He told me that I had to be tired and suggested I try and take a nap. We still had a lot of hours ahead of us on the road. I think he was worried if I didn't stop talking about my mom and our past he wouldn't be able to help himself but turn the car around and drop me right back off on my uncle's doorstep. In hindsight, that might not have been the worst thing.

Upon waking from my "pretend" nap, he had his mind set on talking me through my new morning routine I was going to have to adapt to. My first road trip with my dad, and we basically spoke logistics all the way up to Pretoria. It wasn't an awesome start but at least the music was good. There was always some Johnny Cash, Norah Jones, Robbie Williams or Dixie Chicks in the mix – so I just drowned his voice out with music the fifth time he told me that I was going to have to take my shoes off before walking into the house.

"Take your shoes off before you come into the house!" she yelled as I walked toward the entrance of the place I was about to call my new home. I was still trying to get over the fact that their gate was electric operated by the push of a button. I greeted my stepmom with a hug and a kiss. She showed me around the house, and the second living room area with the white couches I wasn't allowed to sit on unless an adult was accompanying me. I was allowed on the emerald green chairs – the ones I was less likely to ruin.

Back when my mom realized that the cancer was terminal, she made us kids watch a movie about a mom who dies and the dad remarries so they have to get used to life with a stepmom. My mom wanted me to give my stepmom a chance.

She wanted to believe that her and I could have a good relationship, so I was ready to give it my best try the moment I walked in that door. My mom prepared me for it.

"Your dad didn't ask me if I wanted to take you in, he *told* me we were taking you in. I was given no say in the situation. So you're here now, your room is the one across from the bathroom. You can go get settled in."

I unpacked my things out of the boxes and black bags they were in. I didn't have a lot of things - some clothes but mostly a few of my mom's belongings. Her most treasured porcelain doll, with tiny little glasses on, dressed in blue. The book her students made her of their favorite memories together. I put a photo of her next to my bed and slipped on my oversized Eminem t-shirt we bought at the last Pineapple festival in Hluhluwe. I lived in that shirt from the day I bought it. My brother was an avid fan of his, so, so was I. I knew his album, The Eminem Show, back to front before I turned nine. I could sing the whole thing in my sleep. The black shirt hung all the way over my knees, and had a massive Eminem on it, looking angry, and a green marijuana leaf sticking out behind him.

Even in Hluhluwe, people looked at me funny whenever they saw me in the shirt, but it was no big deal to me. I suppose my mom didn't love the shirt on me, but I felt comforted in it and she was fine with whatever made me happy. I didn't have a baby-pink "blankie" or easy childhood to go with one. I had Eminem who sung about father-daughter struggles (Hailie's Song) and found a certain sense of sadness in "Sing for the Moment" I loved losing myself in. Having older siblings, it was inevitable that I would listen to their music, and I wanted to love all the music my brother loved. I used to listen to Eminem with my brother in the big wooden house we lived in. That's also where I watched my brother write his own lyrics and music, turning thin air into brand new songs, magically. I fell in love with the process of songwriting watching my brother express himself with a paper and a pen, six strings and a plectrum cut from an old Clover ice cream tub lid.

"You can't wear that. *You must be joking.*" She pulled a face of disgust at me, flashing the gold filling in her teeth. It wasn't a question - it was an instruction. How I felt about the shirt and why I felt so at home in it, was irrelevant to her. It was going in the trash. I didn't put up a fight. I was here to try and accept her as my new mother figure, and whatever set of rules that went with it. I was determined to impress my dad and get his way of life textbook right.

My stepmom would treat me in this demeaning manner and then turn around asking me what my favorite meal was so that she could cook it for me. She was more friendly at times, making sweet gestures, and then telling me she was giving me so much to be thankful for.

I woke up the next morning to deal with the loss of my Eminem shirt, not realizing the next thing I had to say goodbye to - was my hairstyle. "I've made an appointment at the hairdresser for you. We're going to cut bangs for you, your forehead is *way too big* for you to part your hair in the middle. And the rest of your hair we'll cut into a short bob." The hairdresser appointment was followed by a lesson in front of my dressing table, on how to blow-dry my hair into a neat style. They changed everything I knew and liked about myself, in a matter of a week.

We went to go buy my green and orange school uniform for Totiusdaal Primary School I was to attend where we lived in Waverley. Then the worst thing of all happened – we went shopping for black school shoes. I had to wear shoes to school?! I never had to wear shoes to school in Hluhluwe. Running shoes if it was cold or if I wanted to. Not that this was their fault. I was pissed off regardless.

I traded the sand-and-grass-between-my-toes-life in for knee high socks and shoes that gave me blisters – perfect. And I had to hear how expensive this all was every time she needed to make a purchase.

I could very clearly see that she felt like she got stuck with someone else's problem but that she tried to make it work because it was the right thing to, out of loyalty to my father.

I would say things like "this school is so awesome - the classrooms are so roomy and the playground so big!" I would make any shit up to sound grateful for the new life they were trying to give me. In reality, I wasn't making any friends whatsoever. The half an hour between the time they dropped me off at school, and the bell sounding for assembly – I spent walking alone around and around the school grounds singing to myself. I went from a seven-pupil class in Hluhluwe to a forty-pupil class in Pretoria. In Hluhluwe, my teachers were part of my life outside of school too. They all knew me personally – school was my second home because of my mom having been a teacher there. But nothing was the same in Pretoria apart from the fact that I could still watch the soap 7de Laan every night.

I was a stranger to every new teacher or person I met. I didn't know how to deal with it – in my head, I felt as if my teachers were ignoring me although they were doing nothing wrong. I was just used to teachers being like family to me at my previous school. I was avoiding interaction with fellow students at any cost. I didn't understand that I was suffering from social anxiety. I was always smiling, gave my best in class, and told my dad and stepmom that I was doing great, even though I couldn't get myself to interact with any of the kids. "The kids are all so nice and welcoming." I started lying at my own expense to protect their feelings. I didn't want them feeling like I wasn't appreciative of them taking me in, and I didn't want to do anything to mess up the opportunity to live with my dad.

Away from school, they initially included me in their long-standing-routine-orientated weekly outings. Every Friday afternoon my stepmom and I would walk down the road to the video shop to rent some videos, and we'd meet my dad at the restaurant where they'd have focaccia bread and sangria.

We'd sit in silence, and my dad would look at both of us and say, "Ah, this is nice."

One thing I learned is, if you have to break the silence by saying that the situation is "nice" – then it is most likely not-so-nice.

We stopped at the liquor store almost every day to pick up a bottle of First

Watch Whisky. I thought nothing of it. My mom used to buy cigarettes everyday – I didn't see the difference and it didn't bother me.

One day I started getting the sense that my stepmom was fighting with my dad out of frustration about their lack of alone time, now that I was around.

She insisted I move to the bedroom furthest away from theirs, and after that, I was enrolled in a full time afterschool program. I was at school from 7am to 5pm every weekday and I hated every single minute of it.

I wasn't allowed many visitors at home, so my social awkwardness was even worse because I knew they didn't want me bringing home friends anyway. I took part in the school play, which I don't remember them showing up for. At the end of the school year when it was time for prize-giving, I got an invitation to attend. We were all going to go but my stepmom conveniently felt sick right before we had to leave, so it was just my dad and I.

I had only been at the school for five months at that stage - I did not win any awards that night, I was invited because I was nominated to be part of the scholar patrol team – as voted by the class and teachers. My guess was that a teacher insisted I should be included in the team to help me feel like I had a place to belong. I also received a certificate for the student who had shown the best progress in class. When I was in Hluhluwe, I won at least two trophies every year. Usually for language and math, and arts & culture. Even though I didn't win any trophies at my new school, I was really excited to be included in the scholar patrol team and felt awesome for receiving the certificate for the progress I made.

When the ceremony was over, and my dad and I walked toward the car, he literally said, "well, that was a waste of a night, you didn't win anything. They shouldn't get your hopes up by inviting you for no reason."

I thought I didn't hear him correctly, but then I heard him repeat it to my stepmom at home. I just kept quiet.

We went away vacationing in Graskop when schools closed for the December holidays. They made sure I understood that it was a privilege to travel – but they did it in a way that indicated I was ungrateful by default.

To make me show my appreciation, they made me do the dishes or other chores.

I think it was very hard for her to share her husband with his child. I just said "ja tannie" (yes, aunty) with a smile to whatever was asked of me.

Sometimes we'd play cards and board games together – and things felt kind of normal, but it felt like she was fronting, to try and keep my dad happy, and then she'd be like "okay I'm over it now, go play outside like children are supposed to."

We stayed in plain but beautiful chalets, the camp had a swimming pool with panoramic views of miles and miles of green hills, cliffs and plains. I finally made some friends there, but I stayed out playing with them after sunset and my dad was pretty upset having to come look for me, torch in hand. He was very protective over who I was and wasn't allowed to hang out with. He made it clear to me that I needed to introduce him to anyone I was going to interact with from that point on. To some degree I appreciate that, only, there were times he wouldn't like the way a girl was dressed (amongst other situations) and based on what she wore alone, I had to say goodbye to her and call it a night if he didn't think it was appropriate. No fun activities at the kids' club for me. Looking back I feel like it must have been PTSD my dad was dealing with from the war, I had no concept of what that meant back then – he had to be in total control of every situation, and anything outside of our circle or comfort zone was a threat. I personally feel like that level of control and cutting me off from the outside world was a form of abuse, although I have empathy for whatever he was and still might be going through.

We explored the waterfalls in the area, and they let me do a zipline between two cliffs, that stretched over a canopy of trees below. I loved it. It was all smiles and laughs until it was the complete opposite the next moment. She was likely pissed at my dad for spending money on me ziplining. When we stopped at the gas station, she told me I ought to be buying children's magazines and activity books with my pocket money – "that's what kids at your age should be doing. Coloring in, not ziplining." And with that, she sent me into the convenience store to go and buy myself some activity books.

I never knew where I stood with her. If I spoke too much, I was an irritation. If I shut up for extended periods of time – she'd call me out for sulking and causing an unpleasant vibe.

For the first time in my life, I was in a family who prayed to Jesus Christ and celebrated Christmas. Christmas eve came and so we opened gifts while away on holiday. My dad got her luxury towels and dried fruit from Woolworths as a gift – she freaked out. "Ah!" She inhaled and exclaimed in disbelief, acting totally insulted. "TOWELS! *You have got to be kidding me!*" She would always switch from Afrikaans to English whenever she felt insulted or upset. She was so upset with my dad and explained that she was expecting another gold bangle for her collection. She already had a few on her arm and after that night they multiplied every year.

She decided when the night was over, and ended it screaming and shouting. I went to bed with a hole in my stomach from anxiety over what had happened.

When she got over herself, we continued with our vacation as if nothing happened. New Year's Eve was next – we attended a dance evening in some sort of hall with the locals. I was eleven, and she thought it was funny to order me alcohol. "You're going to have some peach Archers, you're *so* grown up, aren't you?" I had no idea what was going on, I just did as she said. Was she expecting me to say no? What the hell did I know at age eleven? And then she ordered another one – which resulted in me puking in the back of their car. I was drunk for the first time and was made to promise that I would never speak about it to another human being – and I didn't.

When we were back home, I continued to feel like I didn't know where I stood with her. I can't remember if I asked or if she offered, but she let me adopt a cat – I fucking loved her for that. Around the same time, she also asked my dad

41

to ask me to remove the photo of my mom from my bedside table– because it was apparently hard for her to see photos of her husband's ex-wife in her house. I did as they asked – but that really hurt me.

Schools opened for the New Year, and with the New Year came new friendships. I settled in a bit more this time around than I had before – but the teachers must have sensed that something was off about me, because my stepmom apparently got a call from the school to come in and see the headmaster.

My dad was working in Hatfield, he didn't join her for the meeting at the school. To this day I have no idea what triggered the school to call the meeting, and part of me wonders if my stepmom was the one who called for it.

I sat outside the headmaster's office while my stepmom was in there speaking to him. He wanted to see me alone after speaking to her, before seeing the both of us together.

I had no idea what was waiting for me inside that office when she stepped out and I had to step in.

BACKFIRE

(**Backfire, verb:** *[of a plan or action] rebound adversely on the originator; have the opposite effect to what was intended.*)

"Tell me, does your dad and stepmom drink a lot?"

The headmaster was asking me these random questions after meeting her.

"They buy a bottle of Whisky every second day, but it's not like they go wild or anything," I laughed, nervously. Wondering why the hell he pulled me out of class to ask me a question like that.

At eleven years old, I could care less about the amount they were drinking, and I knew even less about what a small or large amount was.

I was used to adults drinking often, when I lived with my mom – it was nothing new to me.

So, when I responded to the headmaster, I wasn't trying to cause trouble, I was just answering a question.

He called her in and confronted her about the amount of alcohol her and my dad consume. She was outraged and immediately started challenging him – and stared me down with that "if looks could kill" vibe. I was freaking out, not understanding how I turned their meeting into a fight. Not understanding why I was being shouted at, and made to feel like I was in massive, massive trouble.

Upon arriving at home, she locked me out of the house and told me to play in the tiny garden outside while she was making calls inside the house – for hours. At some point she called me into the house and started yelling at me that she was going to put me into an orphanage.

When my dad eventually got home from work, I was excluded from the initial sit-down she had with him. I heard her shouting that I went to the headmaster to rat them out for drinking – as if it was something I planned. Meanwhile I had no idea who called the meeting and why I was being asked questions.

When my dad managed to calm her down, he called me into the lounge and started preaching to me about how it is unacceptable for me to "speak out of the house" and that it may never happen again. "What happens at home, *stays at home.*"

He managed to talk her out of her idea to shove me into an orphanage, and negotiated it down to grounding me, taking my pocket money away instead. This was the first time in my life I had ever been grounded.

I cried uncontrollably the entire time trying to explain that it was a misunderstanding – I wasn't trying to cause any trouble, but my stepmom kept shouting at me. The more she shouted, the less words I managed to get out of my mouth – dying from shock, inside. That was the first time I felt like I was a problem for them to have around – an inconvenience.

I was so devastated that I had disappointed my dad. I did everything I could to lay low and get back into their good books, but my stepmom moved on to the next step of her plan – getting me into a new school, hundreds of kilometers away from her.

Before I could blink, I traded in my green and orange school uniform for a dark blue one, in a little town called Bronkhorstspruit.

My stepmom's plan was coming to life. I was in boarding school, an hour-drive away from her.

I was eleven, and this was my new home, Monday to Friday. Those were the days before Facebook or email or a phone to keep in touch. I was shoved to the side, finding myself in isolation.

I had to start over at a new school in the middle of a term. There were very few kids in the boarding school – I don't think we were more than twenty. That first week I arrived, we all played outside after school one afternoon. We sat in a circle and each kid introduced themselves to me by name, followed by the reason they were sent to this boarding school. It turned out that the boarding school was explicitly for "problematic kids." Some kids had alcohol and smoking issues, others were there for stealing, and some just seemed depressed and misunderstood.

My self-esteem dropped tenfold when they shed light on my new circumstances. I didn't understand why I was grouped into the same category of kids who were smoking, drinking and stealing.

Evenings were so lonely. Us kids would talk and cry to each other about why our parents didn't want us home. I was mourning my mom's death - and missing my dad.

I only made one friend at school, she shared her lunch with me because being in boarding school – I didn't get a packed lunch for school. I was always hungry, and the food served at boarding school was either horrible, or never enough. That was what I hated the most. And to this day I am so angry that my dad could let that happen.

My stepmom's attempts at keeping me out of the house lasted a mere three months before the boarding school had to close down due to lack of funding.

I blinked and I had to turn my blue uniform in for a green one – the third school I had to start over at since my move to my dad just over a year ago at that point.

I was back at home, and my dad had just started working abroad again – away, six weeks at a time, and then back for only two, before leaving again.

My stepmom was devastated. Her plan of having me out of their hair backfired. All the changing of schools cost them big time – to the point that my dad had to work away for a better income. At least, that was her version of events – that it was my fault that my dad had to work abroad again.

She was stuck with me.

They bought me a bicycle. It wasn't a gift. It was their way of pushing me into independence at the age of twelve. My stepmom refused to drive me back and forth to school. I was to ride my bike – rain or shine. They bought me a big yellow rain coat to make sure of that. I was back to school and after school programs, 7am to 6pm Monday to Friday, this time, at Rietfontein-Noord.

I don't know what changed, but I made friends with every single person in my grade. I was determined to start enjoying my life. The more I was out of the house, the happier my stepmom was – so I started playing for the girls' softball and mini-cricket teams – which kept me busy and out of the house most Saturdays too. I was part of the school choir and our local church's youth evenings.

Somehow, I turned out to be friends with every single clique in my grade. I wasn't popular whatsoever- just welcome, everywhere.

Maybe the culture of the school was just more inviting, or maybe something in me changed, I will never know, but for the first time since my mom died, I felt sort of okay, sort of happy, sort of like I belonged.

It seemed as though my relationship with my stepmom was manageable – I was hardly home and when I was home, I minded my own business. With my dad being away for six weeks at a time, she would fall into depression. I saw her crying all the time. She starved herself for weeks on end at times. She always played the victim, sobbing at him "why are you doing this to me?"

International phone calls were expensive, so I wasn't given the opportunity to chat to my dad – it was mostly just for her.

Now that I am twenty-six, I look back at some of my failed romantic relationships. I see the patterns of codependency and how I mimicked her behavior of falling to pieces every time my partner wasn't giving me enough attention. It is a cycle I have broken, but one that I have to be conscious about at all times – in order not to fall into.

My stepmom and I eventually bonded over things like listening to Norah Jones in the car every time we went to go and fetch my dad at the airport. He would return with a pile of gifts. Expensive perfume and jewelry for her, and a dirt-cheap box of chocolates for me. The first thing they would do each time he returned home, was close their door and make up for lost time – she'd make sure I heard.

At that point, I was estranged from my dad, again.

The only time we interacted was around the TV when *the Springboks* or *the Sharks* played. I made it my mission to understand rugby and get to know the names of every player – so I could have something to talk about to my dad.

In all of the sports matches I played over those years, my dad showed up to one.

To this day, I don't think of the ones he didn't show up to, just the one he did show up to and how excited I was that he was there. It was everything to me.

All the matches I played without a parent on the sidelines to cheer me on – they taught me to stop waiting for a pat on a shoulder, it taught me to do things for myself, and for my own pride and enjoyment. Not that it was easy – but it served me in the long run.

STOCKHOLM SYNDROME

(Stockholm syndrome is a condition, which causes hostages to develop a psychological alliance with their captors as a survival strategy during captivity.)

Twelve years old, and two years into my new life in Pretoria – I felt like I grew up overnight and lived a few different lives since I left that small town of Hluhluwe behind, along with my innocence.

I had my dad back in my life – for a moment – and lost him again. Each time he went away to work in Uganda and Nigeria, six weeks at a time, I was left at the mercy of his wife, and every different version of herself she switched between quicker than I could change the radio station from Highveld Stereo to Jacaranda FM on our drive to her doctor's appointments.

She had major health issues.

I had seen the insides of 1 Military Hospital more times than I could count, but I didn't mind. I always loved the long drive there, because we passed the massive granite Voortrekker Monument – the only place in Pretoria I had memories with my mom – but I never said that out loud to my dad or stepmom. I just reminisced in silence.

Before my mom died, we visited the monument one December to commemorate "Gelofte Dag" (the day of the vow.) This was one of the high holidays we celebrated in the cult-religion – "The Chosen People" – my mom's family identified as. It is one of the many holidays I no longer celebrate.

The day we visited the monument, my mom and us three kids joined the crowd that stood assembled. We sung the old South African national anthem as the sun crossed the cenotaph. We sung the old anthem, Die Stem, that was only sung in Afrikaans, even though the new anthem, Nkosi Sikelel i'Africa, sung in

45

five languages, had taken its place. It is illegal - and considered disrespectful and racist to sing the old anthem, but our family and cult continued to sing it, rejecting democracy, publicly – back then.

In retrospect, I am always grateful for the one good thing that came from my mom's passing – the opportunity for me to get away from the cult and culture I grew up in, even though at that point, I was taken out of one bad situation and placed in another. Every light at the end of the tunnel was really the headlight of another oncoming train. But what did I know at that age? I was a sponge, soaking up my environment, drop by drop, whether I wanted to or not, just trying to keep my head above water.

Not only did I have memories of visiting the monument with my mom, but my dad had spent a lot of time there as a skydiving instructor, training soldiers for parachute jumps. Whenever we visited the military hospital, I tried my very best to block out reality – the hours spent next to my stepmom in waiting rooms – and imagined my dad walking the halls in his military uniform. I took so much pride in my dad's history in the military. It was his life, and I wanted to love that part of him as much as he did. I had no concept of the possible PTSD he might have been dealing with after serving Special Forces for thirty years, exiting the army as a Major. The only time he seemed truly happy, was when he got to speak about his days in the army. The only time he had something to teach me, it was about how to find your way without a map, by navigating the stars. Or licking your finger and holding it up in the air to tell which direction the wind is blowing, before starting a fire. Discussing code words I needed to remember in case of emergencies, or how to tell who to trust if a stranger came up to me and told me to go with them because my dad or stepmom was in an accident or something.

Even though I was tugged out of my mom's cult-religion, I was living my life in a "controlled environment." One where we only went on routine outings, one where I wasn't allowed to go out with friends or have many friends over. One where any unknown situation, was potentially a dangerous situation. The one lesson my dad drilled into me was "the only way not to get into a bad situation, is to avoid it in the first place."

My dad expected me to be independent, but he bubble-wrapped me at the same time.

I overheard him talking about a mission he was on, where new recruits were instructed to fast rope out of a helicopter while the enemy was attacking. They shot and killed each one of the young men making their way down the rope, and there was nothing he could do about it.

As much as my stepmom was his safe place, I don't think he knew how to function being back home, and back in society. He was always gathered and didn't seem out of place, but he showed no real connection or emotion toward me. When he was offered the opportunity to work in security abroad, away from us, I think it was his saving grace. He could go and live in a world where he could live the only way he knew how to function, not having to hide behind a mask. Being emotionally detached made him a bad father, but brilliant at his job in security.

On the rare occasion that my dad was home, he tried to make things pleasant, and he was usually in a good or neutral mood. He wanted me to start jogging with him where we lived in Waverley. We jogged down the road with all the mansions, it always put him in good mood. One afternoon, his mischievous side slipped through – and he egged me on to steal the neighborhood newspaper out of a couple of houses' mailboxes. We had a way of laughing about absolutely nothing. I can imagine how much fun him and my mom had as youngsters. He liked making jokes that weren't funny whatsoever – like when I asked him if it was Wednesday, he would reply "yes, the first Wednesday of the week!" I thought it was hilarious, and my stepmom would mutter out how stupid it was. I could listen to him play guitar for hours on end, but she would step into the room and say - "I think that's enough now, your guitar-playing is getting a little annoying. Can you put it away?" Something my mom would never have asked him to do.

I don't know what he liked in my stepmom so much. Maybe just the fact that she made his house a home. She sure knew how to kill his vibe. Whenever she got mad at him, she was verbally abusive toward him and threw her glass of wine into the wall if he managed to dodge it quick enough.

When we returned with a bunch of newspapers from our run, she was so disgusted and told us both how childish and disrespectful we acted in taking those. Rumor has it she beats him up too nowadays.

Back then, while my dad was away working abroad for weeks at a time, my stepmom was happy to have me around to help make her life a little easier. Whether that meant carrying the groceries to the car, pushing her around in a wheelchair around the mall, hanging the laundry, or climbing the steps to the milk shop to refill our milk containers – so that she didn't have to endure the physical-pain that came with these simple tasks – and I was happy to do it. I was happy to be there for her – in an attempt to win her and my dad over.

It began to feel like she could tolerate having me around the house. The drama seemed to have died down, and even though I wasn't brought up in a materialistically oriented way of life, I understood that my quality of life had increased, living with her and my dad. Our Mercedes Benz never died on the side of the road, our house was modern, clean and organized. I had a TV and a computer in my room. We traveled occasionally and dined out frequently. And if we ever had any financial issues – I never had to worry about it. It was never discussed in front of me. When they sent me away, I had a taste of boarding school life – the cold showers, and the shit-on-shingles they called food. I didn't want to go back to that. I did everything I could to stay in her good books so that I could stay home.

School and sport kept me so busy, and I was doing well. She let me attend the school dance and came to a few of my sports matches on Saturdays. Then she asked me to start calling her "mom." I couldn't.

We eventually settled on a mom-like-nickname because she insisted on it.

It felt like she wanted a second chance at raising a kid – seeing that she had lost her son and drove her daughter away.

When I started writing my memoir, I wrote down my intentions for telling my story. Very high on my list, I wrote that I wanted to write my story in a way that doesn't harm myself or anyone else I wrote about, but to simply to tell the story in its most truthful way as it happened. It has been hard to find the line between writing about what happened - and how I feel about what happened, but I am doing all I can to honor that intention I set. And with that, I wanted it to be known that I truly believe that some part of her, tried really hard to be a good parent to me, in the best way she knew how. Even when she didn't want me around, she tried to do right by my dad, her husband. So, I acknowledge that part too.

For a while, it seemed like her and I were building some sort of relationship. She took me ice-skating, and out for lunches at Spur, even clothes shopping – although she shopped at Edgars and Woolworths (the high-end stores) for herself - and bought my clothes at PEP-stores – the cheapest of the cheapest stores in South Africa. Even though it didn't bother me, I couldn't help but notice that it was hard for her to treat me like I was worth more than being bought the bare minimum.

She would do things like drive me around Danville, a poor, rundown neighborhood in Pretoria, known for drugs, violence and white squatter camps – telling me that I would end up there because I don't know how to be grateful. But she did it in a way where it was like, in passing. As if she was threatening me and talking down to me, but also doing it because she loved me.

She made me wear gypsy skirts with flowers and glitter, when all I wanted was my old Eminem shirt and a pair of shorts. I had to learn to let that go - and smile with every girly item she added to the cart – to avoid setting off her bad temper.

Every now and again she would throw a "big gesture" my way, like taking me to Sheet Street – wanting me to pick some new pink bedding for my room. I didn't know how to tell her in a nice way that her "nice gesture" was my worst nightmare. I kept circling the boys' section and picked out a blue bedding set with surfboards all over it. It turned into a massive issue for her that I didn't want pink bedding – I was not the type of kid to throw a tantrum, I more or less just said "don't buy me bedding, then. I'm really fine with what I already have." She ended up buying me the blue bedding with the surfboards, just to throw it in my face and tell me what an ungrateful little bitch I was, for days on end.

I often felt like I didn't create problems, I was just dragged into them and then blamed for something I didn't ask for or initiated.

The bedding issue turned into a nightmare. Before I knew it, she was yelling at me that I should get ready to move into an orphanage (again.) She'd make me return any gifts she ever gave me, like necklaces or my watch, throw my cupboard out on the floor saying that I needed to start packing my clothes because I was leaving.

This was the first time this happened while my dad was out of the country.

It started out with her, calmly asking me questions – trying to have a conversation about where I was at in my head. She kept trying to explain to me that I needed to find it within myself to make more space for her in my heart and life. I didn't understand what I was doing wrong. I couldn't understand why we were having this conversation, when all that happened was that I wanted blue bedding, and not pink.

After a long silence, she asked me a question I wasn't equipped to answer.

"Tell me the truth. What did someone say to you, or your mom say to you, to make you hate me so much? *Why* don't you love me?" She asked, as if she was really, really hurting.

"It's not that I hate you, I just don't really like you." I responded calmly – the only genuine thing that had come out of my mouth in months at that time.

She freaked out.

All hell broke loose.

This was the first time she started hitting me and pulling me around by my hair.

She jumped on the phone with orphanages after shouting at me that she wanted to drop me off to live on the street in Danville. She made me stay in my room while calling my dad. I was devastated and still had to go to school the next morning.

In the midst of all this, her and my dad had also cut off all communication between my siblings and I for months at that point – for my own protection, they justified. They were *always* fighting with my siblings over the phone, thinking random accusations up out of thin air. My siblings who were around eighteen at the time needed money for things like toiletries. My dad and stepmom would refuse to send them money saying, "No, what if they buy drugs with our hard earned money?" I overheard the phone conversations many times.

With my dad out of the country and communication between my siblings and me cut off, I was alone and mortified. I want to get sick as I am writing this – it is a hard place for me to go back to.

By some miracle, my dad managed to talk her down from her orphanage ideas over the phone – again.

She still took it upon herself to get to the bottom of "my issues" though – and interrogated me, and explained I needed to cooperate if I had any intention of not being kicked out to live in an orphanage anytime soon.

My stepmom caused a massive amount of damage between my brother and I – having me claim that he molested me – based on her venture of taking me to a psychologist who pulled out naked puppets I was supposed to blush at - but didn't blush at. That night, she had the bottle of Firstwatch Whisky next to her bed whilst telling me about all the times men abused her. She told me that she opened up to me, so it was my turn to tell her who violated me. I kept telling her I had nothing to say. I was also in trouble at school that day for writing a nasty letter with a group of girls, to another group of girls. My one and only time getting into trouble in school. She was convinced there was a reason that I was such a "damaged little girl" and continued asking me over and over who violated me. She was drunk and crying as she kept repeating the questions and her life story to me – all I kept thinking was – I have school tomorrow. Eventually I admitted to a game of truth or dare where a bunch of us kids did "I'll show you mine if you show me yours" – which I figured was a pretty standard thing and no big deal – where I came from. She made it a massive deal, made me write it all out, blamed it on my brother, and kept telling me to "add more details, add more details. No one is going to believe you if you don't add more details. There must be a reason you never told your mom about this. You must have been threatened with your life to keep quiet – write it."

She had the affidavit certified at the police station and told my dad about the whole thing only after he returned home from one of his six-week work trips. She told me to let her handle it alone with my dad and insisted I let her speak on my behalf while waiting in my bedroom.

She felt like she could finally justify why I was such a "damaged little girl" and told me I had another chance to try and be in their lives – "now that they knew what was wrong." She told me I had one last chance to improve my behavior now that she had helped me figure out what was wrong with me. If I didn't change my behavior – she was going to send me to an all-girls juvie school.

She manipulated me into believing I had to be forever grateful to her for saving me from my brother – who she never wanted me to see again, even though I wanted to see him and felt confused about the whole saga.

My stepmom decided to visit my dad in Uganda for six weeks when my school closed for summer break. They cut off all communication with my mom's family at that point - but reached out again to ask if they could ship me to Hluhluwe for the six weeks she wanted to go to Uganda. My uncle refused to have them put me on a bus to Hluhluwe and drove to Pretoria to pick me up himself.

I was prepped before-hand not to "talk out of the house" while I was visiting my uncle and family. My dad and stepmom went over the list of what I was - and wasn't allowed to discuss about my life in Pretoria - with my uncle and cousins. Like a parrot I regurgitated the words to my uncle and his family "I am so happy. I love my stepmom. They are so good to me." The worst part is, I lied so well, that I believed myself. My uncle and his family had their reservations about letting me return to Pretoria - but wanted me to go back to my dad if that's what made me happy. They didn't like that I was celebrating Christmas, and that I was no longer identifying as part of their cult-religion "The Chosen People" and everything that went with that. The fact that I was attending a school alongside people of color was hard for them.

My uncle and cousins were alarmed by what transpired regarding my brother – and disowned him from the family as per my stepmom's request. I wasn't allowed to see him during my visit in Hluhluwe.

During my visit, the "Boxing Day tsunamis" (2004 Indian Ocean earthquake and tsunamis) hit, killing around 230 000 people. My uncle and his family were convinced that it was a sign of the times. For the first time since my mom's passing, I remembered what I grew up with – always being told that "the end of the world was coming" and that God was going to come and take all his children away in the night to save them before hell broke loose on earth. Now that I had lived in the capital of the country, been in three different schools, and interacted with people from all walks of life, I couldn't help but think that my uncle and his family were being ridiculous for praying in fear for God to come and "take them away in their sleep" with the end of the world approaching.

I didn't want to go back to Pretoria where I was being mentally and physically abused, but I didn't want to stay with my uncle and his family where I had to live in a religious cult.

At the end of the day, I wanted to be wherever my dad was – so I fought to stay with my dad at all cost. No matter how hard I had to pretend to be happy around my stepmom. It was a price I was willing to pay, if I could keep my dad in my life.

TORTURE

(**Torture, noun:** *[from Latin tortus: to twist, to torment] is the act of deliberately inflicting severe physical or psychological suffering on someone by another as a punishment or in order to fulfill some desire of the torturer or force some action from the victim.)*

I must have been the only kid who was happy that the summer break was over. I started my final year of primary school and couldn't be happier to be back in the swing of things beside my friends, and away from my uncle's family telling me that the world was ending, and my dad and stepmom, literally making me wish that mine was.

I became infatuated with a boy for the first time – even though there was no chance of me ever gathering up enough guts to even say hello to him. The process of liking him and thinking about him was a much-needed escape from my harsh reality and day-to-day troubles. Thinking about him felt similar to the process of listening to music. My mind wandered and I daydreamed myself out of the warzone I learnt to survive in.

My dad was still working abroad. My stepmom had days that she was good to me, and days when she couldn't stand being in the same room as me. She decided to turn one half of the car garage into a space for me to hang out in, which was her way of keeping me out of the house whilst playing it off to be her awesome way of giving me a cool place to relax in. I don't know who was happier to have me out of the house 90% of the time – her or me. The space was equipped with a desk, the emerald green chairs, a hi-fi and a fridge. I spent every second I could in there, playing the Greenday album "American Idiot" that had just dropped – on repeat. I clung onto the little things I loved about living with my dad and stepmom – like being allowed to eat bacon and listen to American music – two things my uncle's cult doesn't allow.

My most treasured possessions were the two Avril Lavigne albums my dad and stepmom gifted me on birthdays, and the few things I had left that belonged to my mom – photo albums, diaries and her porcelain doll.

I wanted to dress like Avril, so badly. I bought a black eye pencil with my pocket money and tried to mimic Avril's make up. I got into so much trouble – they wanted to take my Avril albums away but let me off with a warning. They tried to give me everything they thought I needed, but when it came to what everyone else had, or got to do – they felt like it wasn't important for me to fit in. I didn't get to experiment with makeup or choose my own clothes. On Fridays – we were allowed to wear sneakers instead of black school shoes - I was the only girl in my grade who didn't have white Adidas sneakers. It was a big deal. Everybody noticed and pointed it out. No matter how I pleaded with my dad and stepmom, they wouldn't buy me a pair, or let me buy a pair with my own pocket money. To this day, I don't know what that was about. My dad got mad and told me that just because the rest of the world is doing something a certain way, doesn't mean that I have to follow or that the same rules apply to me. So, every Friday I rocked up at school with a red face and my adventure-like-shoes - my PEP-stores "tekkies."

They didn't allow me to go out to the movies with my friends on Friday nights, even if my friends' parents offered to drive me. As much as I can appreciate a parent wanting to teach their child that they don't have to always fit in with the crowd – it was pretty hard to always be the girl who was different. I was the girl who walked out of the house with her hair in a neat ponytail and thick Alice band on, only to loosen it up in the school bathroom mirror into a "normal" style once I arrived – so I wouldn't be made fun of. My friends lent me branded clothing whenever it was casual wear day at school, so I didn't have to feel like a loser – the only kid without Billabong or Roxy clothes.

Thank God for the friends I made at Rietfontein North Primary School. I didn't have to say out loud that I was being abused or ill treated at home, they could tell, and they were just there for me, giving me a place to belong. One of the cool kids – my friend Janine – cornered my stepmom one day after school, insisting she allow me to go to the movie theater with her that night. She turned on the charms and explained that her mom already bought the tickets. My stepmom agreed, but as soon as Janine left, she shouted at me for putting her in a corner. I kept on insisting that I had nothing to do with it – and I was telling the truth. But I was fine with whatever consequences were waiting for me the next day – I was sure it would be worth it, because I had my first ever kiss in the cinema that night. Janine didn't tell me she had a double-blind-date planned out for us. Let's just say I didn't get to see a lot of what actually happened in "A Lot Like Love" in the movie theater that night. I loved Janine forever for hooking me up, and making me feel like one of the cool kids for the first time in my life.

With the end of our final year in primary school approaching, the big question was which high school everyone was going to attend - Oos-Moot, or Waterkloof. But as fate would have it, I wasn't going to attend either. My life I was just settling into, was about to change – again. The friends I finally made – I had to say goodbye to soon.

My dad had a job opportunity come up in Botswana - one of South Africa's neighboring countries. A consulate offered him a permanent position as head of their security operations there. They were going to help us relocate and my dad wouldn't have to travel and be away from home anymore. My stepmom could have her husband back, and her home - they decided it would be best to put me back in boarding school for my high school career that was ahead of me.

As tough as my life was, trying to keep my stepmom happy and hardly ever seeing my dad - I loved Pretoria and the little things we did as a family that made me feel like things were okay. Like all the Sundays we drove to the Union Buildings after buying soft serve ice cream at McDonald's and just sitting there in the parking lot waiting for the sun to set over Pretoria. Or driving around in the car with the Sharks Rugby flag hanging out the window to celebrate their victory over the Blue Bulls on Saturdays. The routine and new "normal" I got used to – was about to be yet another memory.

My stepmom wanted to move to Botswana straight away although it was the middle of a school year. She arranged for me to live with somebody she knew – I can't remember if they were related or just friends. Her and my dad moved to Botswana and left me in Pretoria to finish the last couple of months of Primary school.

Apart from the fact that I was living with strangers, I appreciated being away from her, and having some sort of freedom to wear my hair how I wanted to, and rip my jeans without her knowing about it.

I celebrated my thirteenth birthday (the big one) – in a stranger's house. I started my period – in a stranger's house. All of this whilst they were setting up their new life in Botswana and enrolling me in a high school as far away from them as possible. My dad's job set us up in one of the wealthier suburbs of Botswana – Phakalane, situated a few kilometers from the capital city Gaborone. A lot of the expats living in the area put their kids in the local English schools – but my dad and stepmom decided I was going to continue my schooling career in an Afrikaans school in South Africa and only visit home on weekends.

That December over the summer break before high school started, I finally went to Botswana to get settled into our new home, only it wasn't a warm welcome waiting for me. More like a warm beating awaiting me.

The people I stayed with to finish grade seven, gave me pocket money now and again. My dad and stepmom left the money with them. It turned out that money was meant for emergencies only. I didn't ask for the money – I had no idea what the arrangement was.

My stepmom was so pissed about the few hundred Rand she left for emergencies that got spent, she demanded to know every single thing it was spent on. The school dance, airtime for my phone, sanitary pads – but she couldn't give a damn. This was just another reason for her to lay into me, and boy, did she.

They were extremely mad at me, and disappointed in me – for a mistake I didn't even know I was making. She kept hitting me in the face and screaming at me. Eventually my dad took me to the bathroom and beat my ass, back, and legs black and blue with a wooden clothes brush that left me sore with marks for a week.

I wasn't allowed out of my room unless it was to pee. When it was time for a meal, I was shouted at to come and get my plate and return to eat in my room.

They were pissed at me for joining a "dating" chat room on my phone while I was in Pretoria, and also pissed about my baggy pants that had torn between the legs. The cheap PEP-stores piece of crap tore when I got out of the pool one afternoon, but they insisted there had to be more to the story since the tear was between the legs.

They were characters. Hard work, man.

The more I tried to explain myself, the more they told me they were waiting for the truth. I didn't know what they wanted me to say. Eventually they took away every CD I owned and held my Avril albums over the fire pit, threatening to burn them "if I didn't start talking."

They wanted to know if I was smoking, using drugs, and if I broke my virginity. Meanwhile I was just a kid who couldn't scrape together the guts to tell my crush hello. A kid who wanted to be part of the nerd-club running the school newspaper.

They messed with my mind by excluding me from everything they were doing for a week, telling me to play with my old Barbie dolls in my room (like a normal little girl) whilst they were watching movies and having a swim and a barbecue outside.

When I needed roll on and pads for my period – she bought the cheapest possible products – and sometimes I even had to go without, because she didn't feel like spending money on me "after what I had done." Other times she would yell at me to stop talking to her when I wanted to ask for things like pads. I was smelly in the forty degrees Celsius Botswana heat, rolling up toilet paper to serve as sanitary pads. My self-esteem couldn't get any lower. I started lying awake at night, imagining what it would be like to run away – wondering if it would be worth it, and how I would go about it.

Then one day, she woke up, told me to stop hanging out in my room, and was more or less pleasant to be around, again.

She repeated this sort of treatment often in the years after that. One time after punishing me, she bought me a new throw pillow for my bed and asked "do you really think I'd buy you a pillow if I was serious about kicking you out of the house? Come and give me a hug."

She put me to work around the house, hanging curtains, unpacking boxes, watering the garden, and cleaning the pool. I felt grateful to be included in their life again – so to speak. Completely shell shocked after all the physical and mental abuse – I couldn't tell my ass from my face. I was so broken down. I just kept my head down and only spoke when I was spoken to.

Sometimes I wonder if there were things that I did, that were actually really bad. Things I might be blocking out, things I did that could warrant their behavior towards me. Did I really cause that much trouble? Was I really that hard to love and have around? I won't ever know their reasons, or what it was like for them to parent me – maybe it was really hard. But no matter how much I think about it – I can't ever justify what they did to me as a child. No matter which way I look at it, I've come to accept that I was a victim of abusers – and that was very hard to accept as an adult. Because that meant I had to accept how powerless I was. That meant I had to accept that they were bad people, bottom line. And I didn't want to think of it that way. I wanted to be able to fix whatever made them unhappy so that we could be a family again.

They gave me back my Avril Lavigne albums – I had a dance party with my CD player's volume on low – until I ran out of breath. The thought of running away kept creeping in, but I decided to keep trying to be the girl they wanted me to be, and hoped that things were going to get better again.

SOS

*(**SOS, noun**: an international code signal of extreme distress, used especially by ships at sea. An urgent appeal for help. Early 20th century: letters chosen as being easily transmitted and recognized in Morse code; by folk etymology an abbreviation of save our souls.)*

The only thing worse than walking into my fifth new school – was walking into it being a grade eight student. Being the youngest group in the school meant our first week of orientation included carrying the Grade twelve students' schoolbags around, over and above your own. Each school day consisted of seven different classes – which meant you had seven heavy handbooks in your bag – none of the schools I attended ever had lockers, so you kept all of your things with you for the day.

Back at the boarding school, the grade twelve students instructed us grade eights to buy and bring snacks for a party they were arranging as a welcome for us. We had to hand over the candy and any food we brought from home for the week, to them. We kept waiting and waiting as they told us they would call us when the party was set up. They never called us – they ate all our food.

That would have been a funny joke, only, the food that the boarding school served was nearly inedible or never enough – so having our own food and snacks stolen was really devastating.

My new school was located in Zeerust, a town situated in Ngaka Modiri Molema district North West Province, South Africa. It lies on the main road link between South Africa and Botswana.

I heard as much Tswana being spoken in the streets as I did Afrikaans.

Back in Botswana, my stepmom was insisting to move to a new house again as she was unhappy in the big white house with its massive yard and swimming pool. Just as we unpacked every last box, we started packing them again. We didn't move far, just a couple of blocks away, into a gorgeous brick house, more modern than the one before.

Almost every house in Botswana had an outside room on the property – a room for the help or domestic cleaner to stay in. The room was completely blocked off from the main house and more basic, not matching the modern house whatsoever. The room did not have an alarm system like the rest of the house either. Whenever I pissed my stepmom off – she kicked me out of my princess-pink room in the house, to sleep in the worn down outside-room.

Botswana was extremely boring. I kept myself busy with swimming in our pool or riding my bike in the streets. I had no friends at all, my dad and stepmom made no effort to take me to kids' clubs or anything of that sort to help me adjust to life in a new country.

If I was well behaved, my stepmom took me along to the Chinatown market where we always shopped for pirated DVDs. She allowed me to buy the very racy "My Prerogative" music DVD by Britney Spears but didn't allow me to buy Avril Lavigne's live concert DVD. I explained I needed to use the bathroom and went and bought it in the store next door in anyway. I hid the DVD under the clothes I was wearing and found a place to hide the disc in my room once we got home – between the pages of my Bible. Whenever she went to the grocery store, I waited till the automatic gate closed as she drove away and ran to the TV room to watch the DVD until I heard the gate open again. They found the DVD eventually, which got me into trouble, and a night in the outside-room, of course.

The drive between Botswana and my school in Zeersust was two hours each way. I was always one of the last kids to be picked up from school on a Friday afternoon and one of the first kids to be dropped back off on a Sunday afternoon. There was no lunch or dinner served on Sundays, and no breakfast served on Monday mornings. I had to pack myself something to eat from home.

The boarding school didn't have a lot of students, and a lot of us were a bunch of weirdos. One girl was into studying Satanism, with books about rituals. Other girls were Jesus freaks, always praying for God to "protect us in this haunted hostel". My one friends' mom was an alcoholic, and the other one's parents beat her black and blue – like mine did me.

At school - I was back to being extremely introverted again, like I was when I attended that first school in Pretoria – not speaking to anyone and walking the school grounds alone, minding my own business. I fell behind in class because I was too embarrassed to ask for help, having a low self-esteem and always having massive wet spots under my arms because my stepmom wouldn't buy me deodorant, which also made me hesitant to play sports even though I loved hockey so much.

In the hostel, I at least got on with a few of the girls in my hall. Nearly all of them were smokers, and even though I wanted nothing to do with anyone who smoked – I had a choice of staying friends with them or having no friends at all. I was never tempted to smoke – mostly because I felt that my mom's smoking killed her faster when she wouldn't quit after being diagnosed with cancer. So saying no to a cigarette was never hard for me. I had a grudge against them.

I also liked hanging out with the kids who smoked after school, because they were always playing music on their phones – and I wanted to be anywhere the music was. Mattafix's "Big City Life" and Fort Minor's "Where'd You Go" were the two big songs then. One day after school, my friends dragged me along to one of the girls in our grades' houses. She was one of the prettiest girls in school. Rumor had it, she had a baby and left it in the trash – I have no idea if that happened, but I loved her music selection. That's all I cared about We listened to music through massive speakers while chilling in her house.

Visiting kids outside of the hostel wasn't allowed, this was one of the only two times I snuck out of the hostel with my friends.

On the subject of rumors – rumor had it, I was the only grade eight girl who hadn't been fingered by a particular guy in the eleventh grade. I wasn't exactly bothered about it, but my friends kept making fun of me for "being such a nun."

My life in Botswana started feeling like a place I just visited occasionally, and my life in the Zeerust hostel felt like home – my real life. I spent 80% of my life there at that stage – it was inevitable that I was going to adjust to my surroundings. Even though I wasn't going out and looking to cause trouble, I was going to run into it eventually under the given circumstances, and the community I was in.

The general feeling that I got in the town was that parents gave their kids more room to develop their own identity. There were a couple of gay teens, males and females, and they were accepted for who they were by the other kids. Girls dressed however they wanted to and always wore makeup. There was always a party going on, and someone always had alcohol at a sports event or in the hostel. I felt like I was back in Hluhluwe and allowed to develop my own identity. I stated wearing makeup too and let one of my friends pluck my eyebrows. I didn't go the route of getting fingered by the grade eleven guy, instead I loved shower time in the girls' bathroom and occasionally made out with one of my girl-friends when she wanted to "practice her kissing skills."

I started feeling cool. Along with that newfound courage I started acting out and breaking rules. We snuck out of the hostel one day after I found a screwdriver and took the screws out of the window railings of an unoccupied room. We walked to a guy's house in the dead of night and got drunk there – apart from the one New Year's my stepmom made me drink Archers at age eleven – this was my first time being drunk. I wasn't too hyped about the drinking or whether or not I was going to make out with anyone – which I didn't – all I could care about was that there was a piano in their house. I was a real mood killer when I kept insisting that they should turn the music down so I could show off my piano skills. Probably the reason nobody made out with me! We walked back to the hostel before daybreak, drunk and disoriented. Marcel and I locked ourselves in my room, hungover and trying to skip school. The hostel staff noticed we didn't show to breakfast and kept banging on my door to let them in, but I think they just gave up eventually. When we had to face them later that day, we put it down to oversleeping and I don't remember getting into a lot of trouble over it.

There's a chance they gave my dad and stepmom a call, I don't know, but not long after that, my stepmom didn't feel like she wanted me home over weekends. My dad called me to say I was to stay in the hostel over the weekends for the time being. Nobody was allowed to stay in the hostel over weekends. He knew that, and I reminded him, but all he could say was – "what do you want me to do? Your stepmom doesn't want you home, so I am in a difficult position. Just make it work."

I had no other option but to stay in the hostel, against the rules. No food was served over the weekends, but at least I had warm water in the shower because I was the only one there. One Friday, my friend's parents were late to pick him up, and we were both starving. It was late in the afternoon and the last time we ate was around 7am when breakfast – the last meal for the weekend - was served. We walked to the local grocery store even though we had no money. He told me to wait outside, I was confused but did as he said. A couple of minutes later he walked out with two sausage roll pies he stole from the bakery, one for each of us. I thought that was one of the nicest things someone had ever done for me.

On Friday afternoons, I watched my friends' parents come and pick them up to go home for the weekend, one after the other, until I was the only one left – and stayed there alone for the weekend. The noisy hostel hallways died down, like someone turning the radio off. No TV, no computer, no cell phone. Just a payphone at the entrance of the building, that I wished would ring with my dad on the other end of the line, calling to let me know he was on his way to come and pick me up – but not a peep out of the damn thing. Sometimes I picked the phone up off the hook and put it by my ear, just to make sure that it was working.

I sat in the big empty bathroom - its rows of empty showers, my audience. The echo bouncing between those walls made my voice sound loud and heavenly. I sang every song I could possibly remember, to pass the hours late into the night, and it put some sort of smile on my face, for a while.

Back in my room, I started writing and drawing – what I wrote and drew I can't remember. I left the papers scattered on my desk between my schoolbooks – I wasn't very organized. As luck would have it, I had my period, and a limited amount of pads that weekend. Sometimes I'd get blood on my pants or bed sheets because I ran out of supplies, and the folded toilet paper in my panties could only hold so much liquid. Sometimes I washed my stained clothes in the basin, and sometimes I put them in my suitcase instead – left them there out of laziness and low self-esteem.

Friday blurred into Saturday and Saturday blurred into Sunday – the isolation depressed me to the core. Finally - some girls started arriving back at the hostel Sunday night, and I started feeling better again, knowing it's back to school and three meals a day on Monday.

One of the hostel staff picked up that I wasn't going home over weekends and called my dad to remind him that no one was allowed to stay in over weekends. My dad picked me up that Friday. Nothing seemed wrong in our car ride back to

Botswana, but when I arrived home, my stepmom raised hell from the moment I walked in. She got a new puppy, a silver dapple dachshund. She yelled that I wasn't allowed near it.

She threw my school bag out onto the dining room table, and my clothes out of my suitcase onto the cement outside, through the backdoor of the kitchen.

She went through the papers that came out of my school bag, and my dad shouted at me for how disorganized my bag was. They read through the poems I wrote and things I drew, she went to her bedroom and came back with one of my dad's belts. She started hitting me in the face with it.

I don't know if I wrote anything about her in the poems – but I think it's possible, and what might have outraged her.

"I knew it!" She shouted, and then demanded I came with to go through my clothes with her where they lay outside under the laundry line on the cement.

"Smoke! I smell smoke on these clothes!!" She started yelling. Throughout the abuse of the years, I never reacted or put up a fight. But when she accused me of smoking, I got really angry and shouted back at her "I *don't* smoke!"

I was shaking from anger and shock, feeling like I was having an out of body experience, almost in complete denial of what I was experiencing, because it felt like a truck hit me. Eventually she stopped swinging the belt at my face and legs.

She found my blood-stained panties and pants, as well as a used pad between my clothes. She freaked out, telling me how dirty and gross I was and that I wasn't allowed to wash any of my clothes in the laundry machine from now on. She made me wash my mountain of laundry in the outdoor room's bathtub. The water soaked into the clothes making them heavy, my arms went numb from the labor of picking the clothes up out of the water and washing them by hand, and then squeezing them dry before hanging it on the line outside.

I wasn't allowed back into the house, I had to stay in the outside room for the weekend. Whenever they went out, she slammed the kitchen backdoor and locked it so that I had no access to the house – that included no access to food.

At some point during the weekend, my dad left a little chocolate on my pillow when I wasn't looking. He was obviously feeling sorry for me and didn't know what to do. He came to speak with me in the outdoor room, telling me to keep what he was about to say between him and I. He asked me to try harder to stay out of trouble, and out of my stepmom's way, and explained that she had her own issues but that I would be fine if I just did as she said. I said I'd be better, but I was so sad and felt betrayed by my own dad when he defended her behavior.

When I was back at the hostel, my dad called to let me know that I couldn't come back home over the weekend again. He arranged for somebody to come and give me fifty Rand to buy food for the weekend. At that point, I preferred the isolation of staying at the hostel alone on the weekend, over being home in anyway.

My dad's instructions were clear, I was to stay in the hostel and wasn't allowed to visit any of my friends or go home with them for the weekend.

That following week, some girls and I decided that we just about had it with the shit-on-a-shingle-excuse-of-food that was being served at the hostel kitchen. We were set on taking matters into our own hands and made our way down to the local grocery store where we filled our jacket pockets and backpack with food and snacks and walked out without paying. We did this a couple of times more and felt so invincible that we moved on to the clothing store and stole clothes too. I was loading up for the weekend ahead because my dad didn't manage to get money to me.

A couple of days later, my friends went back to town to steal more clothes, but I didn't go with them. That was the day they were caught and put into the back of a police van to the police station. They ratted me out for joining them in previous ventures, and the grocery store pulled footage of us in the act.

My dad was called and had to drive from Botswana to come and see me and the school headmaster, as well as the owners of the stores. He pleaded with them not to press charges, for the sake of my future, as well as his reputation in the security industry. He was so disappointed in me, and I was so embarrassed.

Arguing that he should not have put me in that position of being without food over weekends – wasn't relevant. I just prepared myself for the hiding of my life, but he didn't take me to my hostel room to hit me - what he did was worse. When we drove from the stores back to the hostel, he yelled at me to get out of the car and drove off without saying goodbye.

I walked to my bed, crawled into a fetal position and sobbed my eyes out, devastated that I disappointed my dad to the point that he had no interest in even saying goodbye to me. I felt like a piece of trash that he threw out of the car window at a hundred miles per hour.

Some of the older girls I was friends with came to try and talk to me and comfort me, but I was inconsolable. I was fourteen and experiencing what it felt like to want to take my own life for the first time. I couldn't get myself to move out of the fetal position but kept imagining walking to the fourth floor of the hostel and jumping out the window. I pictured myself facedown, lifeless on the lawn, and wondered if my dad would finally take responsibility for the ways he neglected me, if he could see his own daughter, dead.

CHILDLINE

(**Neglect, verb**: *fail to care for properly. Child neglect is the ongoing failure to meet a child's basic needs and is the most common form of child abuse. A child may be left hungry or dirty, without adequate clothing, shelter, supervision, medical or health care. A child may be put in danger or not protected from physical or emotional harm.*)

I had the hostel to myself again that weekend. By some miracle, my sister called the payphone, and I answered. We hadn't been in contact before that because my dad and stepmom forbid them to contact me and vice versa. My sister knew that something was wrong, and it didn't take long for me to break down over the phone and spill the details of what was going on. She made me write down the number for Childline, a non-profit organization that works to protect children from violence and further the culture of children's rights in South Africa. Although I didn't want to go through with calling them, she made me promise.

I made the call. I told them about all the times I was left in the hostel without food or supervision, and about the physical abuse. I obviously failed to tell them that I was busted for shoplifting the week before.

The idea of them stepping in and reaching out to my dad, terrified me. I would much rather have put up with the abuse than create more trouble, more reasons for them to lash out at me. It took everything in me to make that call.

After my dad and stepmom questioned and shouted at me for hours, they left me home in Botswana for the weekend, as they made their way to South Africa to meet with Childline. I have no idea what transpired in their meeting – and whether or not it even happened. No one from Childline came to check on me or follow up to see if I was actually okay – my guess is they had no jurisdiction to do so since my home address was in Botswana. Because my cries weren't heard, I hesitated to speak up ever again.

When my dad and stepmom returned to Botswana, I was told that I was changing schools, again. I didn't get to say goodbye to my friends in Zeerust, but neither did I have to look my peers in the eye, embarrassed and forever labeled as one of the girls who got caught shoplifting. In retrospect, taking me out of that school was one of the best things my dad could have done for me whether he intentionally acted in my interest or not.

"Botswana doesn't have laws against corporal punishment. You can call the police here until you're blue in the face, but they will encourage me to hit you in this country, so try!" She laughed before she started the slapping, and scratching. Pulling me around by my hair and slamming her fists into the top of my head as I ducked - taking it until she had enough and walked away.

While writing this, I started the process of getting access to the old case files. The folks at Childline have been very helpful and are trying to get to the bottom of why I wasn't aided.

"Children who are abused don't hate their parents, they hate themselves." – unknown.

SURRENDER

(**Surrender, verb**: *cease resistance to an enemy or opponent and submit to their authority. Synonyms: give in, submit, back down, cave in, lay down one's arms, raise/show the white flag, throw in the towel, accept defeat.*)

"What is that glossy greenness in the sausage, does yours have it too?" I asked the person next to me as I cut further into my food, dissecting it with my fork.

"Oh my god, there's a dead fly in my sausage!" I exclaimed, trying not to throw my last few bites back up in my plate.

That was my warm welcome to school number six. High school Lichtenburg. Despite the fly in my sausage, the overall quality of food was significantly better than what I had in Zeerust – but I was never able to eat a meal at my new school without checking it for flies first.

The girls at this school were cool kids, but prim and proper, with hair always done neatly, and they all took themselves quite seriously. Everyone was excellent at something – some in sports, others in academics, and others in arts and culture.

No one was smoking, and everyone was either a virgin – or lied about being one. The girls at this school judged each other harshly when it came to how far you were willing to go with your boyfriend. Practicing Christianity was a big part of our day – we started each morning in prayer after singing worship songs during assembly, and there was a group who got together in a classroom to pray during recess – open for anyone to join, supervised by the school's life coach and the school's ten students who were leaders for the UCSA (Unifying Christian Student Association).

It was a contrast from my previous school – I had to reel in the ghetto.

Whatever rebellious behavior I developed in Zeerust, had to go. My dad signed me up for higher math, accounting, business class and economics, and forbid me from taking music as a class.

Whenever I was upset about something my dad did for me that I couldn't understand – like putting me in hostels away from home or deciding which classes I was to take – he would say "can't you see I am doing this because I want the best for you?" I always had to read between the lines with my dad, I always had to accept that he was hurting me because he loved me. Sending me away to a school away from home was his way of making sure that I didn't have to suffer abuse from his wife every day of the week – it was his only logical solution. As an adult, I had to break the habit of trying to find the good in things every time somebody hurt me, I had to break the habit of trying to read between the lines when someone treated me like shit, I never took people's actions at face value. Instead I kept thinking they secretly cared for me – like my dad told me he did every time he hurt me. I still struggle breaking this thinking pattern.

My dad had a certain type of future planned out for me when he tried to steer me in the direction of laying a foundation for a career in business and economics. I'm sure he thought he was doing what was best for me, but it killed me when I wasn't allowed to study music.

As bitter of a pill that was to swallow, I adapted very quickly, and very well to my new community. Just like my time at Rietfontein North - I was friends with every clique although I was one of the least popular girls. Mostly unpopular because I still had sweat patches under my arms and was almost always red in the face because I was constantly embarrassed for existing, and suffering from low self-esteem. While the other girls were out playing sports in the afternoon, I could often be found writing poems or short stories alone in my room. One night my roommate Elisna asked me to read her what I was working on. I had written out scenes of what I imagined my future life would look like – in this particular scene I was a flight attendant working on the private plane jetting the Springbok rugby team around the globe. I thought I'd work for them one day. I was always obsessed with rugby, mostly because watching matches with my dad around the TV was one of the only things that united us as a family. I also read Springbok coach Jake White's biography in the hopes of having something to talk with my dad about.

So while other girls were worrying about boys, I was worrying about finding a way to work for the Springboks one day – if for no other reasons than to make my dad proud and work for my heroes. Elisna never laughed at my stories, she could never wait for me to write more.

My bed was always the only one in the room that had a massive mess underneath it, and I was usually the last person to get up in the morning. Although, for the first time in a while, my life was just mellow and nothing was wrong, but I still felt like something was missing.

My life changed in a flash one night when I was at the weekly UCSA gathering, and the councilor announced at the end of the event that they were looking for someone who could play an instrument to relieve the full time musicians from time to time. Soon enough I was playing guitar at the smaller gatherings, leading the worship songs before and after sermons. Never before in my life had I felt that feeling of having a purpose until then. My faith grew, and so did my circle of friends. Before I knew it, I was voted to be one of the school's ten students who were leaders for the UCSA – which was seen as a big deal and a privilege by other students. The next year, my peers also voted me hall leader in the hostel.

I went home both times, excited with the massive news. But my dad and stepmom couldn't care less, I can still hear her voice in my head and the words she said while laughing; "do they all know they made a mistake by voting *you* leader of *anything*?" and that was the end of that conversation.

I took part in our school musical "Fame", and although I was just part of the choir singing in the background, I made sure to get myself noticed during rehearsals. Everyone was on a break and we sat in a group on the lawn. There was a guitar lying around so I grabbed it and asked the group what they wanted me to play. "What's your favorite song?" I asked the nearest person to me. I was introverted in every situation apart from when I had a guitar in my hand. I play music by ear which means I am able to play any song that I know, without researching the chords or having to read music. My fingers just know where to go. People kept throwing more and more song requests and I played them one after the other and had everybody sing along. The music teacher in charge of the play took a liking to me and wanted to know why on earth I wasn't in her class, studying music as a subject.

"My dad wants me to take economics. He says music isn't a career, ma'am."

I was failing my economics class despite my efforts of trying to understand

and learn – but I had less than no idea on what the subject was about, how any of it fit together, and why the things I was learning about, even mattered in life.

The music teacher managed to convince my dad to let me swap classes when I failed economics for a second semester. I was in heaven. I got to study music theory and learn about the history of Bach and Mozart for the first time.

Things were finally looking up for me – I found joy in music and Christianity and felt invincible.

Each time my stepmom had a meltdown, I literally turned the other cheek. I felt at peace inside no matter what she did. I had God in my life, and I believed he had a plan for my future.

The better I did in school and behavior-wise, the more intense her emotional abuse toward me became. She sent me to the Valentine's Day ball in a twenty Rand ($2) dress from China town, while all my friend's moms had formal gowns made for them. She also demanded to take the photo albums and diaries I had which belonged to my mom, because she still felt personally offended by my mom's belongings being in her house – even though they were out of sight. She told me to pick one thing to keep of my mom's, so I chose to keep her porcelain doll on my dresser as she took everything else away. She never gave me back my mom's belongings that she took away.

Sometimes I would be watering the garden and she would call me inside where she sat on the emerald green chairs watching TV. She switched the TV off and made me stand in front of her while she screamed at me out of nowhere, telling me that I am a "snotkop kind wat niks weet nie." (a retarded snot-head child) who will never amount to anything. She also made it known that they won't fund my tertiary education if I had any interest in going to college or university. "You're a fuck up! When you hit eighteen, you're out of my house" she used to say.

Each time that line came out, my tears ran. My body always went into a certain type of shock when she attacked me. As a result of that anxiety she instilled in me, I failed to stand up for myself in everyday situations at school, to the point that I couldn't get a word out to state my case or defend myself even if I tried.

In our house, drama was always one whisky away, no matter how good I tried to be, or how much I tried to alter myself to appease her.

Because of my love for music, I read every CD booklet I could get my hands on, from cover to cover, often copying the lyrics into the back of my school books by hand. Studying them, memorizing them, looking for patterns in them.

I became very good at English because of my obsession with words and my interest in learning how to express myself in a language other than my mother tongue - Afrikaans. All my classes were taught in Afrikaans, so improving my English took time. I ended up being the top student in my English class and valued the language deeply because for me, it was the ticket to being able to write and sing in English one day.

Despite the drama back home, I was focused and determined at school, and internally.

I somehow managed to separate the two worlds from each other.

There were times I felt like my dad tried to be part of my life and be good to me, but in reality, our relationship was non-existent.

The school break was coming up and I was very disinterested in being home for a couple of weeks – for obvious reasons. Around that time, my sister fell pregnant. The fact that she wasn't married was unforgivable to my dad and stepmom. They were highly embarrassed and made it clear to her that she was on her own. They even changed my cell phone number so that she couldn't be in contact with me. They sat me down to tell me about my sister's pregnancy and my stepmom laughed, "when she told us she had important news to share, I immediately thought she was going to tell us that she had HIV Aids."

It upset me a lot that I wasn't allowed to speak to my sister.

My stepmom decided that we were going to vacation in Namibia for a week or so, and also invited her cousin along. The road trip was fifteen hours long each way – I knew every Theuns Jordaan, Dozi and Bok van Blerk song by heart by the time we arrived in the picture-perfect town of Swakopmund. After driving through only desert for hours on end, we met the wild Atlantic-ocean, almost abruptly. I couldn't stop staring at the postcards in the gift shops, with their aerial view shots of Swakopmund. Like a line had been drawn down the middle of the page, desert on the left, and ocean on the right. No in between.

We traveled north from town to town on the Skeleton coast. Stopping at places like Walvis Bay and Henties Bay but didn't go up far enough to explore the many shipwrecks further north. In the days before engine-powered ships and boats, it was possible to get ashore through the surf but impossible to launch from the shore. The only way out was by going through wetland, dominated by grasses and reeds, hundreds of miles long and only accessible via a hot and arid desert.

The Namibian Bushmen called the region "The Land God Made in Anger," while Portuguese sailors once referred to it as "The Gates of Hell." But despite the coast's haunting labels - the dense fog hanging over the water, seeping in between the German Architecture on land, made me feel calm. Everything was just so quiet, I liked that.

My dad took me quad biking in the dunes one morning, where we sped past carcasses far into the red-brown sea of sand that I wished we got lost in, never having to return to life as I knew it. I never got to do anything alone with my dad, we were having the adventure of our lives out there, away from my stepmom.

I was on my best behavior but still got shouted at by her, for any excuse. I was a picky eater, so when we dined out, she got pissed at me for ordering kid's meals or French fries, and not wanting to try the local cuisines. She told me with much disgust how uncultured I was – at age fifteen when I didn't even know what that meant.

Back at the accommodation, her cousin and I were relaxing in the bedroom when suddenly we heard my stepmom throwing things and shouting at my dad, accusing him of flirting and trying to sleep with her cousin. It was so awkward.

Her cousin took me out of the house to Kristall Galarie – a crystal gallery in Swakopmund. I was so used to the drama by now, that it was normal to me. In 2018, my stepmom's cousin reached out to me after all those years, to tell me that she was sorry for never stepping in when she could so clearly see that my stepmom was abusive towards me. She recalled things I had long forgotten – telling me over WhatsApp that she could never get the image out of her head of my stepmom making a scene when one of my shoes broke and she needed to buy me new ones. She apparently threw the new pair of shoes at me as she walked out of the store after buying them – I blocked that out and probably so many other bad memories.

The whole vacation turned sour when my stepmom asked me where my watch was that they got me for Christmas. I lied and said I left it at home, even though I knew it was missing. She told me I better hope that it is home when we return because if it's not – she was going to beat the crap out of me. For the entire remainder of the trip I died from anxiety inside, knowing what was lying ahead for me when the vacation was over.

As my dad shut the engine off as we parked the car when we got home, she sent me straight to my room to go and find my watch and bring it to her. I turned my room upside down, praying for a miracle – but the watch was nowhere to be found. I couldn't help but wonder if it was a set-up, if maybe she was the one who took it, just so she could hit me again. Regardless, she was making a massive deal out of something minor; the world was coming to an end due to the fact that my watch was missing. All hell broke loose.

She threw my cupboard out onto the floor and told me to start packing because she was kicking me out of the house. By now this was standard procedure, but that feeling of being shell-shocked never went away each time she did this to me. She grabbed ahold of my hair and tugged me around by it, she threw me around the room and hit me in the face, as she did before. My dad stood in the hallway looking at what was happening. He did nothing.

I sobbed and begged for mercy, but she grabbed hold of my mother's porcelain doll and broke it over my head before storming out with any valuable belongings she ever gifted me.

All I kept thinking was that God was with me, I had nothing to fear. I trusted him with my life and told myself I knew he would provide for me if she really kicked me out and put me in an orphanage this time. I could even picture myself spreading the word of God amongst children who went through the same as I did when I got to the orphanage. And if God failed me, my music would save me. If I could just get myself to one of the big music festivals, I would gate crash the parties till I found one of the bands who would let me go on the road with them as their apprentice, and *one day* I would get my shot to show the world what I was made of.

My mind was racing with irrational thoughts.

But in that moment of chaos, I came to the conclusion that I would be better off in an orphanage, so I took the suitcase and packed all my clothes through all my tears, my body shaking.

She burst in and threw the clothes out of the suitcase onto the floor. "You arrived at my house with your shit in black refuse bags, and that is how you will leave!"

So, I walked to the kitchen to get the black refuse bags and started packing again.

In that moment, I saw myself clearly. It was like the spiritual awakening I experienced when I saw my mom's body the day she died. I was conscious about who I was, where I was, what my purpose is, and where I was heading, even though I had no map of how to get there.

After taking the abuse for five years, the penny dropped, and I understood so clearly that I needed to get away from her and my dad. For the first time, I decided that I didn't deserve the abuse, for the first time, I stopped hating myself for not being good enough for her. I had an epiphany that what was happening had everything to do with her, and nothing to do with me.

In that moment, I wasn't sad about it, I wasn't afraid, I felt like the only thing harder than walking away from the abuse, would have been staying.

My dad came in to talk to me. I was packing frantically, and he couldn't get my attention. For the first time he seemed freaked out about how she treated me. His solution was also that I had to move out of the house because it would be better for my well-being – and even though he seemed genuinely concerned for me, what he said, only sounded to me like he was picking her over me. At that point I couldn't care about what he had to say. It was all just noise to me, it was like I couldn't hear or take anything in.

I was fifteen and life as I knew it, was about to change for good – I was aware of that. I chose that. I chose that it would be the last time she ever had the opportunity to abuse me. I chose it, even though I was unsure how much it was going to cost me, unsure about where I was going next.

I chose to surrender, not to her, but to the need I felt to please her, the monster that ate me alive every time I tried to be my best for her, only to be told that it was still not good enough. I admitted defeat, accepted that she was a war I was never going to win – and in doing so, I felt at peace in my skin, there and then.

I zipped the last bag up and threw it over my shoulder. I looked back at that picture perfect all-pink room as I walked out of it and said to myself, I never liked it anyway. I hugged my cat goodbye and would have her ginger fur all over my clothes one last time.

I got into the silver Merc and kept quiet, waiting for my dad to say something during the forty-minute drive to the border, but he said nothing.

That was the last time my dad drove me from Phakalani where we lived, 10 minutes outside of Gabarone, the capital of Botswana, over to the border where I hitched a ride with other scholars making their way back to Lichtenburg for the school week ahead. "Just lay low for a couple of months" he told me as I was about to get into the other people's car. "Keep going to school and when the hostel closes over the weekend, find a friend to stay with. Your stepmom just needs time to cool down, I will work it out and you can come back home in a couple of weeks. I will call you when you can come back home again."

But he never called.

YOU NEVER KNOW YOUR LUCK IN A BIG CITY
Poetry & Prose

I used to think that New York is like a beautiful blonde Russian playboy bunny.

Nice to look at.

Hard to have a conversation with.

Seductive by nature, and bitchy as fuck if you dare smile at it, thinking for a moment that you were cool enough to try your luck with it.

And I have been trying my luck with this juicy, Big Apple.

And some bites have been more poisonous than others.

And the more I got rejected, the less I tried my luck.

And I tried. I tried so hard to drown out my stepmother's voice in my head, but I can hear it, how she used to say "you never know your luck in a big city!" while scratching out numbers on a LOTTO card in Pretoria, her only reference to a 'big city' & then getting drunk on a cheap bottle of Firstwatch Whisky right before telling me how fucked up I am, at the tender age of twelve.

It took me until twenty-three to look her up on the internet, find her Twitter account and see her vomit her racist political views in broken English to her 16 followers.

I laughed at the ten years I spent believing her, when she told me that something was wrong with me. With ME!

And I laughed because her uneducated opinions on Twitter sounded exactly like her uneducated opinions of me.

And for the first time I understood the saying "take it where it comes from."

And for the first time in my life I realized that I can never take anything someone has to say, personally, ever again.

And for the first time I saw, that people will see you as they see themselves, and you ought to ignore anyone's opinion of you.

And now, not one ounce of my self-worth comes from anyone's opinion of me.

So, I stand before New York today, the city that has slapped me in the face a few times, the way her uneducated, angry fists used to. And I'm looking this city in the eye with a smirky smile on my face. Sipping on my cup of freshly squeezed APPLE juice, saying, go ahead, try your luck, New York. You hit like a girl.

NO MAN'S LAND

*(**No Man's Land, noun:** an area or land that is unowned, unclaimed, uninhabited, undesirable or under dispute between parties or opposing armies who leave it unoccupied due to fear or uncertainty.)*

Fifteen, and waiting for a call from my dad that wouldn't come, I walked into school one morning to find our entire class devastated after one of the boys got ahold of his dad's shotgun and committed suicide. I wasn't friends with the boy, and it being my sixth school, I couldn't relate to the rest of the class who grew up with him and were mourning his death. But I felt closer to this boy than anyone would understand. I envied his bravery for pulling the trigger, I envied the attention he got for the statement he made, the point he drove across that depression is real, that children's feelings are real and should be paid attention to. I wished that my dad could walk the hallways of my school that day, sit in math class with me to witness how no one knew how to function or carry on. I wished he could see the tissue boxes being emptied around me, I wish he had to fight the lump in his throat, to the sound of someone weeping, unable to hold the tears back during the moment of silence for the boy during assembly.

If my dad could just see that he drove me to the point of wanting to find a shotgun and pull the trigger against my own temple too. If my dad could just ask himself if he would be half as devastated as my peers if it was his daughter that died that day.

Even though it had been weeks since I had been home, weeks since I last heard from my dad – I couldn't quite decide if I was hoping for him to call me or not. Part of me kept thinking up fairytale endings of my dad showing up at school to bring me home to a house where he had told my stepmom to leave. The other part of me hated him and found that I felt safer since I was away from them both, I kind of preferred my newfound freedom. Any other kid who had been kicked out of the house would have been having sleepless nights I'm sure, but not me - I slept well for the first time in five years.

My friends knew I couldn't relate to their pain of losing their friend, but back at the hostel I gathered everyone around in the hallway, to give them the one thing that I knew would have helped me to feel better in a situation like that – music. The only thing I felt, understood me.

We sat down on the wooden floor in the long hallway, and I played the boy's favorite song on the guitar for us all to sing along to – The Dixie Chicks' "Traveling Soldier." It was as special to me as it was to them – being able to find common ground through a song and deal with the tragedy through the language that is music. I was trying to bring some sort of comfort and healing to the situation – while selfishly challenging myself to learn how to work an audience, learning what it felt like to have a couple dozen eyes glued to me for three and a half minutes, and liking it. Feeling like I finally found my superpower.

I was lucky to have a couple of very close friends in Lichtenburg. My friends took turns to have me over for the weekends while I was hanging in limbo, not knowing if my dad was ever going to tell me if I was allowed to come back home.

My friends and their families took care of me, without making me feel like it was an issue at all to do my laundry, feed me, drive me around, have me in their homes a couple of days at a time.

It was weird to spend so much time in other people's houses and have them do things for me that my dad was supposed to do, but I did my best not to show that I felt out of place. For as long as someone was giving me a place to feel safe in, I felt like I had no right to dwell in my feelings of abandonment, no right to question these families' kindness, question why they even gave a damn to help me out.

I told myself that in return for their kindness, it was my own responsibility to keep doing well in school and sport and keep my behavior in check. I told myself that I had no right to fall apart, when there were people around me, taking care of me out of the goodness of their hearts, when they could very well have called child services to come and take me off their hands.

The way my friends and their families opened their homes to me, felt like a reality check of life itself, for lack of a better expression. Because I was constantly around different people, with different beliefs, people with different habits, different personalities, I was always aware of everything and everyone around me, fine-tuning myself to fit into their worlds. Not because they asked me to, but because I was trying to make an effort to not be a burden or irritation to them in their own homes.

From family to family, I mimicked whoever they were.

If they went to a catholic church, I went to a catholic church. If they didn't practice religion, I didn't practice religion. If they loved listening to Kurt Darren in the car, I loved listening to Kurt Darren in the car. If they couldn't stand Kurt Darren I couldn't stand Kurt Darren.

But I didn't always have to change who I was, change my heart faster than the skin of a chameleon on a Smarties box changed colors. For the most part, my friends and I were very similar. We liked daydreaming, listening to music, writing poetry and playing hockey. My most treasured teenage memories were made during those weekends in my friends' homes.

From Azaria's parents always buying extra KFC burgers so I had something to eat on Sunday nights back at the hostel, to getting into food fights, covered in flour while making pizzas at home with Michelle and her nephews where they lived in Slurry, a cement factory village.

The unbearable smells on Jorika's dad's chicken farm, listening to her Three Doors Down album till we knew every word.

My twin friends Johandri and Sodé teaching me how to drive on dirt roads.

Lighting the fire pit and watching stars at night after a day spent spotting different buck at the watering hole on their farm. Watching High School Musical over and over until we could act the scenes out by heart. Going to church on Sundays and stopping at the convenience store on the way back home for candy. That was as close to normal my childhood would get.

I spent so much time at my friends' houses, I knew their routines and what to look forward to depending on whose house I was going to spend the weekend ahead at.

This was my new normal for three months until the next school break was coming up. My sister called to let me know that my dad had arranged for me to come and stay with her for the month-long break.

I traveled across country by bus to visit her, and it just so happened to coincide with the birth of my nephew – Jack.

I was excited to visit her, but the concept of having my own family or having siblings wasn't real to me anymore – in a sense, it felt the same as visiting my friends over weekends. We had to work hard to get to know each other as sisters, again.

She lived with her partner in the Inchanga hotel where they both worked. Inchanga is a village situated halfway between Durban and Pietermaritzburg – a place where nothing happens, and I loved it for exactly that. The hotel and old railway nearby were the main attractions in the area. The old Victorian style hotel with its red bricks and green roof became my playground for the holidays, lush green hills stretched as far as my eyes could see.

My sister and her partner gave me the space to just be a teenager and get away from my complicated life back at school. I didn't have to put on a show to fit in, and I didn't have to smile if I didn't want to – and that's what made me feel like I was in the company of family.

She was in the hospital for a couple of days for Jack's birth. During that time, her partner took me around Durban, showing me cool places like Ushaka Marine World, ordering me as many burgers as my heart desired, and allowing me to download as many songs as I wanted to, and write onto CD's on his computer he let me use. They both knew I was going through a tough time and spoiled me every chance they had.

My sister appreciated having an extra set of hands in the house to help with newborn Jack-Jack, and although she was overjoyed with his arrival, I knew the sadness in her heart, neither having our mom, or dad around to be there for his birth.As the end of the school break was approaching, I had to bus back to Lichtenburg, back to hoping that my friends would let me stay with them over weekends, not sure how long this "solution" was sustainable for.

Inevitably, there came a weekend where none of my close friends could have me over. My friends asked their friends from another clique if anyone could take me for the weekend – I ended up going home with a girl I had seen before but had never interacted with.

And that's the story of how I ended up spending my not-so-sweet 16th birthday at a friend of a friends' house.

I was woken up by people I didn't really know, where I lay on a mattress in their TV room, as they sung happy birthday and put a plate in my hand, with the biggest slice of black forest cake I had seen in my life.

I was so grateful to Michelle and her family for trying to make my day special, but they could all tell that I kept staring at my phone, waiting for my dad to call. Late into that night, I eventually called him. Upon answering, he told me that he couldn't speak to me. I said, "but it's my birthday."

He wished me happy birthday, and then hung up. I cried myself to sleep that night.

I had been spending a lot of time with Michelle's family at that point. Her parents were divorced, but they both let me stay at their houses. Her mom cleared out their attic for me to stay in, a small space I could get to by taking a ladder.

It had no walls and was just big enough to fit a bed, my suitcases and a CD player – in my mind, I had everything I needed.

My dad showed up at their house once. He sat down with Michelle's parents for about an hour, but he completely avoided talking about me, or the fact that they had taken me in. He didn't offer any help financially toward the family for the room and board they offered. I don't even know why he was there. It is so hard for me to remember any conversation him and I exchanged. I imagine him asking me something like "how's it going with the hockey, hey?" and then saying, "well I better get back on the road before it's dark, bye."

I don't remember. All I remember is the way I cried when his Mercedes wheels steadily rolled across the bumpy road and spat out the grey rubble rocks leaving a cloud of dust as he drove off and left me there.

I lived with them there in Mafikeng for about 3 months, during which Michelle and I grew quite close. I don't know what would have happened to me if her and her family hadn't stepped in to take care of me during that time.

They were "joking" about adopting me, but I had so little trust in parental figures at that point that I couldn't process what they were trying to have a conversation with me about. I was also scared to stay anywhere long enough for anyone to have any sort of ownership over me again, living in fear that any situation could turn into a threat in the blink of an eye – I didn't know anything else.

The concept of safety, security and stability was foreign to me – something I didn't believe existed.

I was getting used to drifting. Different towns, different cities, different provinces. All the me-time, daydreaming on buses. Traveling back and forth.

Having many homes, but no curfews. Being part of many families, but not having to answer to anyone.

I belonged to nobody.

And I started to like it.

PART FOUR

FROM THE VAAL TO THE DOLPHIN COAST

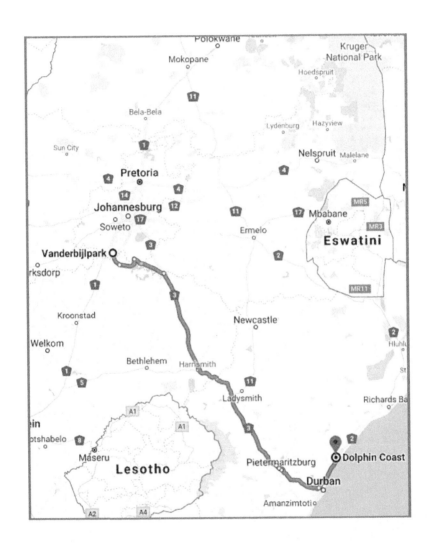

THE WAR IS OVER

I liked two things about Michelle. The way she didn't care about anyone's opinion, and the fact that she almost always had Tracy Chapman playing on repeat. Away with her family on a farm one weekend, she handed me her phone. "This guy I met in a chat room keeps texting me, he is so annoying. Can you just reply on behalf of me, please?" I didn't have a lot of experience with this new trend of chat rooms. If you wanted to be in chat rooms, you needed airtime on your phone – which I never did. I grabbed her phone and typed away to carry on her conversation with this stranger neither of us had ever met. Apparently, I nailed it, because hours of chatting later, the guy wanted to know how on earth him and Michelle (who he thought he was still chatting to) all of a sudden had such a great connection – and we did.

AJ and I kept texting on Michelle's phone for two weeks until I realized that I actually liked him as much as he thought he liked Michelle.

I came clean and told him that I had been texting for Michelle – and that I wanted him to know who I was. All of this, over and above meeting strangers on the internet, was considered shady back then – we're talking 2008.

Being able to communicate with a guy through text was heaven for a girl who was as shy as I was. We lived a three-hour drive apart and had no easy way to see each other – so we didn't. For four months we "dated" online. I had never had any real sort of relationship with a guy at that point, and having met online, I didn't know if I should take any of it seriously.

Little did I know, that what started as a harmless joke of texting on behalf of my friend, would turn into the next three years of my life.

Michelle's mom took us kids to Aardklop - an annual South African arts festival held in Potchefstroom. I always imagined that if I had the opportunity to attend a festival as big and popular as Aardklop – that I would have been gate crashing the bands' dressing rooms trying to land an apprenticeship or cornering an artist and singing for them in the nearest bathroom hoping they would offer me a record deal – I would happily have signed my life away to them.

Well, none of that happened - I was sucking face somewhere between Steve Biko Street and Thabo Mbeki Way, going full on PDA with my internet boyfriend I finally met in person for the first time. Abandoning any plans of sneaking backstage to convince the nearest celebrity that I was a superstar waiting to happen, if only they could mentor me.

For a second, I forgot about my music dream.

For a second, I forgot that I was an abandoned child.

For a second, I didn't have to daydream myself out of misery.

75

My emo-knight-in-matte-black-armor finally showed up and swept me off my feet. We only had a couple of hours together before we had to go our separate ways again. Him back to Vanderbijlpark and me back to Lichtenburg.

Seeing each other in person sealed the deal for us – we wanted more at any cost.

Two weeks back at school, my friend Alicia asked me if I wanted a ride to Vanderbijlpark with her over the weekend as they were visiting family there – I couldn't believe my luck. I said "yes" a thousand times – but we had to keep it a secret because all my other friends would have judged me for spending a weekend with a boy, so I lied to everyone about where I was going, including Michelle.

I got to meet AJ's family and his best friend at the time - Eddy. AJ and I didn't know when we would see each other again, so we spent most of the weekend in his room, in his bed, naked. I kept thinking how my very religious friends in Lichtenburg would have been so disappointed in me if they knew what I was getting up to, and I myself, felt a little guilty for losing my virginity when I also believed in waiting until marriage. But I couldn't help myself. AJ felt like the end to all my pain and problems. Like the war was finally over.

He was in his final year of school, with little idea of what he wanted to do next. He was older than me but not more mature. I was aware of it but looked the other way because having a hot, emo boyfriend wearing Volcom hoodies, was everything to me. We just clicked, loved the same music, and he would make fun of himself just to get me to laugh. Somewhere in the back of my mind I decided that I could be strong enough for the both of us. Driven enough for the both of us – if it came to that.

We spent another two months apart, during which he lost his dad in a tragic motorbike accident. It crippled him further but made our relationship stronger as we grew closer.

AJ's mom suggested that I moved to Vanderbijlpark to live with them and finish my last two years of high school there - and there was nothing I wanted more. I just didn't think it would ever happen.

I visited my sister in Inchanga when the schools closed for the December holidays. She encouraged me to call my dad to ask if I could move in with AJ and his family - to my surprise - he agreed and told me he would drive me there himself when the holidays were over.

I stood in my sister's kitchen, gobsmacked that the call concluded in my favor. My dad was going to let me live with my boyfriend at sixteen, the same dad who wouldn't allow me to go to the movies with friends a year ago. I was confused as fuck.

But I was finally going to get my happy ending.

LURKING

Just in from Durban, I climbed out of the bus in total disbelief that my dad was actually going to be there, waiting and ready to drive me to AJ's house, but sure as hell, there he was.

I didn't tell any of my friends in Lichtenburg about my plans to move to Vanderbijlpark after the December holidays - I didn't mean for it to be that way - but I pretty much left without saying goodbye. The last time we saw each other, I didn't know it would be the last time. They were all pretty pissed at me. The majority took it personally and never spoke to me again - especially after everything they had done for me when I had nowhere to go.

As much as my move was selfish, or for love, it was hard explaining to my fellow sixteen-year-old friends that I was moving so that I could try and find some stability on my terms - not having to move around from friend to friend, having to be a burden to them, living in their shadow, or be worried that at some point something was going to go wrong.

I didn't expect anyone who hadn't walked in my shoes, to understand my decision, especially not my friends who mostly knew nothing but love and stability growing up. I didn't try to justify my decision when friends started fighting, I just accepted that the friendships were over and moved on.

I wished the words would fall out of my mouth, "dad, I'm terrified that this is going to be a mistake, I want to come home." But nothing. Total silence as we turned onto Lewis Carol Street and pulled into AJ's driveway - an Amazon of green. "His dad just died - that's why the grass hasn't been cut." I nervously mouthed to my dad, sinking down into his Mercedes-Benz-car seat in embarrassment, one last time.

My dad had a whole ten-minute long conversation with AJ's mom who he had just met for the first time. He agreed that he would continue to pay my school fees and that he would send a couple hundred Rand for food every month. His mom failed to mention that she was about to move out to live with her boyfriend - leaving AJ and I to run a four-bedroom house alone.

"Well, I better get going," concluded the discussion and off to his car, my dad walked.

Apart from the fact that my dad was about to leave me at a mustard-yellow-house with someone I met off the internet and had only seen in person twice before - the whole thing just felt off to me, as much as I wanted to be with AJ.

I could hardly fathom that my dad was driving away from me, again.

The same way he drove away, leaving me behind so many times before, when I desperately needed him.

No matter how happy I was to be with AJ, nothing could fill the void my dad's absence left in me, but I had to keep my chin up and soldier on, with only fifty Rand in my pocket and my dad's last words to me echoing in my ear "it's better if you don't keep in contact with me."

I walked into my seventh school trying to avoid having to explain to my new friends that I live with my boyfriend. When I eventually had to tell them, they thought it was the coolest thing ever - not one of them judged me. Instead they were excited that we could hang out at my house with no adults around.

It was back to a laid-back culture, kids who smoked during recess, and gay kids out and proud - one of which became one of my closest friends.

I didn't have it in me to try and make friends with every clique, I stuck to the same circle of friends for those two last years of my high school career. None of us were popular, and we couldn't care less. Getting invited to parties or sneaking into clubs with fake IDs like the cool kids did, was the last thing we cared to do. Our idea of fun was getting together at someone's house for a barbecue and guitar singalong.

AJ was happy that I made friends and encouraged me to go out with them often - he quickly realized that living together was a bigger commitment he could have imagined. He was missing his space, and was very vocal about it too. Our first fight ended in him telling me that he wished I never moved in. I was shattered, but he glued my pieces back together when we both got over our frustration and anger the next day. It was hard for both of us to all of a sudden be grownups playing house, but we were happy to be together.

He was still very shaken and depressed after his dad's passing. Most days I would come back from school at 2pm, to find him still asleep in bed. I was trying to be understanding towards him, but I kept thinking "what the hell have I gotten myself into?!"

In the years before living with AJ, I had to fight to survive. So, I wanted to celebrate every moment AJ and I had together - I was so happy to be with my boyfriend and have some freedom. I couldn't wrap my head around the fact that he was depressed and mellow almost all the time. It was hard to have a partner who couldn't keep up with the ambition I already had at sixteen.

I felt neutral about his mom moving out to live with her boyfriend, she always treated me well and I liked her very much. She tried to help AJ find work, because she couldn't support him financially, but he wanted no part in finding a job. He felt it was very unfair that he had to start work straight out of school and wasn't given the chance to study or take a gap year.

I have empathy for it now, but back then I felt like, "what is this dude sulking about? He needs to get his shit together." The truth is, neither of us had any option other than getting our shit together, so I didn't understand why he didn't take getting a job as seriously as I did. We were on our own. I could wrap my head around the trouble we were in financially and started making plans, asking around for work. We went for an interview to waiter together at Spur - a steakhouse franchise.

I was so excited for us to start working and earn our own money when we walked out of the interview being offered the job. He took one look at me and said "I am not doing it. I would rather die."

He couldn't get over the humiliation of being a waiter, and his fear that his slight stutter would surface on the job was a problem to him too - which I got. But because he was my only means of transport - if he didn't work there, then neither could I.

I lost all hope, knowing that we couldn't survive on the few hundred Rand my dad was sending for food once a month.

A couple of months down the line he found work and things started to get better. Through the ups and the downs, we were best of friends, and happy to have each other, because that was all either of us really had - just each other. Somebody's hand to hold. No matter how bad the fights, no matter how hard the times - to quote Eat Pray Love - "during the bad times, we were happy to be unhappy together, if that meant we didn't have to be apart."

Our worlds revolved around each other, and so did our bodies. His older sister took it upon herself to get me packs of government issued birth control pills every month - for which I was grateful for. I didn't have my mom around to give me "the talk" or take me to the doctor for a prescription - I had no idea where to start when it came to birth control, how to get it or how it worked. Even though I sometimes felt judged by his sister for my situation and background, she was level headed enough to make sure I was taken care of in that regard - and even now, I am grateful toward her for that. I know my life could have made a turn from bad to worse if I fell pregnant.

I understand why she hated me the rest of the time. I wore her clothes and used her make-up without asking.

Where I came from - it was a culture of "mine is yours, and yours is mine." My friends knew I had nothing of my own, and after years of sharing everything in hostels - I didn't see any problem with using things that weren't mine. I felt incredibly ashamed for being called out for it, and eventually saw that I was in the wrong and should have had more respect for her.

It didn't help that my stepmom was lurking around every corner of my life - just as soon as I thought I shook her off, she showed up again.

It turned out my dad had told my step-mom he was moving me to a new school to live with a female friend and her mother – "because I really needed a mother figure in my life."

Somehow, my stepmother found these people's contact details, called them up and told them all about how unstable and rotten I am, and that they better watch out for me, that "I was not who they thought I am." In return my stepmom was surprised when AJ's mom corrected her explaining I was living with her son, and not her daughter. My dad told my stepmom that I lied to him about the fact that I was living with a boy - to cover his own ass.

Can you imagine the ambush I walked into that afternoon, when my first love, his mother and pissed off older sister sat me down in their living room to cross-examine me about who I am and what my intentions were? Wanting to know if it was true that I was caught shoplifting when I was fourteen.

I was ripped apart. I couldn't understand why my step-mom still interfered with my life when I did as she asked, when I left home and made my own way. If she didn't want me in their lives, why was she inserting herself in the life I was trying to make for myself? As an adult, I had anxiety about her ruining more relationships I had built, by doing what she did back then, again.

I was sitting on a couch on one side of the lounge, AJ, his sister and their mother, on the other.

I took a deep breath and feeling completely attacked and anxious, started to speak.

"When I was fourteen, my dad and stepmom wouldn't let me come home over weekends for a while because my stepmom didn't want me there. The hostel closed over weekends and no pupil was allowed to stay in over the weekends, but I had nowhere to go. I locked myself in my room so no one would know I was there and climbed out the window so the staff wouldn't see me come in and out. I would walk down to the local grocery store where I stole food because I had no money, and nothing to eat. So yes, I was caught shoplifting at fourteen, it's true." I managed to get out before bursting out crying.

Their angry eyes turned teary and red very quickly as they embraced me and apologized for how they treated me after the phone call from my stepmother. But the damage was done, my stepmom managed to hurt me and make everyone in my new life question me. I was so embarrassed and depressed after that. My stepmom forced my dad to stop paying for my school tuition and to stop sending me money for groceries too. It was a disaster. There were times we didn't eat, or all I ate for a week at a time was an apple a day. There were times the water and lights were cut off for days on end. I kept applying for weekend jobs until I finally found work as a waitress at Wimpy.

It was a blessing when AJ's best friend, Eddie, rented a room in the house - the three of us were a little family. We loved each other's company. We put the bit of money we had together and went grocery shopping together with that every month. Eddie's stepmom taught me how to cook. We'd buy fresh veggies in bulk and she'd show me how to wash and boil them, package and freeze them so we would have enough to last us the whole month.

I cooked for the three of us once I got home from school on weekdays. Eddie would make us pray before eating, he was a strong person. I remember looking up to him and often thinking to myself, I wish my boyfriend was this strong willed, with that sort of sense of direction. But I loved AJ as he was and let it go. I was the man between him and I, and I was fine with it.

After dinner, Eddie would insist the two of them clean up the kitchen. Afterwards, they played World of Warcraft on their computers and I packed lunch for the three of us, for the day ahead - toasted ham and cheese sandwiches - which meant that life was good. The three of us couldn't afford to go out much, so if we had enough gas in the car we drove into town where there was illegal drag racing on certain nights and watched the action - it was the ultimate entertainment.

We didn't need much to be happy.

This was our life for a couple of months.

I was running a house at sixteen, taking care of myself and two nineteen-year-olds, and was happy to.

Eddie always stepped in if AJ and I fought - he had a temper and did stupid things like throw my phone to break into pieces when he got pissed about something. We both had our issues - I was extremely clingy because of my past and never gave him any space. Whenever he pissed me off, I turned to the other extreme and ignored him. I was quick to grab a backpack and disappear to a friends' house for the night without saying goodbye or explaining where I was off to. He found me walking to a friend one day, drove past me slowly, asking me to come back home while challenging me at the same time, shouting rude comments at me. I took one of my high heels out of the backpack and threw it at his car - oh my god he was pissed. We didn't always see eye to eye, but we were so in love.

If I close my eyes, I can still feel that cold, dirty laundry room I stood in day in and day out, washing and drying our clothes, the two guys' work overalls that took hours to get dry.

Taking on as many responsibilities as needed, I didn't care how hard it was, I was so proud of myself for keeping things together, and functioning. I was proud of the life I had, the independence I found, I felt all grown up. I thought I was going to marry this guy one day. "You're supposed to marry the first guy you sleep with." I was taught this from a young age. So, I tried to play my part, cooking and cleaning. AJ tried to play his part too - he helped me to buy a scooter from Eddie's dad that I paid off monthly. He tried to play his part but did it in a way that made me feel like he wanted to have power over me whenever anything went wrong.

I started asking myself what the point of completing high school was. I would have made more money if I could waitress full time instead of weekends only. I had to pay my own school tuition if I wanted to advance from Grade 11 to Grade 12 - and that was the last thing I wanted to spend my hard-earned money on. By some miracle, I continued going to school despite questioning the importance.

The house we lived in belonged to AJ and his sister who inherited it from their father. His sister was never there so decided to rent her half of the house out without really discussing it with AJ first. I just got home from school one day and there was a huge family living in the house with us. AJ was pissed off and fought his sister over it, but I didn't have much say, and didn't get involved.

AJ and I both had sober habits, we knocked back a few drinks on occasion but that was it. All of a sudden there were parties at the house, lots of drinking, screaming babies, and we didn't know what else happened behind closed doors. We were both having a hard time living with the new people in the house, feeling like outsiders in our own space. I grew close to the mom of the family who lived with us, I have fond memories of long discussions her and I had, but it didn't change the fact that we missed having our own space.

We were making just enough money - both having jobs - and decided to move into a smaller two-bedroom apartment - and get a cat who we named Stickly after

AJ's favorite "Attack Attack!" song. Our life was starting to take shape, and I joined a local church band (who let me sing with my own microphone and everything.) My faith and religious beliefs were dwindling, but I attended church just so that I could be on that stage and sing in front of a couple of hundred people each Sunday.

Eddie moved in with us again which helped a lot financially, though we still had rough days when the end of each month approached. One day while the two guys were away at work, I packed all of my best clothes into a backpack and drove around the neighborhood on my scooter, stopping alongside domestic workers who were walking home. I sold all the clothes in my backpack and invited them back to the apartment to raid the rest of my cupboard. It was a good day, because I could buy butter and milk and make pasta for dinner with the money that I made.

"How about the burnt orange, do you like it?" Eddie's stepmom took me shopping for my Matric farewell (Senior prom would be the equivalent in America.)

She paid for it all, the dress, the hair and make-up, the shoes. "What happened to your phone, darling?" She noticed the cracked screen. "AJ got mad and threw it, broke it. But it's okay aunt Marin." I explained. "It is not okay." She responded.

AJ had a wandering eye and couldn't understand that it hurt my feelings. For me it was hard feeling like my first love needed anything else, when I thought I was giving him everything.

He was going clubbing alone with his friends when I was 17 and not allowed into clubs - all these little things added up and I couldn't help but feel ruined and rejected by the man I was trying to build a life with – whatever that meant at the tender age of sixteen, seventeen, eighteen. We were just fighting a lot and we were both very emotional beings.

My friend Bernice went clubbing that same night. I told her she could come and crash at our place when she was done for the night, I knew she didn't want to get home at 4am and have her dad question her for being out late. She was part of the popular group in school - she was gorgeous and was out of my "friend-league" in school, yet somehow, we became besties. "Maiq" we would call each other. (Afrikaans for friend.)

I don't know what solidified our friendship, it must have been the class we took together in business and economics – the class neither of us paid any attention to – I think that was it. Her friend group and mine did not see eye to eye. They were the pretty, party girls. We were the nerdy, dirty musos. But her and I were ignorant toward each of the groups' standards. We were just her and I - maiqs. And we still are, nine years later. Maiq!!! <3

She walked into my house 4am that morning. AJ was still out clubbing. She found me on the kitchen floor where I tried to overdose on the pills I found. She helped me to the bathroom and made me vomit as much as I could.

Night turned to day and at some point, she left. I woke up and AJ was next to me. "I just don't think things are working out between us, I don't think I can be with someone who is trying to commit suicide" he explained.

"You can't do this to me, don't leave me" I cried. The same way I did to so many men after him.

He got over it and before I knew it, wanted to cuddle and of course acted as if he did not say any of those things. But I could not have been more hurt. I had to leave him before he left me, I kept thinking. I can't be abandoned again.

I moved out one weekday while he was at work. My friend Anette helped me get my things and we carried it on our backs some twenty blocks to her house where I stayed for a while. They didn't have much, but they were determined to look after me for as long as I needed and made me feel loved and emotionally supported.

I spent a couple of days at Jo-Anne's house too. They bought me a new phone after AJ busted mine. Her mom colored and cut my hair for me - it was a treat to visit them. I remember her dad getting upset and wanting to phone my dad to confront him about abandoning me, but I think her mom convinced him to let it go when she saw the horror on my face, my fear of how my dad would react. So, he didn't make the call.

One night, Jo-Anne's parents picked us up after a youth evening we attended. They gave us each R200 ($15) to do something fun with. I couldn't remember the last time I held a R200 note in my hand. I spent it all on food. Jo-Anne laughed, she couldn't understand what was going on when she used her R200 to buy new shoes, and I just wanted food. But it all became clear to her and her family as time went on.

I was back to moving around between friends' houses, back and forth, one bed to another, until Jinx and her dad invited me to move in with them. They lived in quite the mansion, a block away from Bernice. I had my own room and we had steak for dinner every night. They bought me new school uniforms because mine were so worn out. Her dad gave us a thousand Rand to go and buy me some new winter clothes. He was really old, and she was dealing with her own depression as her parents were going through a divorce. She spent every other weekend away with her mom, and I'd stay at her dad's house when she was away. She loved having me around to do sister-stuff with, we had a fun relationship and I was grateful to her for giving me a safe place even in her own chaos, navigating her parents' divorce.

I felt like I had to be very emotionally available to her, as if her situation was worse than mine. At the time, I didn't understand her crying when the only problem she had in her life was that her parents were getting a divorce. These thoughts never came out of a bad place, they simply came from a place of looking at how I managed to navigate my disasters over the years, not having food or parents – at all, and her world fell apart because her mom and dad weren't living together anymore. Of course, as I grew older and more mature, I realized that it was unfair of me to low-key judge her in the ways I did. I never verbalized the judgmental comparisons, I didn't give them much thought, but I know they were in the back of my mind. It is hard for me to acknowledge that other people's pain is as real and valid as my own, even if their situations are not as life threatening as mine. They still have every right to have a breakdown - their feelings are as valid as mine. I did my best to be there for her when she was depressed about her situation. We were each other's support system.

"So, he works in security you say? He is a car guard?" Jinx's dad asked when we got the news that my dad was on his way to come and see me – to my own surprise.

"No, no, he is not a car guard. He was Special Forces in the army for thirty years and holds quite a respectable position at an embassy in Botswana." I responded in disgust. My dad - a car guard? He thinks my dad is a car guard standing in the sun all day with a reflectors jacket on, working for change?

And then it clicked for me.

I had my dad on such a pedestal despite all the ways he failed me. Hearing someone else's idea of who my dad was, what he must be doing for a living, that would explain why he couldn't take care of his daughter. People around me thought my dad was a failure, a drunk, homeless, poor man who did not have the means to take care of his daughter - even though I said nothing of the sort to give them that idea - it was their own conclusion.

And there he pulled up in front of their mansion in his silver Mercedes, dressed up in his business suit to everyone's shock and disgust.

He made small talk with Jinx's dad for a while and then rudely jumped to, "can I have a moment with my daughter, do you mind?"

We pulled two garden chairs beside the swimming pool and sat down. "Look me in the eye, have you been having sex?" he fired away. I let the breath I was holding in, out - with half a laugh and confusion on my face. "What do you mean? I was living with my boyfriend - what do you think we were doing?"

He didn't say much. I wasn't trying to be rude or disrespectful, I was just genuinely completely puzzled by what he was even doing there. It had been two years since I'd been home, he stopped supporting me financially, none of it made sense, but I had no way of communicating my feelings to him. I was shell-shocked that he was in front of me and even though he was fighting with me for things I couldn't understand, I really, really just wanted to see him.

"What are you doing living at these people's house?" He wanted to know. I tried explaining to him that it didn't work out with my boyfriend, and that I needed to get out. I told him how hard it was to support myself, work over weekends to pay my own school fees. I told him I wanted to go back to Hluhluwe and live with my mother's family. They said they would take me in and put me through university. "Under no circumstances!" he exclaimed.

"How can you forbid me from making a choice about my future when you haven't been part of my life these last few years? At least they will take care of me, feed me. I want to go to Hluhluwe!" But he continued, "under no circumstances will you go back there, do you hear me?"

I didn't understand it. I listened to him though. That was the last time I saw my dad.

I was visiting different friends over weekends again when one of their dad's told me to come and sleep next to him in his bed one night after dinner. I tried to politely decline but he insisted. "I won't do anything to you. Just lie next to me and we will hold each other."

Well, it happened. I didn't know how to get out of it. It never happened again, and I had no idea how to tell anyone about it. I was in contact with AJ at that stage and decided to move back in with him after the incident.

We tried to forgive and forget, and we were fired up for each other having spent some time apart. We drove around and ended up at a casino, it was dark and rainy when AJ parked the car. The parking lot seemed empty, and we couldn't resist getting it on in the car, but after a few minutes there was a knock on the window.

AJ's first response was to speed away in angst. I kept insisting we just apologize to security, but he was in his own head and couldn't think straight. We almost had an accident - he didn't see a speed bump and hit his nose on the windshield - blood spattered all over. We kept driving around the premises until the security cars surrounded us. I was so pissed at him and was crying uncontrollably.

In the security office, they wanted to call child services because I was under eighteen and after questioning me, they were concerned about the fact that I didn't live with my parents. They explained they had to take us to the police station unless I called a parent they could speak to. I called my sister and asked her to pretend to be my mom - luckily my plan worked, and we were just banned from the casino instead of having to go to the police.

The fights got worse, and trust was broken. At some point, AJ told me to accept the fact that he was always going have a wandering eye, to accept that he will never change for me. It was such a big issue for me - mostly because I was a teenager and it made me feel like I wasn't enough. I was so young, he was my first love, my heart was broken, and I was told that I was being unreasonable.

If he could have his fun, then so could I - I thought. I ended up sleeping with one of my girlfriends a couple of times. I never told him about it, and I didn't feel bad about it either.

It wasn't long till I realized that it was never going to work between AJ and I, and that I had outgrown him. He wanted to just be twenty (which in hindsight, he had every right to be,) but in my mind, I was a married thirty-five-year-old. It was no one's fault that we grew apart.

A few days after I graduated from high school, I packed my things and got on a one-way flight to Durban without saying goodbye to him.

I left no goodbye note, no explanation. I knew he would try to convince me to stay if told him.

Eddie drove me to the airport at 4am that morning while AJ was still sleeping. It was my first time on an airplane - I felt like I could conquer the world when those wheels left the runway.

I slapped a smile on my face and changed my number. Eddie sacrificed his friendship with AJ to help me get out of a failing relationship and my dead-end-waitress-future.

My sister waited to receive me on the other side of the gates at King Shaka International. We both cried. She cried because we hadn't seen each other in a long time. I cried because I just left my first love to wake up in an empty bed with no one next to him. As much as I was the one who left him, I had to break my own heart that day, too.

HEY, DAD. I WON'T BE THERE.
(Song written in 2010 on the day that I matriculated/graduated from high school.)

Hey dad do you remember what day this is?
It's the day that I'm supposed to spread my wings
But you forced me to fly some time ago
And then you said that I can't come home

Sixteen was supposed to be sweet
Seventeen was difficult indeed
You weren't there when I turned eighteen that day
And this is what I have to say

You're making me wonder what I'm worth
When a father don't remember his daughter's day of birth
Guess I was never that special to you
It hurts but it's the truth

So, when you decide that it's time to make things right
When you wake up crying in the middle of the night
When you finally miss me and realize you were wrong
I will be gone

You are the reason that I'm holding everything inside
You are the reason that I cannot sleep at night
You are the reason for my nightmares and my tears
The reason I can't face my fears

You are the reason that I'll never know what mom was like
She was sick, she was dying – still you chose to fight
She just wanted to make things right
And say sorry to you – before she died

Now I know why you didn't pick up the phone

86

As she called you from her deathbed, she was all alone
It's because you knew that you were guilty from the first day
So now I'll be just like you in my own way

  Because when you decide that it's time to make things right
When you wake up crying in the middle of the night
When you finally miss me and realize you were wrong
I will be gone

When you're lying on your sick bed and you're calling me up
Or even if you're calling just to see what's up
When you're blowing out your last breath of air
I won't be there
And I won't care

I won't be there
Because you never were
It should've been you
Instead of her

When you decide that it's time to make things right
When you wake up crying in the middle of the night
When you finally miss me and realize you were wrong
I will be gone

When you're lying on your sick bed and you're calling me up
Or even if you're calling just to see what's up
When you're blowing out your last breath of air
I won't be there

TERRIE THE LION

As an adult, I put Terrie down to just being a figment of my imagination. I thought I remembered him from a bedtime story my dad once told me – the only bedtime story he ever told me. When I kept recalling the same memories, I Googled the bits of information I could remember until I finally found an article that would prove Terrie didn't only exist in my imagination.

www.imagemag.co.za - "Celebrated as an Honorary Operator in the South African Special Forces decades ago, Terrie was a lion born in captivity at a zoo in South West Africa. Having been adopted as a cub by the Operators, he went to be their mascot at Fort Doppies in Namibia, where he eventually led the life of a wild lion.

Terrie adapted well to his double life at the Fort and in the bush and would always be there waiting for the men before or after their training or deployment. During the harsh and hazardous duty served in the South African Border War of the 1970s and 1980s, the men's morale was boosted by this powerful but friendly lion. The Operators let him have free run and go outside the Fort, feeding him every day or every other day, sometimes shooting game for him and sometimes feeding him meat scraps from the mess hall. Frequently they invited him to a braai."

STORIES ABOUT TERRIE
Lyrics

I do remember a story or two
That's about all I remember of you
I do remember asking you questions
You told me you didn't have the answers to

I do remember as young as I was
You said they took away your youth
But war is the only thing you trust

Stories about Terrie
And "I told you so's"
And you said sometimes that's just the way it goes
You said, "kid you're an army brat, do what you must, and don't let them turn your heart into dust."

The orange redness of the camping fire
And stars that tell us where to go
You said, "the places I've been to and where I'll be tomorrow, these are the things I don't know."

I do remember as young as I was
You said they took away your youth
But war is the only thing you trust

Stories about Terrie
And "I told you so's"
And you said sometimes that's just the way it goes
You said, "kid you're an army brat, go out and do what you must, I'm afraid they've turned my heart into dust."

LONELY SOLDIER CRY

Lyrics by my brother

Rainy starless night
All alone you fight till dawn
Until the sun of early morn lies
Shiny brown across your weathered face

Lonely soldier cry
Your tears aren't wet
But your pain is real
You can't believe you've let them steal
The emotions that you once possessed

The world would be a better place
Without humanity
Small at first, it always starts
Following you
Growing
Gathering speed
Gathering strength
Until it catches up with you
And you start running
Oh, there's no escaping life

Remember the helmet you wore
The webbing
Ammunition belts
Born to kill
But you would die to live
Looking back
You feel alone
These restless dreams
They won't leave you alone

The firing shots
Are ringing in your ears
The world is on fire
And you may not die
Your wife and child on you they rely

The tracers flying
Coloring the sky

The screaming of a comrad dying
Oh why did I survive?

Lonely soldier cry
Those were the days
Those were the times
Those were the men
Our nations pride

You bare the scar
Deep down in your heart
And your flag still flies
In our mind's eye

The firing shots
Are ringing in your ears
The world is on fire
And you may not die
Your wife and child on you they rely

The tracers flying
Coloring the sky
The screaming of a comrad dying
Oh why did I survive?

DRUNK TEXTING

"I don't get why people find drunk texts annoying. You're the only person they're thinking of when their brain can't even function properly." - **someecards**

The bottom half of my face was celebrating with a massive smile, and the upper half of my face was drowning with sad Niagara-Falls-sized-tears falling from my eyes into my Mango Airlines cup of coffee. I felt like either halves of my face belonged to two different people on my hour-long flight from Johannesburg to Durban.

My mind was blown by my first flight experience, I paid attention to the flight attendant demonstrating the safety instructions like it was bible - she was after all, doing the job of my dreams second to a career in music. I wanted to be her so badly. I got annoyed at the rest of the passengers who were scurrying around not listening to what she had to say. But it wasn't their first flight and they had probably seen the demonstration so many times.

Not sure if I was running away from something, or running towards something new, I couldn't stop the tears from streaming down my face as I felt my heart breaking, flying away from the first person I ever loved.

We took a short drive from King Shaka International Airport into Ballito where my sister moved to since the last time that I saw her. My nephew Jack-Jack shared his room with me while I stayed with them.

The glitter and confetti on Sandra Street had barely been swept clean after the 5fm New Year's Eve party - the posters reading "DJ Fresh, Euphonik, Jack Parrow" hadn't been removed from the street poles yet.

It was a new year, a new place, the smell of the ocean hanging in the air - the perfect setting for a brand-new start. The fresh air was a nice change from the black smoke streaming out of factories in Vanderbijlpark I was used to seeing hanging in the air.

Ballito being a holiday destination, was quieting down as the summer holidays came to an end. It didn't take long for me to meet a local sun-kissed surfer to help me forget about all my sorrows. He was the breath of fresh air I needed, but one too many tequilas landed me passed out in my sister's empty bathtub - a habit I developed when she still lived in Inchanga. You could tell how good the party was by whether or not you had to wake me up in the bathtub the next morning.

Sadly, one night, instead of passing out in the empty bathtub, my scrambled tequila-drenched brain cells managed to puzzle together AJ's number on my phone. I hit the red button a couple of times before trying the green one.

I asked him to visit me a couple of weeks later. My emo-knight-in-matte-black-armor rose to the challenge - he climbed on his super-bike-horse and rode the N3 for an eight-hour long journey - judging by his enthusiasm, my guess was that he hadn't gotten much action since I left.

The trip he made was a very dangerous one, but he didn't want to buy a plane ticket, so I told him to suit himself. It was unfair of me to start things up between him and I again, I didn't want to take a step back when I had already offered up so much to move forward, but I didn't have closure.

During one of his visits we decided it was a great idea to get tattoos of each other's first letters. I still have the "A" on my left wrist to prove my impulsiveness.

It couldn't have been two weeks later, that I woke up one morning and realized that I was over him. I visited him in Vanderbijlpark one last time, really just to get my guitar from his house, and called it quits - for good - after that.

I walked into King Shaka International Airport again, guitar in hand, ready to really start my new life in Ballito this time, freshly inked ex-boyfriend's tattoo on my wrist and all.

Tarryn - a friend of a friend - got me a job as a part-time babysitter before my brother in law helped me to find full-time work. I decided to juggle both jobs - during the day I was a receptionist at a high-end furniture store - Whetherleys - and some nights I babysat. I knew less than nothing about furniture and had to make a really big effort to study different material, styles and lingo. I was grateful for the opportunity. If I put my heart and soul into it, I would have been able to make a good living in that field - but I really hated it.

When the family I babysat for offered me a full time live in au pair position for the same amount of money, I handed in my resignation after a mere three months of working there. My sister and brother in law were understandably pissed at me for quitting a job they worked hard to help me get. I moved out of their house to my new au pair job. Once again my move seemed selfish to the people around me. I tried to explain that I was grateful for their help but that I couldn't say no to an opportunity to have my own bedroom again, firstly, and a job that gave me more freedom and flexibility to pursue creative projects in my free time.

I gave up on trying to understand the difference between art deco and vintage, antique and retro - and traded in my 9-5 for a half-day job where I could live in a world where hard work meant scrubbing paint off tiny hands, and making sure she didn't scrape her knee during our nature walk in search of Winnie the Pooh.

PART FIVE

FROM BALLITO TO JOHANNESBURG

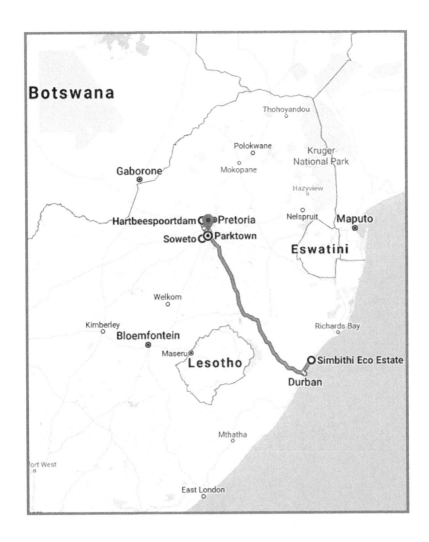

ADOPTED AT EIGHTEEN

She pulled another card.

"Hmm. Children. Your journey involves a lot of children, but not your own."

And another card.

"Spiritual teacher. You're going to teach the world important things through your music and words Lylie-loo."

A couple more cards.

"Oops! Oh well. It looks like you and I aren't going to get on very well in about two years from now. We are not going to see eye to eye. But we will reconnect when you're older."

I told her she was wrong.

She was my mom. My third one.

We didn't mean for it to be that way.

A few weeks before she did that tarot reading for me, I was still "the au pair" when I went out with some friends one night. But the guy I was seeing carried me back into the house not even an hour after we left to go out. My drink had been spiked and I was unconscious.

"What did you do to our daughter?!" they shouted at him as he burst through the door with me in his arms. And that's how it happened. They decided there and then that they were my parents going forward. They took me to the hospital, put me on their medical aid, and we decided that I would take on their last name when I decided to change my name to "Lyla" later on.

Stepping into that au pair job, none of us could ever have anticipated the pain that was lying ahead. But contradicting to almost every other situation in my life, this one got a whole lot better before it got a whole lot worse.

I went from sharing a bed and cupboard with my four-year old nephew for months, to having my own room in their apartment that had a balcony with an outdoor Jacuzzi and 180-degree views, overlooking the Indian Ocean and Dolphin Coast. All my singing in church bands was paying off - I finally made it to the Promised Land.

Till this day I believe that Jesus had my back the day my stepmom abused me for the last time and I left that house for good at the age of fifteen. He was the voice in my head that said, "you need to get out of this situation, I will walk with you no matter where you go, don't be afraid to leave."

He is still with me. We have lost and found each other a couple of times along the way but; we talk, in our own ways.

When I took the au pair job in Ballito, the family accepted me as I was and how I chose to see the world. Our connection was deep, especially after they adopted me as their own daughter.

For the first time I was encouraged to think for myself instead of accepting other people's ideals. For the first time I experienced emotional and spiritual freedom, and healing. I learned what it was to be at peace with myself - my new parents helped me to work through the pain of my past and to be in love with my fate and future.

My mom was completely bonkers - in all the best ways. If I said: "let me try to think out of the box" she would reply with "there is no box, Lylie." She was the first person to ever look me dead straight in the eye and tell me that all my wildest dreams were one hundred percent possible - and meant it. She was also the only person who knew how to call me on my shit without hurting me in the process.

She encouraged me to keep working at my relationship with my sister, but my sister was beyond pissed at me for moving out, changing my name, and no longer identifying as Christian. She was at a place in her life where she couldn't see eye to eye with me and the more that she fought with me, the more I told her not to be in my life if she didn't like the way I was choosing to live it.

I had a strong sense of identity and it got in the way of many of my relationships. Because of my drama-filled-past, it was no big deal to me if people walked out of my life if they couldn't accept me. I didn't know how to compromise - even if I wanted to. I wasn't interested in fighting with anyone to prove any point - I was just fine without them, fine without the drama.

I was in a safe space, well taken care of emotionally and financially, but something was still missing, something felt off. For the first time in years I had the space to just be a kid, a teenager. I wasn't fighting for survival anymore and all of a sudden, I had the freedom to just act my age, but I didn't know how.

My mom encouraged me to get a second job, one where I would meet more people, hopeful they'd be about my age. On weekends I worked as a hostess at a popular pub & grill at the oceanfront called "Hops Ballito." As expected, it did help me to make friends more or less my own age. Ballito is one of those small coastal towns where there is a major age gap between residents. You can either afford to live there because you are over forty and successful, or you are a youngster who moved there to work "holiday jobs."

For 90% of the year, it was a ghost town. But boy did Ballito come alive for Matric rage in December, the infamous New Year's Eve street party Gareth Cliff often DJ's at. The "Ballito Pro" is a surfing festival where celebrity Liezel van der Westhuizen usually emcees. This was another time of the year where the area came alive. My first big performance was on the entertainment stage for the Pro back in 2011, but I remember how it felt so lame being up there. Performing sometimes still does. I don't get it when musicians post a picture of themselves being on stage and caption it "my happy place." Or "this is what makes me feel alive." That may be true for them in their journey, but I can't really relate to that.

If performing was "my happy place" or the thing that "makes me feel alive" - I feel that would mean I am using the stage for my own amusement, my own fulfillment. I don't walk onto a stage looking for a feeling of joy. If I leave the stage feeling happier than I was before getting onto it, that is great, but being on stage isn't the be-all and end-all of my existence.

I was born to create and express through literature and music, it's in my DNA. I don't know anything else. I write to communicate, not to entertain. I have problems communicating in person, and I believe it is rooted in childhood abuse. Writing and singing isn't something I chose, it is something that "happened to me" at a young age and kept me alive. Like medicine. Like a cure. It happened to me so I may function, whether what I write gets performed or not, gets heard or not. The fulfillment happens when I sit on my bedroom floor and piece the song together, when my feelings find a place to belong, a place to exist. The fulfillment happens when the shit that keeps me up at night finds its way into words, and into melodies, and I can finally call it out and call it by its name. Clench it with my fists and feel it exist.

Getting to perform is just a bonus, seeing people respond to it is just a bonus, the Facebook likes are whatever to me. I wish that wasn't a "thing," because as much as I don't care for it, it's still nice to see.

But all of that comes after I have felt fulfillment already.

Till this day, whether I'm sitting in the lounge, singing for one person, or in a stadium singing in front of thousands, I know the music coming out of me has the power to make them feel something, something they need to feel, and I am burdened by the need of fulfilling that process again and again.

My fondest memories in music are not the ones from big events.

It is sitting beside the bed of an elderly person and singing their old time favorite to them.

It is meeting Hloni in Maboneng and singing "Weekend Special" together on the park bench next to the street vendors while I play the guitar, and we're harmonizing as if we'd been rehearsing for years when we really only met moments ago.

It is serenading the cleaner in Central Park that my friend Kishan (who makes bubbles in the park) introduced me to.

When he got out of the garbage truck he drives around, we all stood around trying to keep warm in the November wind. "Welcome to Central Park, you sing?" he asked and encouraged me to come and sing in the park more often. I said yes and asked if I could sing him one.

I remember it clearly, his yellow reflectors jacket, and how I was looking him in the eye while singing Ed Sheeran's photograph. "It will get easier, remember that with every piece of ya." I sang. And I think I needed to hear that as much as he did.

I have such a long way to go to fulfill my destiny in music, but no matter how far I get, I hope I will never forget what it really feels like to communicate through music, and never forget why I do it.

My new family in Ballito understood that about me, understood that music was a language to me and that I was okay if my only audience was the four walls of my bedroom - but they helped me to think bigger, to think beyond the mental abuse I suffered, think beyond my stepmom's voice that told me I would never amount to anything. They helped me to be able to say out loud "I want to be a successful musician one day" instead of allowing me to just act like it was all the same to me whether or not it turned into a career.

Living with my new family; my new "mom and dad and baby sister" in Ballito played a big part in me becoming self-aware and brave enough to choose to pursue my music and radio aspirations. Christmas gifts were electric guitars and amplifiers, and the hours and hours of time spent waiting in Idol auditions lines were spent with them holding my hand, every time.

But it's true that new "problems" always show up as soon as the ones you have, disappear. My friend Boo once pointed them out to me as "higher caliber problems."

I had a lot to be grateful for, but life continued to be hard for me to cope with emotionally. The life I built in Vanderbijlpark with my then-boyfriend, all the roles I took on from housewife to breadwinner at the age of sixteen and seventeen, all of that was suddenly a distant memory. I went from functioning like a thirty-year-old to being told I can now be "eighteen" again, and that my needs would be taken care of for me. I tried going to Shakers and Crush (dance clubs in Ballito) but found no joy in it.

All my high school friends were still in their same friend groups as they moved on to University, partying it up in Potchefstroom and Tukkies in Pretoria. I was on the other side of South Africa, meditating. I was on my own mission, captivated by being exposed to higher frequency thinking and trying to reach my higher self from the moment somebody told me that such a process exists. Finally, I found others who were infected with the "disease of meaning." It was delusional and fantastic, and just what I needed. I was living in my own world.

Needless to say – and how could I blame them – my high school friends and biological family did not take it very well when I changed my name in 2011. The guy I was dating thought I had lost my mind. But my attitude toward people not accepting it was simple. If they couldn't accept it and support my decision, I didn't ask them to. I didn't need anyone to stay.

I wanted to work in music and radio, and my Hebrew-Afrikaans name was not exactly the way I wanted to be known or remembered. I was convinced that cultural perceptions of an "Afrikaans meisie" (girl) would hold me back, and something about hearing that name reminded me of my dad, and I wasn't ready to deal with that pain.

Changing my name gave me some sort of comfort that I didn't have to deal with my painful past. I was no longer the Afrikaans girl with all her issues and the horrible past, no. I was just Lyla. Lyla who is here right now. The present moment and future that I was trying to build was all that mattered to me. I swiped all memories of my past clean - the good along with the bad - gone and forgotten as if none of it ever happened.

I made the decision to trust my new parents wholeheartedly - they gave me no reason not to. My dad worked in aviation and spent a lot of time traveling between Johannesburg and Durban, so a lot of the time it was just me, my mom, and baby sister at home. When my dad was away, we had girls' nights at home - painting nails, mud face masks and all. Chugging shrimp shell chips, and glasses and glasses of dry white Fat Bastard wine while watching Eat Pray Love on repeat.

They introduced me as their daughter to both sides of the family when we flew to Johannesburg for family gatherings - not everyone understood or approved but my mom was like a lioness over me if anyone made me feel left out. All of a sudden, and for the first time in my life, I had uncles and aunts, grandmas and grandpas. Some relationships were stronger than others, but before I knew it, having a big family was my new normal. They did a really good job at helping me to transition into my new life. When I looked in the mirror, I saw Lyla Illing, who had a mom and a dad and an extended family - without having to think about it - I immersed myself in my new life completely - because they did.

There was a death in the family - my mom's uncle (her cousin Neil's dad) had passed. She flew to Johannesburg for the funeral and happened to sit next to someone on her flight who worked in media. She asked his advice regarding careers in radio after telling him the story of when I went for an Idol audition and ended up acing an TV interview Minnie Dlamini did with me in the line. After that my mom was convinced that I was supposed to work in radio. I developed a love for entertainment news. I wanted to become an entertainment reporter. The man on the airplane told her about NEMISA (the National Electronic Media Institute of South Africa). My mom believed in fate and that everything happened for a reason. I immediately applied to the college even though I had no way of paying for it, and even though it was in Johannesburg and we lived at the coast. I didn't understand why I was applying, but she told me not to question it, and flew me to Johannesburg when I was among the forty shortlisted candidates for the radio class - only seventeen would get in. During my interview they asked me to name and talk about three current event stories that were trending in the headlines. I didn't even have a single one. I could tell them who was on the red carpet at what event, and what they wore, but when they asked me to talk to them about Marikana - I just gave them a blank stare - completely puzzled by what that even meant.

The Marikana massacre, which had just taken place, was the most lethal use of force by South African security forces against civilians in forty years. The incident took place on the 25-year anniversary of a nationwide South African miners' strike - and I didn't know about it.

I had no interest in current events, I wanted to get as far away as possible from anything political - firstly because I wasn't raised with an understanding for it, and secondly because it seemed like drama. I was happy in my dream world, the bubble I lived in to escape my painful and abusive past.

I got into the school, solely based on my audio production skills. I had no training but had a natural feel to how audio worked, how to read sound waves, how to write scripts, how to edit an interview from forty minutes down to five so that it told a story and sounded natural too.

As fate would have it, my dad had to move to Johannesburg for work, so we packed up our life and drove out the gates of Simbithi Eco Estate one last time, all the way to Hartebeespoort Dam, a resort town an hour's drive north of Johannesburg.

My dad was battling with some sort of anxiety issue - blaming it on the pressure of the aviation industry. I was blind to it, as it did not really prove a threat to me. The worst thing that would happen was that he'd ask me the same question twice, not remembering conversations we had. My mom tried to help him through it, hopeful that the move to Hartebeespoort would reduce his stress levels.

EYES ON THE PRIZE

It had been three years since my parents adopted me, I was studying radio at South Africa's Electronic Media Institute in Parktown North, Johannesburg, only going home to Hartebeespoort Dam on weekends. I was halfway through my school year when my dad lost his job. We had to move in with my grandparents.

Financially it was easier if I didn't go home on weekends. I preferred it, because I started interning at the University of Johannesburg's Campus Radio station, under a former NEMISA radio student, AB Dacosta who graduated the year before me. After my 9am-4pm five day a week classes, I woke up at 4am on Saturday and Sunday mornings to catch a minibus taxi - or if I was broke, walk five kilometers - to the radio station to produce the three-hour weekend breakfast show that nobody knew existed.

AB was working night shifts in TV at the time and traveled directly from his night shift to do the morning show. We were two kids barely getting by, working for free, driven by ambition to turn a hardly-ever-listened-to campus radio show into a show that went on to compete with commercial stations across the country. I used to get so pissed at him when I spent hours producing a segment and he wouldn't air it because it wasn't strong enough. He made me a better producer by pushing me. It helped a great deal that I had a crush on him - it kept me from kicking his ass at times when he was hard on me.

In no time, we were promoted from weekend breakfast, to the weekday breakfast flagship show of the station. Now I was getting up at 4 am every weekday morning, producing a three-hour show, running from work, late for class at 9am most days - but it won us a radio award!

I was the only kid in class who worked while studying, and my lecturers did not like it. They made my mom call me to try and talk me out of it - and she was pissed at me for being late to class - but there was no way they were going to keep me from that show. We were hosting the likes of Jack Parow, The Parlotones, Prime Circle, Locnville and Proverb for interviews. I was one hell of a producer already, managing to get high profile guests onto a campus radio show, and AB was one hell of an interviewer, with each celebrity walking out of there thanking him for "the best interview they had done" in years.

My parents couldn't help me financially, so it was up to me to decide to use my little bit of monthly grocery money for transport to the radio station, instead of buying food. It kept me skinny, so I was cool with it.

Back at college, I was killing it despite my divided attention and confused priorities. When the time came to produce an audio documentary in class, I decided to document the role music plays in war. I focused in on the times music was used as propaganda, as well as the times music was used as a plea to end war. Something beautiful happened when I interviewed my grandpa who was an army vet - he opened up about how music was a form of escape during the violent times, and aptly brought up Springbok radio that had an all request show back then. "On Saturdays we all gathered around the radio to hear if our sweethearts requested a song for us - it was the greatest feeling in the world when your name was read out on the radio and a song was played, just for you."

"And did someone ever request a song for you?" I asked.

"Yes, my sweetheart who I went on to marry." He smiled back at me with a tear in his eye, reminiscing.

It was moments like those that made me feel like I had finally found my calling - being able to tell stories. I started caring less about celebrities and entertainment reporting and fell in love with the true power of radio. The power of telling real people's stories. The power of being able to orchestrate an event in someone's mind without using pictures. The power of playing devil's advocate, leading a panel discussion between people with opposing views, knowing just what to say to get them to evoke and challenge each other - all while staying neutral as the presenter, not picking sides. I was good at it, and nothing scared me.

I had to land a weeklong internship in order to complete my radio studies, and my lecturers wouldn't allow me to use my experience at UJFM since I was basically working there already. So, I got cocky and emailed one of the biggest names in radio, who was in his prime - Gareth Cliff at 5FM. I had no expectation of hearing back, but his producer Damon Kalvari invited me to spend a week shadowing their morning show.

It was the equivalent of landing an internship with Ryan Seacrest in America. I couldn't fathom reality - I knew this internship would change my life forever. And it did.

"Hi, I'm Jen Su! What's your name?" The most gorgeous, friendliest, well dressed person I had ever seen walked up to me and started chatting. It was my role model, one of the most well-known entertainment reporters in South Africa - she was at the station to do her Hollywood report on Gareth Cliff's show. She didn't have to give a shit about who I was and why I was there, but she kept asking me all these questions. "I want to be a reporter for E! Entertainment one day," I answered.

"I've done some work for them in different countries," she explained. She encouraged me to chase my dream. "There's something special about you." She said.

I believed her and was more determined than ever.

Equally driven - it was only right that my UJFM partner, AB, was my radio husband, but I found love in the real world again. I hit it off with a singer from Malawi. I dated interracially for the first time, and my parents were supportive. At that stage, I was on speaking terms with my older siblings, but they stopped speaking to me for about a year after I told them about my new boyfriend - because he was black.

He rented a place in Melville, a stone-throw away from where I was studying. I fell in love with him the first day we met; we couldn't stay away from each other. When I finally scraped up the guts to invite him for Christmas dinner at my grandparents' home, he couldn't make it. I didn't realize he had a wife and daughter somewhere else until she contacted me years after we had already broken up.

I spent Boxing Day and New Years Eve in bed, crying myself into 2014 over this guy who just all of a sudden no longer wanted me without giving me a reason why. The only time I managed to wash my face and get out of my pajamas was when my grandpa took me to sing with him in his church band that he played guitar in.

I cried myself asleep in my mom's arms more times than I am proud to say - but she gave me the space to do that. I was her twenty-year-old-baby, only ten years younger than her, but it didn't feel like that.

Having graduated from college, I was back home, so to speak. We were still living with my grandparents and times were tough. My mom was putting pressure on me to get a real job, as UJFM wasn't paying me (or any of their producers.) Eventually AB took it upon himself to pay for my transport costs when the station started paying him.

I was losing more money than I was making, depressed after the breakup, and all around, in a bad place. My mom was putting more and more pressure on me to get a job. I applied anywhere and everywhere but couldn't even find a simple waitering job - I was told, "we can't employ white people at this time with *BEE* laws."

Black Economic Empowerment is a racially inclusive program launched by the South African government to redress the inequalities of Apartheid by giving black South African citizens economic privileges that are already available to Whites. It is a form of Affirmative action.

I was starting to feel like a burden to my parents who in reality, were young, and young parents to their own four-year-old, trying to get their own lives together too.

I turned to a site similar to Craigslist in the US, to further my job search. I sent out nearly a hundred applications but the only response I received was from a modeling agency - or at least that was what they called themselves.

A bunch of photographers responded to me with high paying jobs. They were looking for models for X-rated shoots. It was the only work I had been offered after months of searching, and as the time passed, I felt like a bigger and bigger burden and disappointment to my parents who were down and out and depressed themselves. I was strongly considering the gig, so I didn't have to rely on my parents financially. Ever since my dad had lost his job, there was a weird feeling hanging in the air and between my mom and I - like the days of her being there to protect me around every corner were over and that she was being hard on me for my own good. I didn't know how to deal with that, and I needed it to stop.

I decided to look into the X-rated photo shoot work out of desperation.

My mom found the emails when I was away working at UJFM during the day and demanded to know if I was taking drugs. It was the only way she was able to wrap her head around the fact that I was even considering the gig. I explained to her that I was just trying to help financially. She told me I never, ever had to put myself in that position to try and earn an income. What I did made them feel like they were failing me even more.

I was so embarrassed by what had happened that I fell into a deeper depression than I was already battling. I couldn't get myself out of bed for days on end. One morning, I woke up and wanted my mom, my real mom, so badly. I walked to the bathroom with a pair of scissors in my hand. I stood in front of the mirror, remembering my mom after her chemo with no hair. I just wanted to look like her. So, I started cutting my long hair off, tears rolling down my face with each sound of the snip the scissors made.

Snip.
Snip.
Snip.
But I didn't look like her.
And now I didn't look like me either.
I didn't know who I was anymore.

A SINNER'S PRAYER
Poetry & Prose

What is the worst thing you have ever done?
Don't read the next line before answering yourself first.

So, what is the worst thing you have ever done?
Can you think about it - without dismissing it?
Can you sit with it - for a minute?
Can you be vulnerable enough to - despite the threat it poses?

The threat it poses -

Having to acknowledge what you're capable of as a human being.

Having to acknowledge the part of you that almost got you killed.

Having to acknowledge the part of you, you hide from the rest of the world because you are not so sure the people who are in your life would stick around if you spoke about the things you did, openly.

Having to acknowledge the part of you, that you try to kill - god knows I've tried. My fist gripped around my own throat, only to find out that I can't kill that part of myself without killing all of me. My fist gripped around my own throat, only to find out that I can't erase that one memory, without erasing the ones that make me - Lyla. My fist gripped around my own throat, only to realize that I can't bury a piece of me without burying myself completely, six feet below.

What's the worst thing that you have ever done?

Can you go back in your mind to that time, look your past-self in the eye without falling apart?

Look your past-self in the eye without self-hatred, without reliving the shame that's self-imposed.

Will you choose to go there, despite the darkness it brings out in you?

Will you dig it up out of the soil you tried to bury it in when no one was looking - brush off the dirt, hold it close to your heart and care for it, forgive it?

Will you try to heal from it? I know your entire body is fighting against the mere thought of having to try.

What's the worst thing that you have ever done?

Can you sit with it - for a minute?

I wouldn't blame you if you couldn't.

Because I can't sit with mine.

5FM MORNINGS
Letter of Recommendation

"To whom it may concern,

This is to confirm that Lyla Illing interned here, at 5fm, on the Breakfast Show, with Gareth Cliff.

Lyla is definitely the most diligent intern I have ever dealt with. Lyla shows a genuine passion and interest in radio, unlike most interns that I have had the misfortune to encounter. It was an absolute pleasure to have had Lyla with us.

Sincerely,
Damon Kalvari – Content Producer – 5fm Mornings"

NO ONE

"Becoming No One takes much more than just losing identity. When one loses their identity, it also means that one finds who they truly are." - **Game of Thrones**

In order to become a qualified radio producer, you take a test where scoring 99% means you failed. If you don't score a solid 100% during your practical exam - it meant you pushed the wrong button, spoke while your mic wasn't switched on, played the wrong ad, ended a song abruptly, panicked and caused two seconds of dead air because you were too overwhelmed to know what to do or say next. It meant you just cost the station money, it meant you just pissed one of the million-dollar-paying-advertisers off, and it meant you just got fired.

Being a radio producer, is a little like being an air traffic controller. Nothing can be out of place. Nothing can be a second late, or a second early. Six things are happening at the same time and it's your job to make sure they don't clash or that you don't forget one. It's your job to know what four things are going to happen next, it's your job to function on the fly for three straight hours, function on the fly without having to pause and think about it first - and do so effortlessly, calmly. As a producer, it's your job to orchestrate your presenter, your guest, your sports and traffic announcers, the phone line - you are leading a team, you are thinking on behalf of five people, and any mistake they make, is your mistake - a plane crash that YOU caused.

Somehow, God decided to give a girl who doesn't know her face from her ass, the super power that is radio producing. It's the one thing I can do with my eyes closed.

I was twenty-one with two pieces of paper - one that said I am a qualified radio producer, and the other, a reference letter from the biggest station, and the most well-known presenter in South Africa, singing my praises. Still, I just couldn't seem to get a paying job, and my mom just couldn't seem to be understanding.

The radio bug had bit me. I had a taste of something bigger than myself. I had a taste of success. I had a taste of the media industry that was once far out of my reach. I had a taste of what it felt like to overcome every soul-crushing label my stepmom glued to me when I was younger. I had a taste of what it felt like to be the person I worked so hard to become - but all of it meant nothing.

I was back to distributing my resume to restaurants, hoping for a waitering position to get my mom off my back and make enough money to carry on traveling back and forth to the campus radio station - but nothing. No job offers. I nervously started the search online again, trying to avoid anything that got me into trouble with my mom the first time around - but it was easier said than done.

The only time there was a job offer, I either needed to already own a car - which I didn't, be a size zero for promo work - which I wasn't, or the job offered - was a scam. I received ridiculous email inquiries - a nudist family looking to employ an au pair, or sugar daddies looking for a girl to travel with. Even though the trend of sugar daddies caught on very quickly in South Africa during that time, coining the term "blessers" and "blessees" and being a widely covered story in the news - it went against everything I believed or wanted for myself. It was never an option for me.

Our country's biggest online classifieds job search section was a rabbit hole of grossness - and the worst part is that no one made a big deal about it because of so many people's desperation to find work.

Finally, one day I came across a job that seemed more or less legit. A spa was looking for girls to train as masseuses, and they were located a stone-throw away from the UJFM campus radio station. The pay seemed oddly high, so out of fear that I was going to get there only to find that the spa was really a brothel - I didn't tell my mom about the interview.

"We will train you for free. You will have to advertise your services independently online and if you get a client, you keep 50% and we keep 50% of the money they paid for the massage. If you want to offer them anything else over and above the massage - that's your choice and you can keep all the money."

My fears were confirmed.

I stuck around after the interview trying to talk to the other young girls who were working there. "No one comes here for just a massage," they reaffirmed. "But do you want to get a job at McDonalds and sell burgers and fries for the rest of your life?" one girl asked as I was about to walk out.

I told my mom I landed a job at a beauty supply store in Campus Square shopping mall - she hardly asked any questions. To this day I don't know if she knew the truth or not.

With my new income, I went clothes shopping for the first time in months - a much-needed black winter coat from Identity.

I could finally afford the ten Rand fare of taking the minibus taxi into Soweto to see my friends and record music with them in their room over weekends.

Because I lived on the edge of Parktown and Hillbrow the year before where I studied radio - I was used to being the only white girl in sight. The only white girl in class. The only white girl taking public transportation - minibus taxis. I had to have thick skin because I was stared at and cat called in those areas - but so was every other black girl. I wasn't going to let it get to me.

My friends in Soweto formed a music group called Pantagon - and I couldn't wait to join. The three guys - Nick, Leslie, Tebogo - and I shared a room and one bed for a couple of days. We had just enough money to eat once a day. I trusted them completely - they were my brothers. They were stared at funny too, for walking a white girl around on the dirt roads between shacks and other houses.

In one backyard, I saw a full-grown dog, chained in its small cage. Nowhere to go, no space to run. That was where it lived. I didn't understand the purpose of someone owning a dog only to do that to it - but there was nothing I could say. It's something that has stayed with me forever.

My friends and I produced and recorded a bunch of songs we were so proud of - it was the ultimate escape from the racy spa. For a while I could be a creative and forget about what I became between that spa's four walls - everything my stepmom told me I would end up being. I couldn't look myself in the mirror because I saw what she saw, all those years back - and now I understood it. She was right all along - so I embraced the darkness inside. Nothing mattered to me anymore - I was no one, I was nothing, I was hollow - but I didn't let it show.

Back home, I managed to be the Lyla my family knew. No one asked questions, no one noticed anything different. I was the only one who knew I was no longer the girl they knew and loved.

I was juggling two personalities, two different realities, two different sets of morals. I still wanted to be the girl who could fall asleep on my mom's lap after Eat Pray Love, despite the monster I had to be outside of home - it seems I pulled it off, and for a while, what I had become didn't seem so bad anymore. I could live with myself if I didn't think about reality for too long - somehow, I never felt the need to use drugs or alcohol - I felt like it would only make things worse.

After a three-hour radio show, and both functioning without getting a minute of sleep the night before, AB finally did what I wanted him to do for the past year - he kissed me, but it was just a little too late. I felt nothing, because I had been numbing myself at the spa for weeks.

His kiss was a moment of impact, a moment that shattered me. A moment that reminded me who I was. I felt everything and nothing for him at the same time - and I couldn't deal with that.

I wanted to tell him about the spa.

I struggled to look him in the eye and asked: "what is the worst thing you have ever done, partner?"

He walked me through his rock bottom over a coffee at the campus café - but I couldn't get myself to walk him through mine - being in the midst of it.

Without question or reason, we stayed - just - friends, and the kisses stopped, because I couldn't.

I couldn't stop being who I had become.

His kiss was my first wake-up call, but I ignored it.

At some point my mom reached out to him without me knowing - she was concerned about me and asked him to keep an eye out. He told me about it, so I knew I couldn't tell him the truth without it getting back to her.

Valentine's day morning I walked from the spa where I had spent the night, to the radio station to produce the 6-9am show.

It was past 5am, the sun was up just high enough for it not to be completely dark anymore.

Just before reaching the Barry Hertzog and Empire road intersection - four men came at me from different directions, guns in hand. I froze when I realized what was happening. They took my backpack off my shoulders and emptied my pockets - there was not another human in sight. I am not sure how they just walked away from me after that, I am not sure why they left me unharmed - because in South Africa, most stories don't end that way.

I ran the rest of the way, up the hill to the radio station, massive Valentine's Day card for AB in hand, and covering my bald head I recently shaved, the wig on my head - the only two things they didn't take from me.

In radio we have an unspoken rule - maybe more of a courtesy towards coworkers. Maybe more of something founded out of respect for the listener, or maybe out of protection for yourself.

No matter what is going on in your personal life - when you walk into that studio, you are no one. You are nothing but a radio producer in those three hours. You don't feel anything outside of that studio, you don't give it space to take up thoughts in your mind for those three hours - because being distracted could cause one unforgivable mistake that could end your career. Being distracted is the difference between a good show, and an excellent one.

For three hours, my coworkers couldn't know what had happened. For three hours, I wasn't the girl who got mugged at gunpoint minutes ago. For three hours, I wasn't the girl who no longer had a phone, an ID, a bankcard. I was just a radio producer - an excellent one too.

The show was over, and I finally got to breathe out the breath of air I was holding in, and with that, tears. AB gave me money so I could get myself back home on the bus - I fell apart in my mom's arms telling her about the mugging. She gave me something that helped calm me down and let me sleep it off.

"Where was my guardian angel?" I kept screaming in my mind. "Where was my mom, my real mom, my guardian angel - when I needed her?" I was angry and depressed, and even though this was clearly my second wake-up call to stop what I was doing - my anger was clouding my judgment - and I went back to that godforsaken place with its red and white towels and décor.

After the mugging, my mom suggested I visit her cousin Neil who played in a band, to do some music stuff to get my mind off the trauma. I arrived at his door, guitar in hand - with only three out of its six strings still in-tact. I couldn't spend money on getting it fixed, and happily taught myself how to play on it using only the three strings.

After about half an hour, he told me to get in the car. He used the last hundred rand in his account to buy me a new pack of strings. We made music for hours on end - stopping occasionally to eat the toasted sandwiches his girlfriend made us. He was eighteen years older than me and he was introduced to me as my mom's cousin - my uncle. I had only met him once since my parents adopted me four years before that - so we were really strangers.

We bonded over our interest in music, and just loved each other's company. We laughed at everything and understood each other in ways no one else had understood us - ever.

I was invited over, all the time - and as time went by, I found myself secretly happy when his girlfriend wasn't over for a visit too, until one day it seemed clear that he didn't want to have her over with me around anyway.

It happened by mistake, in a split second where we both dropped our guard. The fireplace crackling beside us in the lounge made every stolen glance between us more intense. Like gravity, some force pulled us into each other no matter how we fought it.

We kissed.

We made love to the sounds of Lana Del Rey.

And then we both cried.

We were sure that it could never happen again - and it made us want it even more.

We stayed away from each other, we promised to try.

I could hardly get myself out of bed with all that was going on in my life - I stopped going to the radio station. One day, AB just said "you're not coming back, are you?"

I was gone, in more ways than I knew how to say.

I tried to continue my job at the spa but dark thoughts made it harder and harder to fight the urge of wanting to just take my life instead.

I had no fight left in me to say no when Neil asked to see me again - despite the fact that I knew what I had become, despite the fact that he had a girlfriend, was eighteen years older than me, and my adoptive mom's family - she would never forgive me.

He picked me up from Campus Square Mall, confused with my choice of location because he knew I quit my radio job. I just told him that he didn't need to know the whole story - and he tried to leave it at that.

I couldn't take my clothes off that night without telling him first - telling him the truth about the spa, telling him what I was capable of, and that he ought to walk away now. I tried telling him that I was no good. I tried telling him I was all the things my stepmom labeled me. I tried telling him that there was nothing left of my soul.

He held my face in his hands, and the more I looked away, the more he made me look at him. The more I cried, the more he kissed the war inside me away.

He told me that he loved me, that night, and the god-awful thing that I had become, was no more. I never went back to that place - how could I, after being loved so deeply for exactly who I was.

I used to believe the worst thing I had ever done, was hurt my body, hurt my heart and mind, abandon my sense of self in order to earn an income. I know now, the worst thing I have ever done, is keep what happened - to myself, keeping quiet about it for five years, saying nothing about it, when I should have been speaking out.

Keeping quiet about it - is to be part of the problem and not the solution. The problem that young girls like me are being preyed on every day, lured into life threatening situations out of desperation for work. There is a difference between choosing to work in such an industry and having no other option than having to. And I know there are women who feel what I feel, went through much worse than what I did. Women who don't know how to move on from that. So I should never have kept quiet about it. I won't anymore.

"Finally, a girl is no one." - Jaqen H'ghar, Game of Thrones

So, what's the worst thing that you have ever done?
Can you sit with it - for a minute?

CONNOR-VALERIE

"Might as well break all the rules, since I'm going to hell." - **Stephanie Meyer, Twilight**

Neil: "Ly...I've been doubting my feelings for her since long before you came into my life...don't blame yourself."

Lyla: "If anything I just made it worse, and all for nothing. What we're doing isn't fair to any woman."

Neil: "There's one friend at work who's convinced there's something going on between us, but I haven't mentioned anything. I've been trying to remain aloof, remain detached. But like today, when I answered your message in the morning, and you only answered hours later...I'm distracted and diffused... I'm more afraid of not being able to see you than I'm afraid of people talking about us... The way that you start conversations with people in bars... And I position myself close to you, just in case you need me."

Lyla: "Yes I noticed that. Like, what the hell? Lol."

Neil: "Lyla...you are the only thing on my mind these days...and I don't want to scare you away. I'm so afraid of that. Listen, I know it's hard...I know it's weird, even...and I don't know where we'll end up with this. But all I want to do is carry on, and make music together...if for no other reason than one day I'll be able to say to people that you once loved me...in some small way..."

Lyla: "It's hard. I'm a mess to begin with. And I'm trying not to break your heart in the process."

Neil: "Ly, if you could break my heart, it would be a privilege."

Lyla: "I can never be to you what you'd need. In the bigger picture. I wish it wasn't the end but it has to be. We have to try."

Neil: "So when do we start..?"

Lyla: "With?"

Neil: "Ending it."

Lyla: "I don't know."

Neil: "Can we maybe start later..? Like in a few years..?"

Lyla: "Funny."

Neil: "Let's not kill it right away..? Let's just let it ride its course...when we've got over the urgent need to be with each other all the time...then we can make that decision...can't we..?"

Lyla: "I want to say no. But, okay. Telling you that I want this to end now would be a lie."

Neil: "I want to tell everyone the truth...Not that I will, of course..."

Lyla: "Why do you feel the need to tell people though?"

Neil: "Cos, I'm not ashamed."

Lyla: "And?"

Neil: "And I want people to know how I feel, and I want them to share in my happiness..."

Lyla: "Nobody is going to be happy, I hate to break it to you."

And they weren't.

I had barely put myself back together after the spa saga - I was still having hour-long breakdowns behind locked McDonald's bathroom doors occasionally. But Founders Grill finally called and offered me a waitering job, and my parents both found employment too - we moved out of my grandparent's house to an area not far away. Neil and I had been seeing each other secretly for months. My mom noticed that him and I grew close and tried to warn me against getting too involved. "He drinks a lot, I don't want you around him that much." But I knew when she said that, that she had her suspicions - I am sure she was praying that she was wrong. I wished I could tell her about the spa-mess I was in until I fell in love with him and how he healed me, but I was twenty-one and she - thirty-one. Both her and I were going through our own personal drama and I knew she wanted to be there for me, but I felt like a burden, like I was in the way, even more so when they went away for the weekend without inviting me along - for the first time.

In the back of my mind, I felt like she wanted a chance to just be with her husband and biological daughter alone - no part of me wanted to deny her that - but it was just so confusing to me. I was twenty-one but needed a mom and dad more than ever, and she was giving me the opposite of that all of a sudden. Because I lied to her, she had no idea what turmoil I just went through with the spa. She thought she was doing the right thing by being hard on me - but it just pushed me away. Our relationship was at the lowest it had ever been, but I was hopeful that it would work itself out.

Neil broke up with his girlfriend, and we were fed up with having to sneak around, having to make out in the Rumours Lounge bathroom behind closed doors. We knew that telling our family about us - meant risking losing them. It wasn't a decision we made lightly.

We started with my grandparents. My grandpa tried to be understanding but

111

my grandma was so pissed at me. After that, we drove to my parents' house. My dad wanted me to do whatever made me happy, but my mom wouldn't talk to me - putting it down to incest even though we weren't biologically related. I understood why it was hard for her. She needed time and told me we could revisit it after a few days. Neil's mom was happy for us, genuinely happy. She had lost her husband just two years ago and told us that life is too short not to spend it with the one you love. Neil's ex-girlfriend wanted to punch me. "I'm sorry we hurt you, but I love him," I told her, feeling her pain and wishing she could know how much I meant my apology.

"You're twenty-one - you don't know what love is," she cried before driving off.

The very hardest of all, was telling his two teenage daughters who were only six years younger than me - and who I had developed friendships with.

We used to sing along to Taylor Swift songs on the guitar together, and now all of a sudden, they had to deal with their new reality of having someone they call a friend, date their dad.

They cried, and it was so hard for both them and us to deal with, but they were great about it - I was thankful to them for being mature beyond their years about it.

They were living with their mom, and only visited Neil on weekends - but I knew it impacted them greatly regardless.

We were like two puppies, we followed each other around everywhere. We couldn't imagine our lives without each other. In no time I had my own drawer in his cupboard, and we were planting flowers and giving them names - we were a little off our rockets around each other.

My mom begged me to end things with him. She told me all would be forgiven if I just walked away. She got my dad to have a meeting with Neil, but my dad kept telling her there was nothing they could say to us, and that she should find it within herself to make peace with it - but she couldn't.

She was so embarrassed, she felt like she let the family down, she felt like she failed me. She felt like it was her fault - she could hardly look at me, but she tried to love me anyway.

We drove down to Durban for the weekend - I went to visit my older sister since it was my birthday, and my mom, dad, and little sister visited friends in Ballito. My mom and I got into a fight over text after they were changing the travel plans around without warning. My sister baked me a cake and we had my birthday all planned out, only for my mom to text me that they decided to leave that night - a day earlier than planned, meaning I would not spend my birthday with my sister.

That was the first and only time I ever threw my phone. I was beyond upset and felt like she was trying to hurt me on purpose - even though in hindsight I feel like I was stupid for even thinking that.

"False alarm. We're still leaving tomorrow." She texted after I had a full-blown breakdown in my sister's kitchen. "Do what you want to do, I will make my own way back by plane." I responded. Talking to my mom like that was completely out of character for me. She had a go at me for being disrespectful - which I deserved - but it felt like she was holding out for an opportunity to have that go at me. I was hurting badly, knowing that our relationship was on thin ice and feeling like I didn't know which way to turn. If I broke up with Neil, I'd make her happy but hate myself. If I kept on dating him, it felt like her and I would always be walking on eggshells around each other - but I never imagined a world without her in my life.

My sister took my phone and sent my mom a bunch of awful messages out of anger, seeing how much I was hurting, but not signing her name at the bottom. My mom thought I was the one who sent it - but it was too late to try and explain. She told me that my belongings would be packed into boxes and ready for me to pick up once I returned to Johannesburg. I broke.

I couldn't believe she would do that to me, do what she knew my stepmom did to me. Something flipped in me and I lashed out at her for abandoning me when she was the one who healed me from how my biological dad abandoned me when I was fifteen. She vowed to protect me, but we both made promises we couldn't keep, and I think it broke her heart as much as it did mine. We hurt each other badly, but she gave me more than I could ever have expected from another human being - she gave me four years of having a mother again - and I choose to remember her like that, I have to remember her for the good things, for the love she gave me. She will always be part of the woman I am today. And I will carry the name she gave me - Lyla Connor-Valerie Illing - for the rest of my days.

PART SIX

JOZI - THE CITY OF GOLD

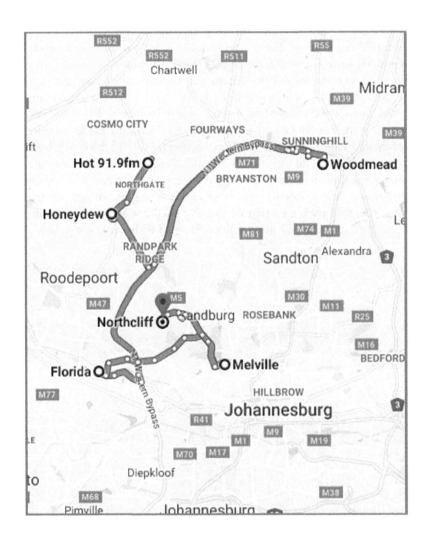

ONE GOOD YEAR

He took his belt off to playfully spank me with - I ducked for cover, falling into a fetal position, covering my face with my hands, managing to squeal out a distressed "don't."

"Baby what did I do?!" He was so upset with himself for the way I reacted. My reaction had nothing to do with him, but everything to do with my stepmom and how she used to belt my face.

Neil got to know every scar, every dent in my soul by heart - he was medicine.

He made me talk about my demons for hours, especially when I didn't want to.

I liked that he was in touch with his feminine side - it made him a good man.

I was never allowed to do the laundry - that was his Wednesday nights.

I was never allowed to pack the dishwasher - because he was convinced that he knew how to, better.

He could name any bird by the sound it was making, he could name each flower in the garden.

Sometimes I'd get up from playing his piano, only to turn around and find him with his head leaned against the wall, staring at me, having stood there listening all that time without me knowing so.

Other times, I couldn't get halfway through playing a song without him snuggling me from behind until I couldn't play the notes in the right order anymore, giving in to him.

My mom kicking me out of the house, left us no other option but to live together. It was too soon, but it also wasn't.

Life wasn't just bearable with him by my side - it was full of joy. I was happy, truly happy for the first time in so long. I had energy. I wanted to get up in the mornings.

With my new lust for life, I remembered who I was. I had lost so much of myself before that - cut off my hair, lost my family, lost my dignity, but I was still a radio producer - I still had that. I just forgot.

I worked my waitering job at Founders Grill every chance I had, 11am to 11pm some days. It was exhausting, but my need to be in a radio studio again was the force that drove me. I applied for radio internships anywhere and everywhere for a couple of weeks until I landed an interview. Neil drove me to it himself.

You misspelled "Matric" my interviewer glared up from my resume in his hand, with a look similar to that of The Joker. His eyes and mouth never told the same story, but I could read him - he knew that, because he could sense I wasn't intimidated by him, and everyone was.

Maybe that's why I got the internship. The six-month-unpaid internship with no guarantee of employment.

For half a year, I made my way to the radio station to work for five hours in the morning and rushed back to waiter late into the night at Founders. My waitering job paid for my transportation costs to the radio station, and splitting food bills with Neil.

The trip from where I lived to the station - should take a half an hour by car. Most days it took me three hours to get there because I traveled by public transport minibus taxis. I had to switch taxis three times and walk in between to get to my destination. Because there was no direct transport to the radio station, I had to travel into the Johannesburg CBD, and from there to the station. I was once again the only white girl between the masses of people traveling through the Noord and MTN taxi ranks. It was intimidating because of the staring and catcalling, but I knew thousands of black girls dealt with the same thing every day. If they had to live their lives this way, what made me any better? What gave me the right to give up? They don't.

I didn't care what anyone thought - I knew what I had to do to get what I wanted. People at work didn't know my situation but sometimes saw me walking alongside the road - some would stop to give me a ride the rest of the way to the station, and others looked the other way - most times I was happy when they looked the other way, so I didn't have to face the embarrassment.

Neil drove me back and forth every chance he had, and my co-workers Mazz and Ashleigh drove me between locations if we had to travel on the job.

At the station, some of my colleagues dismissed my existence completely because I was different than them. "I don't understand why you are talking to me," one used to say. It was a small price to pay in the bigger picture. I was working alongside and learning from Jeremy Mansfield, Ian F, Naas Botha, Kurt Darren, Hayley Owen. People I only knew from TV. I lurked in shadows, barely interacting or contributing to office banter. I took myself very seriously and was a misfit by nature. The only time I wasn't shy was when I was face to face with an opportunity to learn. I pestered everyone to let me shadow them, let me try new things, let me improve. I understood every person's role and tried to teach myself how to do their job so they could always call on me. If there was no job waiting for me at the end of my six-month-unpaid-internship, I wanted to make sure I learned everything I possibly could, so I was ready for the next one.

Our station merged with HOT 91.9 FM.

Ashleigh, the breakfast show's junior radio producer, fell ill and had to take a couple of days off work - I knew her job back to front - only because she wasn't intimidated by teaching me everything she knew. She had no ego, she didn't treat me like other people in the industry who wouldn't teach me, out of fear that I could replace them one day.

Thanks to her open minded-nature - I was able to do her job flawlessly - and people noticed. Our social media guru, Mazz, was the same, she taught me so much. Pretty soon I was transcribing audio interviews and writing articles for our website, helping to run competitions, ticket giveaways, interacting with the winners, clients and show contributors.

Mazz and Ashleigh quit within a couple of months of each other. I was offered full time employment as the new junior producer and shared social media responsibilities with Matt who replaced Mazz. I kept waitering at Founders at night so I could buy a scooter, I finally had my own transport. Things were coming together, I landed my dream job. I had every reason to be in love with my life.

Someone was only ever a split second away from throwing a flip file at the other if they messed up, it was a miracle if a three-hour show passed without someone being shouted at. It was just the nature of the job, the studio is a stressful environment, and we all had an understanding that whatever happened in that studio, was over the second the show was. We could never take anything personally - understanding that, was harder for some people than others. I didn't like being shouted at, so I became brilliant at my job instead. Our station MD held a meeting with our team out of concern about how much our team fought in studio - but we insisted "We know when something clicks, and we know when it doesn't. Our team clicks, it works. The way we clash is the glue that holds the show together, the way we clash off air is what makes us brilliant on air."

Working with our team was like being in a beautiful, chaotic episode of Grey's Anatomy.

The radio scripts - the pre-op.
The microphone - the ten-blade.
The cue to go live - the first incision.
The crossfade between songs - the stitches holding body parts together.
The advertisers - the board we had to keep happy.
The ad-libbing - the gossip around the operating table.
The music bed - Meredith and Christina's thirty-second dance party when tensions are high.
The mixing desk channels and cables - the body's different veins.
The channel faders being moved in different directions - doctors operating together, giving way for each other.
The red and black digital clock - the heartbeat spiking on the monitor.
The dead air - code blue.

Every day was a miracle - making radio out of thin air. It's what I lived for.

When the presenter had to take time off work, I had to produce multiple stand-in DJ's to fill his big shoes. It was my job to make sure they knew how to do theirs. I was thrilled to be entrusted with the major responsibility of having to pull that off - but it made me cheeky. I picked fights with people who were dying to fire me - and I gave them every reason to hate me.

I didn't have to tell the presenter about the contrast - my life in ruins the year before, versus what it had become after I started working for him - but I think he could see it on my face and as a result fought to give me every opportunity to prove myself. At least that's what I'd like to believe.

I knew I was the best on air producer he had ever worked with in his career - because he told me so, and he fought to keep me on the team when I pissed other authority figures off. He promoted me twice after employing me. I wasn't the same shy, fragile girl I was when he initially took me under his wing. I was confident. I pushed boundaries and blurred the line between not knowing my place and having rightfully earned my territory.

BORN TO DIE
"These violent delights, have violent ends, and in their triumph, die." - **Stephanie Meyer, Twilight**

The smell of his black leather jacket as he pulled me closer. His ashtray mouth and brandy breath. He was bad, fist fighting his own demons, trying so hard to be good, every girl with daddy issues' dream.

I bleached the hair that grew out of my recently shaved head but wore wigs sometimes still - it had been over a year, but my hair just wouldn't grow.

"I'll love you until your hair is long again - that's how long I'll be by your side for." It was our inside joke. Neil's way of being romantic, because at that point it felt like it was going to take decades for it to grow back.

I asked my Founders Grill co-worker Zanele to take me to Soweto to let her sister sow hair extensions into my own hair. "Why are you getting a weave, you're white?" - was almost every one of my black friends' question to me. Never out of judgment, more out of surprise that I broke cultural rules that were made generations before us. I didn't see why I had to abide by society's stigmas. I missed the gap of being born into the "born-free" generation by two years (the growing population of South African youth born into a free and racially undivided South Africa, post-apartheid) but felt part of it in every way. I was even more-so driven to be an equalizer given my upbringing, desperate to end the cycle. Twenty-five-years post-apartheid, it had become less of an adjustment for white communities to accept people of color into their circles and activities, it was more-so an adjustment for people of color to receive whites into theirs - something that is not pointed out often. It's not that my friends didn't welcome me into their homes or gatherings - they were just not used to a white person showing up and treating them like a best friend who wanted to be part of their lives in such a way. At least, that was my experience. It was foreign to them. I was often stared at for doing things like attending my friend Shorty's kids' graduation - again being the only white person in the hall and after-party. Despite the surprised looks, I was always welcomed and never turned away. These interactions, these experiences, the relationships and conversations that grew out of them - were necessary to me, something I wanted in my life.

"I wasn't joking when I told you my other name is Sibongile" I teased my

African friends back. Sibongile is a popular African girl name and means "Thanks" in Zulu. A fellow student, Rozario, gave me the name when I was studying radio production at NEMISA, he didn't want me to feel left out because I was the only white girl in class and said - "Thanks" - "for being you" - when he gave me the name. It caught on among students and stuck with me all this time.

I took less and less shifts at Founders as my responsibilities at the radio station grew and grew. Even after a long week producing radio, I loved spending Friday nights serving drinks to the regulars alongside my bar-buddy, Nicole. Fridays weren't complete unless I saw Ross and Sol, and a firefighter whose name I can't remember - in my two years at Founders I grew up before their eyes, they could never wait for me to tell them what crazy thing I got to do in radio that week, they made me feel like I accomplished something for not just being a waitress like I was when they met me. They cheered me on. I had so many wonderful people in my life, whether they worked in the kitchen burning steaks, or hosted some of South Africa's favorite radio shows - they were all equal to me.

I was a social butterfly in my element having so many different circles of friends - I loved the space it was taking up in my life.

Neil and I hosted a spit-roast at our house alongside the swimming pool - our friend Sol provided the meat and we provided the spit. There was some drama when the company we hired the spit from bailed two days before our event. Neil had an anxiety attack and crawled into bed, a mess, feeling like our big party was a fail. I didn't understand his reaction. To me it was as simple as picking up the phone and calling every other company to arrange for a new spit. I didn't understand the severity of his depression - the disease was attacking him from every corner, and it started to affect our day-to-day lives. His shrink upped his med dosage and gave him sleeping tablets, but nothing helped. He was drinking a bottle of brandy a day, isolating himself from the outside world and me. We were fighting every day. I got into his sleeping tablets and acted out whenever he wanted to go somewhere without me - it all turned unhealthy really fast.

To add to his stress levels, his ex-wife was going through something and couldn't have their two girls live with her anymore. They moved in with us permanently. Neil and I were overjoyed to have them move in, but it was like I was the only one between him and I, who realized that our personal relationship as we knew it, was about to change.

It was different never being alone anymore, having Neil's priorities shift completely - as they should have. He was being the best father he knew how. He put them first every opportunity he had - something my father could never do for me. I respected him for it but didn't always know how to deal with him giving them something I never had.

I was twenty-three and back to playing house again, trying to stick by my partner's side while he was in an out of rehab for depression. I fought with his psychiatrist, telling her that they need to admit him for alcoholism, not just depression, but she told me that his drinking wasn't as big of a problem I was making it out to be. He admitted to being a functioning-alcoholic, even in front of her, but told me to accept that he wasn't going to do anything about it, he didn't want to try and change.

The medication turned him into half of the person I fell in love with. He still loved me but whether or not I chose to stick around - it was all the same to him. The side effect of the meds killed his sex drive, and with all that was going on, I didn't know what else to do but take it personally.

We had some good days, but our relationship was falling apart. I thought a trip down to Durban to meet my siblings would save us, and for a while it felt like it did. They instantly loved and accepted him, they could see how much we loved each other. He stayed in touch with them more frequently than I did, to the point that it annoyed me. It didn't take long for our Durban-romance to wear off, and we were at each other's throats again in no time.

My personal life had taken a knock, but I was still killing it at the radio station. I was promoted a second time and could afford to quit my waitering job. I used my newfound freedom to attend events and write articles and reviews for an online music magazine. With my status as a radio producer, it didn't take long to land invites to red carpets and award shows. I was interviewing some of my favorite bands and getting VIP passes to festivals and theaters for free.

Neil was the perfect wingman at events, it was the one time we didn't fight - the events became a space for us to "date" and get to know each other again. He held my purse countless times while I snapped photos of the latest who's who.

I tried to overlook the rift his brandy brought between us, but I had my own temptations, and gave into my own moment of weakness. Desperate for affection, I cheated on him with someone I had long-standing unfinished business with. I couldn't look at him after that, I had to tell him what I had done. He chose to forgive me, but it was clear, we were not the same two people we were when we fell in love, the same two people who fearlessly took the world on and would have fought anyone so we could be together. We had grown apart. All the obstacles we initially had to overcome meant nothing anymore. He was just a guy who didn't know how to make me happy anymore, and I was just a girl who lost her family for a guy who changed his mind - that was how I felt, but even then, no part in me could imagine a life without him in it.

I turned to a co-worker at the radio station, Michaela K, our resident psychic and spiritual healer. She helped me see myself clearly amidst my chaos, and whenever I was around anyone that spiritual, I felt close to my adoptive mom who opened my heart and mind to that world.

Michaela helped and healed so many souls before we lost her to cancer a year later.

I walked out of her home that day, my future still unknown - but with a clear sense of direction, and a certainty in my heart that I was going to be okay - and that was all that I could have asked for.

It wasn't long after my meeting with Michaela that Neil and I called it quits, on Valentine's Day of all days. I rocked up at my friend Mags' house - suitcase in one hand, and a bunch of red roses in the other. It was Sunday so she was cleaning her house, sipping on a straw in a curios-looking cup - she confirmed my suspicions later - she was drinking wine out of a sippy cup! She gave me a space to catch my breath, we became each other's "wife" - a nickname we took on after all the crying and laughing through episodes of "My Perfect Wedding." I stayed with her and Sihle for a couple of days to figure out my next move.

I loved the charity work we got to do on the breakfast show, helping those in need twice a week. Paying for medical bills, paying for weddings, paying children's school fees - I was part of something bigger than me and it changed something in me. I started my own list of charities I wanted to work with, causes I wanted to raise awareness around.

I had my first opportunity to be one of three organizers for a charity event - "Rocking for the Paws" - a music benefit concert for the animals of Roodepoort SPCA. I finally felt like I could even the score, for feeling helpless when I witnessed a dog chained in a small cage - knowing it was his life till the day he dies. I arranged for press at the fundraiser and performed along with about twenty other acts across three stages at Rumours Lounge. We raised thousands of Rands along with a mountain of animal food donated by guests.

The next charity I played a set for was Plushy Fest, a music benefit concert for the Jacaranda Children's Home - the orphanage my stepmom threatened to leave me at all those years back. Even though I managed to dodge that bullet, I knew very well that I could have been one of the kids in that orphanage, so I felt a very personal connection to the event and cause. It was poetic justice.

I had a taste of what it felt like to use my passion for good and loved playing shows so much that I started playing acoustic solo sets in bars and restaurants twice a week just for the hell of it. When I decided to venture into radio years before, I did so with the main purpose of meeting the station's music managers and the musicians I knew we would be interviewing - the goal was to get closer to people in the music industry, through radio, in the hopes that it would open doors for a career as a singer-songwriter - but I forgot about that completely once I had a taste of what it felt like to produce a radio show. Radio was all I wanted to live and breathe once I stepped into it.

Then on some random day, between performing at charity gigs and attending concerts on behalf of the music magazine I was writing for - I remembered. I remembered that I ventured into radio because of the music in me. Music was really what it was about for me. I tried to dismiss the thoughts, but they kept itching at me - I wasn't at peace until I gave as much of me to the music as I did to radio.

I rehearsed with my friend Beer's band "Amber Light Choices" - although I never got to perform with them, it gave me the chance to hear songs I had written come to life with a full band. My coworker and friend Lindsay McGuire took me under her wing and let me open at her shows and before I knew it, Fred, the owner of Rumours Lounge asked me to be an opening act for Ard Matthews - aka Nelson Mandela's adopted grandson and lead singer of one of South Africa's most well-known bands "Just Jinger."

I landed interviews at local radio stations and was written about in the local newspapers - the support grew naturally and more rapidly than I had expected. I wasn't exactly standing out among other local artists, I was as good as the next person who was doing well. Hell, I was worse, but to me, it was like the impossible became possible, like what I always wanted but never thought would happen - happened. I knew I was going to have to work hard if I wanted to become a better musician and try to stand out - I had a long way to go - but given my childhood struggles, I had surpassed my own expectations of how far I thought I would get. The fifteen-year-old girl inside of me, who had to consider running away from an abusive home, wanting to track down musicians and go on the road with them as an apprentice and sing my way out of my own personal hell - that little girl in me was fulfilled and had stars in her eyes, and a heartbeat echoing the words "what's next, what's next, what's next?!"

WE WERE FIRE
Poetry & Prose

We cried together often.
We cried when we made love.
We cried because we were so happy, and that was a brand-new feeling for both of us.

He was twice my age in human years, but it didn't count because he was not from here.
My mother warned me and in response, I told her she didn't know what she was talking about.
But I knew exactly what I was doing, what I was getting myself in to. So did he. And we cried about it often.

We cried because we started something neither of us knew how to keep alive.

Fire. Oh god. We knew how to make fire. And we fueled the flames and burnt our fingers and laughed the whole way through the blaze and we laughed as we watched our walls burn down.

We laughed because we were sick of crying about god's sick sense of humor, sick of crying about the law of attraction, sick of crying about what society demanded from us. So, we laughed at everyone who told us we would never last. We laughed in their faces.

We stopped making out in public bathrooms behind closed doors. We started arriving together, hand in hand. He opened the car door for me. We kissed right there in front of them, and I can't quite describe how fucking rebellious but

122

necessary that felt. Our fire was so wild, they all knew to stay far, far away from it. No one bothered us anymore, but when there was no one left for us to fight with, we fought each other and put it down to having fun, until neither of us were laughing anymore.

Through the kid-like laughter and the gut-wrenching cries, we were on fire. Fire. Oh god. We knew how to make fire.

We became so good at making fire we didn't notice that we were burning holes through each other's souls. And now there's nothing left but ashes, and an abandoned home, and voices that whisper: "we told you so."

SOMETIMES I PICTURE YOU
Poetry & Prose

Sometimes I picture myself, standing at your gate, suitcase in hand, again.
And although I can't remember the street name, oh wait, now I do.
Number 505? 703?
It's been two years, and I can't remember. But I would still find my way back, even without a map, if I allowed myself to try.

Sometimes I picture myself, standing outside your house, heart in hand, again.
And although you took my picture off the wall, you can still see me there, can't you?
It's been a long time, but you still smell me on your sheets, don't you?
Like that smell of the wood we burnt. That you can't wash out of your worn-out couch cushions. I still linger in the air, around you. I know. I don't mean to.
And all the memories we made there, between your four walls, you're stuck with them, and they are stuck with you.
You'd think I wouldn't have that problem, now that I'm someplace new.
But I do.
I still run into you.
On the corner of Chambers and Broadway.
In the middle of liquor stores and walkways.
On the insides of music shops and ashtrays.

Sometimes I picture you, standing at my door.
I live on the 12th floor.
But you've never been here before, and you don't know what the C train means, and how to get on it.
And all of me knows, you don't have it in you to even try to make sense of a subway map. I don't even know if you would call a cab.

And even if you made it all the way
To JFK
There's a chance you'd get on the first one way back.

You've never liked a challenge, I always liked fighting your battles
For you
It gave me something to do
But I can't fight myself
And I'm thankful that you never asked me to

So
Even though
I know for sure
I'll never find you
Outside my door
Where I live on the 12th floor
25 hours away from you
I just wanted to say
That to me
You are here, already.

PART SEVEN

F O U R W A Y S

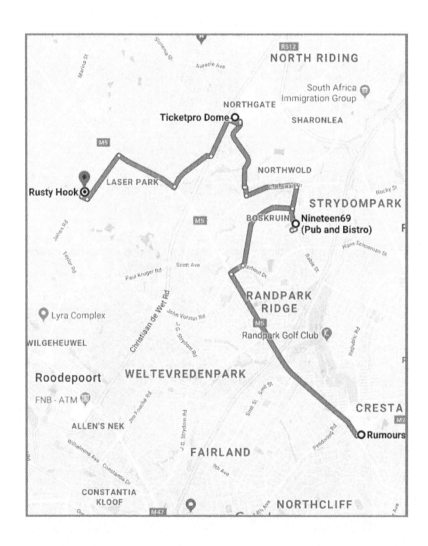

CARPET BURNS

"And this next one was supposed to be my wedding song, but we can't always get what we want, so." I announced before singing my next song on the Rumours Lounge stage - Radiohead's "High and Dry."

I had one too many Caste LITE beers twirling round my stomach when my ex, Neil and our friend Miles walked in and took a seat among the rest of my friends who were there to watch me perform. Him and I were both hurting from our breakup - I sung every hurtful and hateful song I could come up with when he walked in, uninvited. It was my goal to see him walk out, crying, and he did.

That very space - Rumours Lounge - it was the place our romance was born in and bloomed in once - I could hardly go there or walk into any other live venue around Johannesburg without bumping into him and his band, or some of our mutual friends. But I took some comfort in knowing people any and everywhere I went.

I'd never lived anywhere long enough for that to happen - to bump into people I knew around the neighborhood, until then. Even though I no longer had my man by my side, I still had a life - a very full one. Because of my radio job - I had no other option than waking up at five every morning, I had no other option than meeting new people every day. Attending events every weekend and carrying on with my life - but with all of that going on, there were still times I drove home at 9am when our radio show ended, locked myself in my room and just cried myself to sleep until I got up at five again the next morning,

I always thought that being in love was my super power, the thing that made my life extraordinary - all of a sudden, it was the things I got to do in my career, that blew my mind. Being sent up in the air by helicopter for our special election day broadcast - being tasked with having to produce the news reporter for the live broadcast from Lanseria airport. Coming up with solutions under pressure when we were experiencing technical difficulties broadcasting from the helicopter - making sure that the show carried on. I managed to steal a second for myself amidst the chaos, taking in the aerial views of the Soweto Water Towers, the Union Building in Pretoria I used to visit with my dad and stepmom on Sunday evenings. Appreciating the contrast between my past and present. Being conscious of where I came from and where I ended up - finding peace in those stolen moments - moments I could hardly believe, myself.

Our show had grown into the unimaginable. Every day was surreal - from meeting Joost van der Westhuizen and a string of other ex-Springbok players I grew up watching and cheering on alongside my dad when I was a teenager, to taking pledges on air for an hour, fundraising in honor of Nelson Mandela - building a house for Julia and Sihle who called a shack - a few plates of metal -

home, before that day.

From team build trips in Cape Town, sand boarding down the dunes in De Hoop - near Cape Agulhas - the southern tip of Africa, to the HOT cruise - when our station partnered with MSC cruises and sailed from Durban to the Mozambique Islands.

Life was wondrous, more so than I could ever have imagined or have asked for, but there were days I had to fight for my place in radio - I was one of the youngest employees, working for men who had been in the industry for ten, twenty, thirty years. They grew up in the day and age where they interned unpaid for seven years before being granted an opportunity to prove themselves and get onto the payroll. I appreciated that. I ate dirt for what felt like a very long time, until somebody reminded me it wasn't the 1980s anymore - and that working unpaid for seven years in today's world is probably illegal - so there was no shame in not feeling guilty that I managed to get myself into a respectful position at such a young age. A lot of my friends in the radio and TV industry felt exploited, but I felt like I had gotten as far as any other twenty-three-year-old would have gotten in the industry - and that was enough for me. I had peace with my tiny paycheck - I had everything I needed, and I had never been happier, doing the work I was doing.

I was living a three-minute drive away from the radio station, sharing a house with seven friends. The three coolest things about our property was, having a pool, an outdoor pizza oven, and a peacock roaming around the grounds freely - I called her Katy Perry. I lived on the Horn & Phillips breakfast served at the radio station, and sparkling water and chicken-mayo sandwiches at home.

Life was busy, but simple. And then I went and changed that all by trying to date again. I had guys mad at me for not putting out after they paid for the movie, others falling in love with me when I really didn't want them to. I fell for girls whose boyfriends fell for me - it was just a mess all round. And then I met him. The only one who managed to take my breath away after the hardest breakup of my life.

The night I met Sam, I thought the girl who was hosting the get-together - invited only me over. I thought I was heading over to her house to sweep her off her feet, but I clearly misread the message. I arrived to a small crowd - she was playing matchmaker and aced it. Sam was sweet, gentle, reserved but knew what to say to throw me off - just so he could be there to catch me. He spent summers as a diving instructor at Sodwana Bay - the beach I practically grew up on a stone-throw away from Hluhluwe - I felt like I already knew him.

A few dates turned into sudden plans of wanting to travel together internationally. He was the brave one between the two of us, he tried to include himself in my future, but I couldn't see the wood for the trees. His attempts went over my head because I was used to Neil who communicated a certain way. I was used to being fought for and begged to stay. Sam wasn't like that.

I didn't want to give up the independence I had found after Neil, and I was too proud and scarred to be vulnerable. I didn't know how to let Sam love me, and I hated him for it, but somehow, I couldn't keep myself away from him either.

Our highs were so high, and we didn't even have lows, just silences in between. Just silence every time we were apart.

I started looking into work opportunities abroad, to which he started looking into new women to date - only, I was the only one who was open and honest about my new ventures. Our mutual friends knew that he was two-timing me and didn't say anything.

I wish my mind could remember to list his flaws, but they escape me. My heart has always said "but, but, but..."

But he let me sleep in his shirt.

But he made me bacon for breakfast.

But he put on a collared shirt to take me out on dates, and for a while, he wanted to move to California if I did.

He gave me all that, and all I could give him was an unspoken, but definite "I don't need you."

Sitting in his T-shirt, cross-legged on his kitchen barstool - the same place we first kissed - with one too many pieces of bacon crunching between my hung-over jaws, I tried explaining why I wasn't in bed when he woke up that morning. "The whole America thing, I have a feeling that it's really going to happen. I feel a little anxious, I couldn't sleep, have you ever felt like that?"

He knew I had never traveled abroad before, so he told me about his diving ventures in Asia and what he learned from going away and coming back.

"You should go. Johannesburg will still be here when you decide to come back, I will still be here when you come back. You should go. One day if you decide to come back you will come back only to realize that nothing changed while you were away, changing." I was pretty sure he read that in a book somewhere, but thought it was sweet coming from his mouth in anyway.

I hadn't made my mind up about leaving yet, but he knew that I was going to, before I did. Six months before I left for the States, he knew I was going to get on that plane. He knew I was just that kind of person, even when I wasn't sure that I was. He started making peace with it, by slowly disappearing from my life as if he thought I wouldn't notice. I noticed. And I wasn't ready for it. I asked him not to walk away.

I ironically had a really bad motorcycle accident right after that - ironic because Sam is also a paramedic. He was the first one I called, where I stood on President Fouché Drive with skin scraped off all of my right side and both my knees - no longer as tipsy as I was a few minutes before the crash - but he did not answer my call. Neil raced from his music gig to pick me up and took me to the ER. That was single-handedly my most embarrassing moment of being a human-being. I had to take two weeks leave from work, which bothered me more than the fact that I could have died. I couldn't stand the thought of anyone being disappointed in me - even though they were there to take care of me, not mad at me for my mistake. The people around me weren't just my friends, they were my parents because they knew I had none. I felt like I failed myself and every one of them.

Sam eventually came around, it was the only time I wasn't pissed at him for smoking weed - instead I joined him for once - to ease the pain from the accident. When he left that night, he left me for good. I lay there high off him, and high off whatever we smoked, listening to some Alanis Morissette song, thirsty on my bed after he had gone, hearing every word, every instrument, separately, clearly, and slowed down, with all those somethings rushing through my bloodstream.

One morning I just woke up to find a girl posting about their amazing romance all over his Facebook wall. I fought with our mutual friends when they eventually told me that he moved on, only for them to remind me "Lyla, you're leaving, He is trying to protect his own heart. It's not easy for him."

It's like I hadn't even heard what he said weeks before that moment. "Lyla, I love you too, but you're leaving."

I didn't even have a successful job offer in the States yet, I didn't even have a visa yet, I was months away from those things even being a possibility - but he was clear.

LINES
Poetry & Prose

Do away with your lines of blow
Replace them with these lines I wrote
It's a different kind of high
But you'll understand
Once you had a whiff of our personal brand

We seem like a good batch you say as you taste it
Time's not on my side so don't you waste it
I treat each time as if it's the last when we have it
Cos God knows I cannot afford this habit

Every time that you kiss me goodbye
It's like hitting a low after being high
And every time I have to play hard to get
It's like having to turn down another hit

I'm shaking and I'm sweaty as I'm coming down
I call your name you're no longer around
Lying on the floor waiting for your call
But every time I check my phone – nothing at all

But every time that you tell me I can snarf it
I try to find a way to fit it into my budget
If this is my only chance to cope
Then fuck it I don't mind being broke

Every time that you kiss me goodbye
It's like hitting a low after being high
And every time I have to play hard to get
It's like having to turn down another hit

I haven't eaten or slept in five days
But I feel so satisfied
You gave me more than I could handle
And it took away more than my appetite

Every time that you kiss me goodbye
It's like hitting a low after being high
And every time I have to play hard to get
It's like having to turn down another hit

So, do away with your lines of blow
Replace them with these lines I wrote

SO NOT SEXY
Poetry & Prose

I'm a little lost
And a little hurt, today
Kicking myself for the things I did
And didn't say

Running out of tablets
This heartache is a headache that won't go away
Guess I'm the loser
In the game you made me play

Now I'm making New Year's Eve plans
In November already
Cause I don't want to wake up
All alone in January
And all the time I spent alone in my life
You made up for in one night

We're so in love
But something is so not right
We look at each other
With caution in our eyes

Cause I think it's so not sexy
When you light up in your car
Pushing weed around with your credit card
You think it's so not sexy
That I have so many ghosts
And it's so not sexy when I choose to show my soul

Well there was a time
That you showed me yours
There was a time
That I called you beautiful

And at times
You let me have it all
Scared the shit out of me when I realized
You were letting me go
You're so fucking predictable

We're so in love
But something is so not right
We look at each other
With judgment in our eyes

Cause I think it's so not sexy
That you're always stoned
And that you can't even wait
Until we get home
You think it's so not sexy
That I have you all figured out
And it's so not sexy when I choose
To show myself

I'm a mess at 24
But if you want me – I'm yours
I'm a mess
And I'm having fun
And if you want you can keep me around to keep you young

You're a mess at 39
For a moment you were all mine
Loved you the way that you were
But I'll get over you in time

I think it's so not sexy
That getting high is the highlight of your day
And you think it's so not sexy
That I have so much to say

I wanted you to be happy
So, I tried to love the things that made you happy too
It wasn't enough
I'm too fucking much
It's time that I fall
The fuck – out of love with you

MEET ME IN INDIA
Lyrics

It's been a year
Since you left me for another woman
I should be mad at you
But all's forgotten and forgiven

And I try my hardest
To remember the good times, only
But I still remember
All the promises you made me, baby

So, won't you meet me in India?
Because after all this time
I'm still into ya

Won't you meet me in India?
And remind me
Just what I mean to ya

I saw the pictures
Of your December vacation
The one we planned together
Instead you took her with ya

She sure looks good
In your diving equipment
Looks like the two of you
Have made quite the commitment

But won't you meet me in India?
Because after all this time
I'm still into ya

Won't you meet me in India?
And remind me
Just what I mean to ya

I won't forget
What you said
That night in the parking lot

When it rained
And you explained
The rules of the roads
In India

I won't forget
What you said
That night in my bedroom

When it rained
And you explained
That you loved me too

So, won't you meet me in India?
Because after all this time
I'm still into ya

Won't you meet me in India?
And remind me
Just what I mean to ya

Meet me in India
Meet me in India

FOURTEEN ORGASMS
Poetry & Prose

I once slept with a girl, who claimed she had fourteen orgasms before I had one.

I did not believe her.

But it seemed she believed herself - so who was I to argue?

I still did.

"Do you really know what an orgasm feels like?" I asked her.

Because I thought she had to be mistaking tofu, for bacon. A split-second tingle, for the minute-long body contractions, loss of control over muscles, mind - blank for a second - kind of pleasure.

The internet says that many women don't have those kinds of orgasms till their thirties, forties.

I thought maybe that applied to her.

It bothered me, didn't leave me. I thought about it often. At first, I didn't know why.

Then it hit me one day - I was afraid. Afraid that I was suffering from a similar delusion.

AJ? I loved him, in chaotic, unhealthy, life-threatening ways.

AJ's best friend? I loved him like a lover I could trust with my life.

Neil? I love him, in drastic, painful, beautiful ways.

Sam? I love him, I would still tell him that now, I'd still say, "come and get me."

Willem? I spent less than seventy-two hours with him in total, three years ago - but I love him, and I am not over him. I can't sit in an airport without the thought of him overpowering me, numbing me. I look for him everywhere.

"Do I really know what love feels like?" I asked myself.

Am I mistaking tofu for bacon?

I didn't love every next one of them because the previous one had left me, I loved them despite it. I have not loved every man I've laid with, I have not loved every man that I liked - still, do I know the difference?

I'd like to say I do.

So, who the fuck are you to argue?

I once slept with a girl, who claimed she had fourteen orgasms before I had one.

I did not believe her.

But it seemed she believed herself - she seemed to be content, satisfied.

So, who was I to ask her if she knew what she was talking about?

I still did.

PART EIGHT

SANDTON

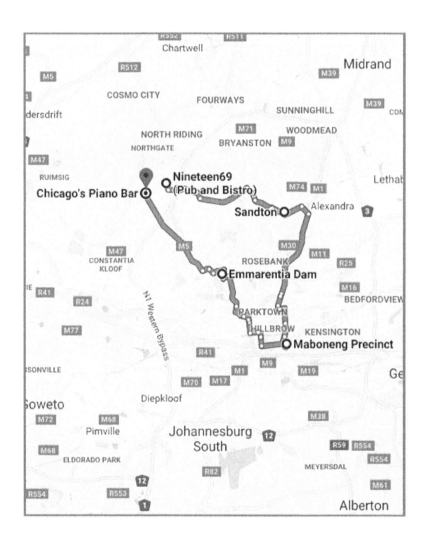

ABSTINENCE APP

"Since I was fifteen, I've either been with a guy or breaking up with a guy. I haven't had so much as two weeks just to deal with myself." - Elizabeth Gilbert, *Eat Pray Love*

At the age of twenty-four I had eight years of serious relationships and more than a few short-lived romantic encounters behind me. The reality was that I needed to take a moment for myself, although I loved myself, knew myself, knew what it was to be alone - I needed a moment to "update" what I thought I knew about me, about love, about life. So, after a November night at a house party where Lindsay broke down her own bedroom door to get to the other side – me, in bed with someone else's boyfriend – I thought that maybe it was time to take that moment, take that breath, give myself that break.

After picking up the screws and door handle off Lindsay's floor, and swallowing a strong cup of coffee on her couch that morning, I started my one-year journey of abstinence - Abstinence App in hand - trust me to find one and download it to my phone. My friends thought I was losing my mind - but I was actually having a really hard time.

Yvette had been going on Tinder dates - I had no idea what Tinder was or how it worked. She was genuinely looking for long-term relationships on the app and her ventures seemed promising at times. As per her request, I often third-wheeled when she went out to meet someone new.

Our team took a month off work from the radio station for the December holidays, maybe I was bored - I was a couple of days into my year of abstinence, I don't even know why I downloaded the Tinder app - trying to swipe myself into a sexless-committed-relationship? Perhaps I thought it was possible, oblivious to what people really used it for - hook ups. I didn't know any better, but I also couldn't be bothered to chat with anyone I matched with - it was all very weird to me.

Friday night hit, and what was supposed to be a trip to the grocery store for chicken, turned into drinks at the local dive – as Friday nights do, when you put Yvette and I in one room. Going back to Nineteen69 that night was quite difficult for me because Sam used to take me there, but I figured it had been long enough.

Yvette and I bumped into a few familiar faces there, and as they went off in their own directions one by one, there Yvette and I were left, innocently sitting by ourselves at a table by the bar – we ordered something to eat. I almost choked on my chicken wing, opening my first-ever Tinder message notification.

Willem: "Hey Lyla… tell me where and when, and whether or not I should bring a nice bottle of wine. I can drive to your humble abode after I finish my Wagyu Ribeye piece of delicious beef. Does 20:30 ETA work in your world, my ooh-la-la friend?"

I thought; first of all, who the fuck still speaks like that?! Are you Edward Cullen? Is it 1920? Is this guy trying to be a gentleman? Is he trying to get laid? Is it supposed to sound creepy? Is it supposed to sound sexy? If I have one more tequila, will it maybe sound sexy?!

He went in for the kill the minute he walked through the doors of '69. Face in my neck. I didn't even have to be brave, he swept in at full speed, giving me no time to even think about it.

He walked into Nineteen69 as if he owned it, he unapologetically kissed the hell out of me 10 minutes into our first date, in front of everybody. I wasn't dressed for the occasion; I didn't even plan to show. I just happened to be in the area because Yvette and I were gonna go to the Checkers to buy chicken for dinner.

I agreed to stay for "one drink" to humor this guy who wanted to "get to know me" - I was so tipsy by the time he arrived.

Maybe it was the whiskey, or his cigar mouth. His collared shirt unbuttoned or his French tongue. We couldn't stop talking, stop laughing, stop touching. I thought I'd be funny and spoke a bit of Afrikaans to him, he replied in French - neither one of us understood the other, but our eyes told another story, we could read each other without relying on language, without relying on words.

My hair was up in a ponytail and my shirt didn't match the rest of my outfit, I felt like a mess. But he put his jacket on me and took the band out of my hair, letting it down, pushed his fingers against the back of my head and didn't break eye contact until he knew he had me.

He had me.

Instant attraction, instant gratification. We couldn't stay away from each other. I was almost - in love, and he was having fun.

He won, a game I didn't know we were playing. He was the car I couldn't see in my blind spot, the impact I felt when he T-boned me and ran me off the road. The tar that scraped my skin off like a hot knife spreading melted butter on bread - all over again. He was an accident. We were an accident.

He begged me to ride back with him to his Sandton penthouse - and it took everything in me to decline.

Driving away from Willem… I was staring out the window of my Uber with blurry vision thinking… What the fuck just happened, am I supposed to be happy, am I supposed to not care, will I ever hear from him again because I didn't put out, is he the one, what will our wedding song be? Luckily Yvette and I stopped for ice cream and toasted sandwiches on the way home, so by the time I got into bed, I was kind of sober.

I woke up the next morning with one question on my mind: What do you call the morning after, when neither of you took your clothes off the night before? I was kind of happy, I really felt good, until I reached for my phone and opened Facebook - first mistake of the day.

Scroll... scroll... scroll...

Tears... tears... tears...

I ran into Yvette's room handing her my phone before sticking my head into a pillow screaming.

There were photos all over social media of Sam on his way to his scuba dive workation at the coast, with the new girl by his side. I allowed myself two tears, and then I got up, Joburg Live Loud media passes in hand - I met Bernice there for a music fest. As we walked through the festival gates at Emmerentia in Greenside around noon, the first teenager who fell victim to "too much fun in the sun" stumbled out the gates with his own vomit all over his shirt.

That was all I needed to decide not to drink that day, I kept in mind that I had to go straight to my gig at Chicago's after the fest, and on to Yvette's dinner party at Tony's Spaghetti after that.

The day continued with the smell of sweat and sunscreen all around, a sniff of weed here and there, the sounds of Matthew Mole, thousands of people around...but I felt alone.

It usually wasn't a big deal to me to go to events flying solo, but even hanging with a few familiar faces and taking advantage of potential networking connections, was another level of difficult for me that day. My head was stuck somewhere between Harrismith and Sodwana Bay, tangled up in the thought of Sam and his new girlfriend road tripping, on their way to go and do the things him and I were talking about doing.

During the day, Willem and I touched base again on WhatsApp, and he invited my friends and I over to his hotel, after Yvette's dinner party.

10pm came and went, most of us had had dinner, others had just arrived, some were keen on the idea of heading to Sandton and others not so much. I had a long day and figured: everyone was going to go home with their other halves by the end of the night, so I didn't feel too bad for sneaking off and jumping into an Uber to Willem's hotel, for a little fun of my own. My Abstinence App was irrelevant at that moment – like nonexistent. The accumulated twenty days of abstinence was enough of an achievement to me after the day I had.

On the road it was a bit of an inner battle, the twenty days I had been avoiding men for, had left me feeling really good about myself, but I also felt like I clicked with Willem at Nineteen69 the night before, and I definitely felt very attracted to him. Also knowing that he was leaving the country for who-knew-how-long, came the break of dawn, I kind of justified the fact that I was probably going to put out with the pressures of not having time on our side. Either way, if

I was going to break my twenty-day streak of abstinence – for this guy - I could totally live with myself. Especially because, for the first time in a while, I could tell the difference between really enjoying someone's company and feeling attracted to them, compared to just wanting to fill a void, by being with an ex or even a friend's boyfriend - which is what made me download the abstinence app in the first place.

Finally, at the hotel... We met and of course... a kiss hello. I totally loved it – the way he was dressed in flip-flops, trunks and some sort of restaurant branded T-shirt that must have been a freebie. I felt a little more comfortable - wearing flats and a red dashiki, having messy hair, sunburnt shoulders and being dehydrated from the fest - not how I pictured myself walking into a two-story penthouse – but his kid-like excitement to show me the city lights from the rooftop and share his thoughts on the architecture of the building distracted me from any self-consciousness I might have built up on the drive over. And of course, that kiss against the ledge, the breeze against my skin and the stars above us, just put me in a different headspace. I wasn't exactly expecting a romantic night, I actually had no expectations at all - but I was with a Frenchman, and I suppose one can't expect anything less when in the French's company. Ooh-la-la indeed!

Stone cold sober, overtired and a little guarded, it wasn't too hard to be a toned-down version of myself, which is what I wanted to be in his company. Partly because I wasn't quite ready to show my whole self again to someone, only to feel absolutely rejected if things were to go south, and partly because I often felt as though I am too much for one man to handle anyway. Too crazy, too mischievous, too talkative, too sarcastic, too flirty, too philosophical, too indecisive, too adamant, and, too focused on getting my shit together, when I am so distracted by my habit of being so happy-go-lucky simultaneously.

I ended up showing more of my personality than I wanted to - in his company, it was hard not to. I was quite thrown by just how many of my above-mentioned characteristics Willem possessed himself. For once I felt like a guy was actually quite a lot for *me* to handle – and this is absolutely what I would order if men were on an IHOP menu and I could take my pick. I just had no expectation that the perfect candidate would ever come across my path – or that he existed for that matter.

A little low on energy but high on hormones, there I was, as usual being a really bad listener, because I knew I probably already had that exact conversation with another version of him, and I also really struggle to retain information even when I am really intrigued by the conversation, but he was happy to talk and I was happy to listen.

I got so lost in all the things I liked that came out of his mouth, just staring at him with a blank look on my face out of awe, that on more than one occasion, he stopped to ask if I needed clarification on what he is talking about. I jokingly laughed it off, asking him if he needed me to acknowledge that I understood the things he said, after he finished every sentence.

His manner of conversing made it easy for me to tell that he overthinks everything, and constantly analyzes and questions everything in his mind. The best part to me was, if that was how much he was letting spill out of his mouth, imagine all the things he talks to himself about in his mind that I don't know about yet – how attractive is that?

Willem seemed like a bit of a "clicker" – a lot like me – we get on with people and we are accommodating, smart enough to know how to handle any situation and conversation, to get out of it what we want and still be accommodating towards the other party's needs. But I wanted to believe it was more to both of us than just "playing the game." More than just a rush to get to the… "c'est dans la poche" part, to him (French for - it's in the pocket, a done deal).

I can say what I want, but I knew when I made the decision to leave Yvette's dinner party and head towards Willem, that I was going out for a hookup, a one-night stand. Perhaps I can only speak for myself, but even in times when we are fully aware of what we are walking into, a "no-strings-attached" hook up, I can arguably say that 99% of the time we still get our hopes up, subconsciously sometimes, hoping that, this might be it, secretly hoping for the night to go better than an average date, and for it to potentially lead somewhere profound.

Being a workaholic, I was so used to knowing what I would get out of my projects when I knew exactly how much effort I had put in. Trying to use the same mindset in a relationship was such a mind fuck. I realized that I had been painting the two scenarios with the same brush – in vain. I thought that in relationships I could calculate the risks and predict the return on investment, when in fact, I had no say in where the other person was at, in their journey, so calculations and predictions were pointless. And, thinking I would get out what I had put in – that just wasn't guaranteed. In my experience this reigned true in long-term relationships as well as short-lived flings. After Neil and Sam, I was no longer disappointed when I didn't get out what I put in. I lost all hope in love - I wasn't sad about it, just done with it.

I had friends complaining about months of Tinder dates gone wrong, and second dates that never happened, guys who were slacking at making a move – so my friends applauded me for "winning at Tinder" within a week and acing my first "Tinder date", saying they wish they could just come across someone they could also just click with so instantly, or a guy who actually showed some interest.

But what I had to stress was that I didn't get lucky, and I was not "winning at Tinder." What use was it to find someone I instantly got on with, someone I could be myself around, and feel accepted by? What use was it to click with someone and have a few moments of absolute honesty and absolute passion, and elevating conversations, only to watch him watch me drive away in an Uber the next day, probably never to call me again. Having to honor the unspoken rules of a one-night-stand.

I think that it was one of the hardest things I had to learn to do in this jungle of a dating scene - that we all want to have a piece of. We want to experience it all, the good, the bad, the short-lived, the commitment, the excitement of something new. We want a taste of all of it – on our terms. We're unapologetically heartless by choice, running around with an appetite for something real, yet when we find it, we say it can't be and we carry on with our lives, and onto the next hunting trip.

But I kept reliving my time with him, over and over in my head.

Willem: "What happened to your skinned-knees?"
Lyla: "I don't want to talk about it."
Willem: "How long has it been since you had sex?"
Lyla: "Twenty days."
Willem: "That's specific. Why have you been counting?"
Lyla: "Because I am only just starting to enjoy my own company."

He breathed out an amused laugh, trying to figure me out - like he was getting some enjoyment out of me not letting him get very far with his quest. Like it was bothering him that he couldn't put my pieces together.

He had been traveling the world for years, stepped foot onto half the globes' countries.

He paused.

"You know, I often meet someone gorgeous, a model-type girl, someone who seems like the whole package on the outside, someone I think I am going to have fireworks with, only to sleep with them and feel nothing."

I stared at him in silence, my eyes begging him to say what I thought he was about to.

"What happened last night? The way you reacted to me? The way I reacted to you? I didn't expect for it to feel that way between us."

I had no words, I had nothing to say back to him. I was taken back, my mind running wild thinking; when you've seen it all, at what point does "rough around the edges - Lyla" become more appealing to you than the model types hanging around because you have cash to burn?

At what point do you allow yourself to let your guard down, and when you fall, how do you put your pride aside and put your heart in the hands of someone who might just break it again? At what point do you let that person know that you think they are captivating and that you want more of them – because, apparently, that is just "so not sexy".

Everything I went through with Sam taught me not to lay my heart on the table. I was trying to play by an old set of rules that didn't apply to Willem's world - but I didn't know that, back then.

I think the bad habits we fall into when we are constantly looking for "the one" – is that we only look for the good in people, we are quick to decide what we like and we downplay the things we see that we don't like, staring at hazards with a smile on our face and winking at them through rose tinted glasses. Quick to start the negotiations with ourselves on which areas we are willing to compromise our beliefs or "rules" on and what the other person will simply have to live with, if they want us.

Finally meeting someone who could handle all of me and ticked so many of the right boxes - that right there, was like opening a whole new can of worms to me. I always felt like I dated men who turned out to be weaker than me, less ambitious than me - for the first time, I met my match, someone not even I, could keep up with.

I looked back a week later, asking myself if was it worth an inner battle during the confusing 15-minute Uber drive to Sandton? I thought "yes." It was a night that changed quite a few of the ideals I had previously lived by...Influenced my way of thinking and changed a few aspects of what I wanted in a partner... Yeah, it was worth it. And if it was only one night – I guessed it was true what they say - that one moment could in fact hold the power to change you forever. They say that, sometimes, forever is just a moment.

To think that at one point in time a fifteen-minute Uber drive was the only thing that stood between me and this "perfect candidate." And I couldn't help thinking, what if, just maybe, those fifteen minutes were not quite over yet.

NO-NO NOMAD'S MATING CALL

Lyla: "Do you know anyone I can sell my bed to?"

Yvette: "Why would you want to sell your bed?"

Lyla: "Because I'm moving in with you until I leave for America."

Yvette: "No, you're not moving to America! I thought that was just a weird phase?"

Lyla: "I've made up my mind."

Yvette: "It's because of Willem, isn't it?"

Lyla: "What?! No?! What are you even talking about?"

Yvette: "You want to be like him. Haven't you seen yourself, heard yourself lately? Ever since you met him you can't sit still. It's like you are becoming him or something. You want to travel all the time. You've started leaning Italian for God's sake. What's that all about?"

I thought she was being crazy, but in hindsight, I might have been more. I didn't have a job offer in the States yet, and without a job offer, I couldn't apply for a visa yet either.

I had seen my life coach Dom at 27 Boxes in Melville a few days before that. She told me that it didn't matter that I didn't have a job offer yet - if I wanted to move abroad, I needed to act like it was already happening, I needed to give up my lease and quit my radio job. "The universe will follow your lead," she told me.

It sounded pretty legit to me.

For a split second I wasn't sure I had the balls to do that, but as soon as I got home after seeing her, I started packing my bags. My landlord nearly killed me for not renewing my lease for another year, she was so pissed that she didn't want me to stay for the last month I was legally entitled to still stay there for. She threw all my belongings out of the room I was renting - my roommates packed it back in, and she threw it back out again. She was a piece of work. I just took her reaction of having the house staff pack my stuff in garbage bags, throwing it into the garage - as a sign from the universe that I needed to leave, more than ever.

I stayed with Yvette January into February. She tried every trick in the book to talk me out of my big plans - impromptu trips to Durban, Sushi dinners at YuMe, she even attended my gigs she never showed up for in the past. She was the only one who knew that I was trying to move abroad - and it literally killed her because we worked at the same radio station and she couldn't let my secret out.

I told her I could see it - I'd be happy in the States. "You're probably going to visit me and get yourself an American boyfriend there before I do," I joked.

One night - late February, I finally received the call I had been waiting for.

"Four kids?! You are telling me you are quitting radio to go and look after four kids in New York? Are you sure you are doing the right thing?"

She didn't want me to leave, but more than anything, she didn't want me to make a decision I'd regret later. I fought with her "for taking my life choices so personally" so many times - but she knew me better than anyone, so I got it.

I signed my new work contract and scheduled my visa appointment - my agency warned me that they have had plenty of visas declined and that it could happen to me too - but I chose not to hear that part. My visa appointment was two weeks away but if it was successful, I didn't want to leave my radio team high and dry, quitting without any notice. I made the decision to drive back to the radio station, to resign there and then, despite the uncertainty of not having been granted a visa yet.

Telling my team that I was leaving was one of the hardest things I've ever had to do, I almost couldn't get the words out of my mouth when I stood opposite them on the station's balcony, but I knew if I didn't leave, I would forever be an interviewer and never the interviewee. I'd forever be adjusting the studio mic for guests and watch them perform on air, and never be the one behind the mic, singing my guts out. And the music forces inside begged me to change my own future - take a chance. Telling the music in me "no" wasn't an option anymore, it was grabbing me by the hair pulling me in new directions - I almost felt I had no control over it, but wanted to honor it.

They told me I'd be stupid to turn down an opportunity to live and work in New York - but I knew it probably took everything in them to say those words to me with an encouraging smile after all the effort they put into my career – but they still did. "You have your visa, right?" they asked staring me down - knowing full well I am the type of person who'd naively quit my job before having my papers in hand. I lied. I couldn't say no and give them the satisfaction of being

146

right. Thank God it worked out.

Yvette booked us a getaway for the weekend - I had to quiet my mind with all that was happening, and she wanted to spend quality time with her bestie - she finally made peace with the fact that I was really leaving.

We were an hour or two out of the city - in the bush, in the middle of nowhere, I had a moment to think about what she said about Willem. I started to wonder if there was any truth in her accusation, if I was subconsciously trying to be him.

I took out my laptop and typed this diary entry –

If you could travel the world, see a hundred different countries, experience every different culture, and get laid in a thousand different mind-blowing ways - wouldn't you want to?

So, when I meet Nomad, however much I'm inclined to, how could I possibly fault him for having this mindset, and, a mating call that is so animalistic, so instinctive, and so hard to decline?

Away for a couple of days glamping (glamour camping - check it out, it's a thing) and as surely as I watch the male Weaver bird weave new nest after new nest, as his female rips each one to shreds in dissatisfaction, just so, Nomad will say and do what needs to be said to get to the ultimate state with me – naked.

As simple and sweet, and as black and white, as picking a partner is in the animal kingdom, just so, things progress as naturally with Nomad. And I almost feel a little bit in love. But.....in love with him, or in love with his lifestyle and mindset? If I could live like him and experience romance after romance, all over the world, would I? The idea is still a little much for me to wrap my head and heart around. If I am ever able to though, one thing is for sure, when I grow up, I would want to be like him – even if it is for just a little while.

But I can't help but wonder if Nomad is capable of truly loving, or experiencing love, even when it is shoved in his face or served to him on a silver platter. A different bed every week, a different cherie every couple of days… doesn't it get old? Isn't the ideal situation one where your partner knows you inside and out and is by your side come rain or shine?

Nomad isn't a shallow person, so, surely he must have emotional thoughts. I wonder when last he cried. I wonder if I ever cross his mind in his most quiet moments...as he crosses mine...

Perhaps Nomad's love is truer than the rest? Having seen more than most, and living his life like an open vessel, dishing out generous helpings of himself, and dishing up knowledge, stories and experiences to satisfy his healthy appetite - he seems captivated by every moment, authentic and sincere. Or perhaps these are learnt skills he uses to his advantage?

I suppose it comes with being worldly - Nomad acing the mating call. Is it even surprising that small-town-girl-me has fallen victim to this primal experience?

147

As naturally as the female Weaver bird decides that she is ready to mate with her clever little nest-builder - when she is now happy with the humble abode he has built - that is how naturally I fall into Nomad's sheets when I decide he has now said all the pretty little charming things that I want to hear.

And as instinctive as it is for some geese to up and leave a continent for another seasonally, just the same way, nomad carelessly hops onto his business class flight the next morning, and carries on with his life, elsewhere, until further notice...no excuses, no explanations. Just a natural state and progression.

In a world where I've had to wonder where I stand with my partner, or a person I am "seeing' (but we are not labeling it) – how refreshing is it to skip the games, the small talk, and just be myself with Nomad? At least for a little while. To give in to impulse instead of reason, to show all of ourselves honestly, unapologetically giving in to the attraction, and acknowledging that our romance might not go beyond this weekend – bittersweet - but the honesty is refreshing.

People say one-night-stands are complicated. They're not. Nomad has it easy. No-strings-attached encounters aren't difficult, commitment is. Being in a relationship is. Being married is. Forgiving your partner when they cheat is. Trying to keep romance alive is. Growing apart is. Staying together for the kids is. So why do we enter into relationships when they are such hard work? Is it because we don't want to be alone? Or because "it is just the right thing to do?" Or maybe it is just because we are human and not animal, after all.

I can almost say that I can wrap my head around Nomad's lifestyle choices. But what does Nomad get up to when there is no one catching his eye on Tinder, or at the local dive tonight? Does Nomad ever get lonely and depressed like the rest of us?

Why do the rest of us ache for relationships so desperately when Nomad is seemingly doing everything to avoid them?

Why does it feel more comforting me, to wake up next to someone I am in a committed relationship with, (Even though we have our problems and probably aren't compatible in the long term) but who knows all of me, and knows what to do when things go wrong, without me having to even ask?

Do we long for companionship or romance? Because nowadays it seems that the two are worlds apart.

(Diary entry ends)

She was right. I had him on a pedestal. Something in me changed after meeting him that December - and I didn't even know it until I sat down and typed it out. It's like we kissed all the way down the elevator ride to my Uber where he bid me farewell that December morning - I drove away to Maboneng and Hayley Williams' "Airplanes" played on the radio - I blinked and now two months later, I gave up my apartment, quit my job, and was moving to New York. It was a long time coming, but he changed whatever needed changing in me - for me to actually make the move.

I even forgot that, back then, New York was his dream, not mine - after mistaking a raw egg for a cooked one, he broke it open on the coffee table only for it to splatter everywhere. We finally contained our laughter and he told me he just bought property. "I wanted to buy in New York, but I could only buy one spot in a parking garage with the money I had! So, I bought a house in Nigeria instead."

I wanted to tell him about everything that changed in my life since we met - but instead, I only managed to get two letters out of my thumbs and onto my screen to him - "Hi."

MY WEDDING NIGHT

"Darling I'm a nightmare dressed like a daydream. So, it's gonna be forever, or it's gonna go down in flames - you can tell me when it's over, if the high was worth the pain. Cause we're young and we're reckless - we'll take this way too far. It will leave you breathless, or with a nasty scar." – **Blank Space, Taylor Swift**

"Hi from two countries at the same time!" Willem replied with a photo of him on a ski trip, with one foot in Italy and the other in Switzerland. I melted like the snow under his boots - completely disintegrating.

He was excited to tell me that he would be back in South Africa soon - I told him I was leaving for a trip to the States. I didn't go into detail.

He suggested we host a send-off party together before I left - I barely finished reading the whole message.

"I'm getting married! I'm getting married! I'm getting married!" I yelled on full volume running around the radio station telling my friends that they were invited to my wedding night - it was a huge joke - I loved making my friends laugh by playing silly, they went along with it of course - we worked in entertainment - what can I say? Dramatizing the ordinary was part of our daily job, and in our DNA.

I had big plans of kissing the hell out of him when I arrived at his Sandton apartment, instead I showed up late by mistake - my friends had already arrived and I froze. He was right there in front of me, like I wanted for so long - but I couldn't look him in the eye. My heart was skipping more beats than was probably healthy - but I couldn't think of anything to say to him. He took care of the catering - all I had to do was show up and provide the other humans - which I did - my friends were there to offer me emotional support on my wedding night (they were also there for the free, French wine.) I eventually lost track of which friends of mine were coming and going through his doors.

He asked how many weeks I'd be traveling in the States for, to what I explained that I wasn't visiting, I was moving to New York. Judging by his facial expression, he didn't see it coming. I kept emptying my wineglass into my stomach - he kept pouring me more - I wished he would just pull me aside, kiss me, tell me he missed me - but I couldn't get myself to be the one to do it either.

While Willem was outside puffing on a cigarette with Yvette and a few others, one of my friends decided to throw their buff arms around me in the kitchen and give me the kiss I was waiting for Willem to give me - I didn't know what to do - I should have stopped but I didn't. We disappeared out the opposite door of the apartment until I finally managed to pull myself together. I wasn't sure if Willem noticed but then he commented on it, complimenting my friends' big arms in good humor. I fucked up so badly. We always spoke about freedom and sharing and being open-minded - but I shouldn't have. Not there, not then, not like that. We were all fairly drunk, he was jetlagged - what I did, didn't seem to have changed anything. My friends left and we finally had the apartment to ourselves - we could hardly keep our eyes open, we kissed until we fell asleep on the couch. I made the mistake of insisting that we consummate our marriage in our drunken state - my body couldn't keep up with my big bright idea and I had to excuse myself from the act - throwing up all over the carpet. I wanted to crawl into a corner and die. I sat in the shower kicking myself for every stupid little thing that went wrong that night - but we got to make up for it in the morning.

He made fun of me for making the night romantic by throwing up, I made fun of him for asking me if pineapples grow on trees - we were even. It was like the first time, for a moment, only, I didn't know how to walk away from him this time without breaking down. High heels in my hand, I walked out his door barefoot, barely one flight of stairs down from him, the tears just streamed down my face, and all the way in the Uber ride, and all the way into Yvette's house. I threw my arms around her, sobbing. She isn't big on hugs and tried to shrug me off. "You smell like vomit."

"I know" I cried - muffling into her shoulder.

I had made a mess and tried to rectify my mistakes with a long voice note to him - but there was nothing I could say, nothing could make it right. The more I tried to fix it, the worse I made an already sour situation. The worst part was, I felt like I couldn't blame him if he never wanted to see me again.

He was off to Swaziland, and I off to Durban to say my goodbyes before leaving for the States - not exactly a honeymoon.

FOR AS LONG AS I'M SAD
Poetry & Prose

The problem is, I know what it feels like to have a second chance to hold you now.

I know what it's like to fight sleep to stay awake so I can be aware of you next to me before the sun rises in an hour and you will tell me to leave again.

I know what it's like to see you again after months of acting like I don't care that you never called, or that it took you this long.

The problem is, I know what your hair smells like after a long night drinking with our friends.

The problem is, I know how you like your coffee and that you will drink it even if it's cold, because we were preoccupied, tangled in each other, when it was still hot.

The problem is, I have seen your messy bedroom after you had to find your cleanest dirty shirt in a suitcase that has been in a luggage cabin for way too long.

The problem is, I let you into my world for a night and you looked like you belonged.

The problem is, I have taken the time to remember what it looks like when you open your mouth to laugh, because you never open it for pictures.

The problem is, you make me question life and that makes me fall in love with you, every time.

The problem is, I like the sound of sadness in my voice when I sing now. The problem is, it will fade when the memory of you does.

This was not the plan. Now I am sad in the city. The problem is, I think I like it.

The problem is, I don't want to stop missing the idea of you. As long as sadness surrounds me, the thought of you will live here.

I don't want to forget the color of your eyes or what your mouth tastes like, and how many buttons you always leave...unbuttoned.

The problem is, my time will be spent on another soon, and there will be no need for me to allow myself time to think of you.

Next time, I might fall for his gin & tonics in take away cups. If I can just find the time to forget about you. But I will.

The problem is that one day I will forget about you as naturally as the sun will set today, and I won't even notice, because I will be too busy falling for someone new.

The problem is, your time of being on my mind is running out, because I will be happy again soon.

That's why I wake up every day, hoping I will be sad, a little while longer.

I have missed seventy-seven sunrises. I can't let myself miss one more. Good morning, New York.

SALA KAHLE

(**Sala kahle** - *a phrase used in a number of African languages in South Africa and Swaziland to say goodbye/ stay well.*)

My soul mate Kwanele and I drove up Sandton roads windows down shouting out in the melody of Frank Sinatra's "New York, New York" - "Bum-bum-ba-da-da, bum-bum-ba-da-da!"

"Thank you for being brave, Lyls. Thank you for leaving." She said to me over a cocktail - our last one on one hangout. She always saw things differently to other people, she saw things clearly, and always meant what she said, even when it sounded like a mistake at first.

It was the day of my big farewell at Joshua Tree - my very last gig in Johannesburg opening the show for Lindsay McGuire that night. All my friends from the radio station, all my friends in music, all my ex boyfriends and their new girlfriends filled every corner of the place. I tucked myself in between my friend Gavin Singh's arms for a moment, had to stop myself from kissing Calvin again, comforted a crying Andy who wished she was the one leaving the country, until I eventually cried with her because she was always supposed to have left before I did. Neil stood almost out of sight in a corner the entire night, we stole a few glances, shared a few tears - but more smiles. He told me he didn't mean to crash my party, but that he just wanted to be around in case I needed him and that he wanted to be there to say goodbye - I didn't want it any other way.

Carel was trying to get me hammered but I really wanted to be sober for as long as possible - I wanted to remember everything. He had the bright idea of suggesting we auction off my guitar during the night to fundraise - my friends wanted to send me to New York with some money in hand for my new music ventures. Lindsay made it happen, raising the bid and overall donations to fourteen thousand Rand. The managing director of the station - Lloyd Madurai won the bid and I signed and dropped my guitar off at the station the next day. They hung it on the wall that all the celebrity guests signed their names on when visiting for interviews - it was the biggest honor of my life.

I visited Benjy Mudie at his Vinyl Junkie store to say goodbye and thank him for being one of the first set of ears to play my rugged-demos to. From there I visited my friend Boo Prince at her house for the night, she made me sign her guitar and wanted to record an interview with me in her home studio - if for no other reason than to help me see myself clearly at the end of my one journey and the start of another.

We decided to title our conversation "Lyla before New York."

With all my Joburg-goodbyes said, Yvette and I road-tripped down to Durban to spend a week at the coast and so I could say goodbye to my sister and nephew.

I fell in love with a piece of material one of the beach vendors were selling next to the road - it was a Lihhiya - the Swaziland Flag with King Swati on it - the same piece I'd seen Kwanele wear before. I didn't know why - but I just had to have it. I put it on immediately after buying it, and we stopped at the Elangeni hotel to have sundowners on the rooftop. There I stood in my royal blue Swaziland flag wrapped around me like a skirt, Indian ocean in front of me stretching as far as I could see, puffing and coughing my way through a menthol cigarette, wishing I could share it with my mom. Smoking is something I never do

- but Yvette and I felt the need to.

At that point, I didn't know that my mom was born in Swaziland and not South Africa - my sister only found that out mid 2019 and told me. My mom must have told me about it when I was little, perhaps some part of my subconscious remembered without me knowing so - because I was attached to that Lihhiya like nothing I'd been attached to until then. It had to come with me to New York - I didn't care what I had to leave behind so that I had space for it in my luggage.

My sister begged for me to spend more time with her while I was at the coast, but my sense of family was long gone, I had been on my own for so long. I saw her for two days and said goodbye as if was all the same to me.

"This is not just another goodbye. You're leaving the country, the continent. It could be years before we see each other again." She cried and pleaded with me to spend more time together before I left. I reminded her how many times we spent years without seeing each other after my mom died - it was normal to me. It was something I didn't know how to cry about - even if I wanted to. "I'm sorry, but I am going now." I left.

I could never have anticipated how much I'd miss her in the States, and that I'd regret not spending more time with her during that trip.

Yvette and I arrived back to Johannesburg the day before my flight to New York. I hadn't seen my brother in a couple of years either, he decided last minute to drive in from Lydenburg to come and see me, to come and hug me goodbye. It was during that hour I got to sit next to him at Seattle Coffee in Montecasino that I realized, made peace with the vast amount of damage our mom's death and dad's absence and neglect did to our relationship as siblings. He showed up to be my brother that day, when for years it just wasn't a priority for either of us. That hour we got to sit there for, and just be brother and sister - it changed everything in our relationship, it made us strong. I was no longer a little girl - his baby sister running around Hluhluwe following him everywhere in an oversized Eminem T-shirt. I was a woman, headed for New York - but inside, still the same girl who learned to write and play music by watching my brother write songs out of thin air when he was a teenager, and I loved him so much for inspiring me from such a young age to do the same. I looked him in the eye and told him so.

Well, Yvette couldn't deal with me leaving. She got a new puppy to replace me, distract her. He fell asleep in my open suitcase on her living room floor, I had to kick him out because the car had arrived, it was time to head to the airport. Joining me at OR Tambo was my wolfpack - Yvette, Kwanele, Andy and Bernice. I emptied the Rand out of my purse. "Take my last change, lover." I handed over the handful of silver and copper coins to Kwanele and gulped down a crisp and cold Castle LITE draft for the last time.

I was in complete disbelief that I was actually going to board that plane. I kept thinking "something could still go wrong at any point."

"It's happening, Lyla. You are really leaving." I stared at Kwanele with a blank face, eyes interlocked as those words came out of her mouth. I had to repeat it out loud to believe it. She put a letter in my hand and told me to read it on the plane.

After a last group photo, they walked me to my boarding gate, all of us barely hanging on, crying off our makeup. "I love you guys so much" I managed to get out as I had to turn away to walk to my plane. After about ten seconds of walking away from them, I stopped. I couldn't let us remember each other in tears, sad faced. I turned to yell "snapchat me that pussy!" A private joke and phrase I used to drop like a bomb at the most random times to break silences. They burst out laughing and so did I. I wanted them to remember me that way.

LYLA BEFORE NEW YORK
(Interview by Boo Prince)

Boo: "Tell me about your phone's new wallpaper?"
Lyla: "It says - you did not waste your love ever – I don't know. Because people are so afraid to admit when they feel something that sometimes you think that your love that you gave them, like, it has gone to waste. But I don't want that to stop me from loving, even if it's for a night."
Boo: "Do you understand that for me, as a voice geek, looking at you up on stage singing your own words, proudly, strongly, saying this is who the fuck I am – look at me. It's the ultimate. You know? Using your power through your voice, using your voice as your super power. Speaking your truth. You're not a cover queen, that's not your thing. You're an artist in your own right."
Lyla: "The more honest I am in my songs, the easier it is for me to sing them, because the easier people connect, and I've learned that the hard way."
Boo: "What you have just said; that's the quote. That's Lyla. You know? The girl who jumps in and does the hard thing, and lives in her truth. That's amazing Lyla Illing."
Lyla: "Speaking of names and expressing individuality, or rather identity – just hearing you say Lyla Illing – you know I've only had to use my birth name for the first time in four, five years when I was applying for my paperwork to go abroad now. It's just been such a reminder. To remember when I decided to change my name and the power in it and how it gave me confidence. I was feeling that I don't want people in the entertainment industry to meet me as a Hebrew-Afrikaans girl. I want my name to sound like a name that carries some sort of energy and power and I don't want them to think oh this is an Afrikaans girl. I've been denying that I'm Afrikaans for the longest time because of what I believe goes with it – people's perceptions. Looking back, I was nineteen and I just decided life was too short for people to know me by any other name than Lyla. I think people must think I'm fucking crazy when they hear I changed my name, and they want to know why. I think people in the entertainment industry understand it more, but a lot of people don't. My family still calls me by my

154

Afrikaans name but it's only been in the last year that they've made exceptions – like my brother, he tagged me on Facebook and for the first time, he addressed me as Lyla. I also remember the first time my sister introduced me to her friends as Lyla, because she always made a point of making me feel like I'm crazy for wanting to change my name, and I'm throwing away my identity and where I come from – when, well, that's the fucking point. I don't want to be reminded of that part of me. Like, that's what I've been wanting to put away. And I'll deal with it when I am ready to. But I remember when she started introducing me as Lyla, and as much as I try to be hardcore about it and act like I don't care – it meant the world to me that she acknowledged it and she let me be.

Boo: "So, we had a start of a very interesting conversation, when you talk about being reminded of being your past self – Afrikaans girl, and I said to you, is Yvette Afrikaans, and you said yes absolutely, she is Afrikaans and I said I thought so. You guys are close, you go away together, you've been staying at her house. Are you speaking English to each other or are you two Afrikaans girls?"

Lyla: "For the longest time, we were speaking English to each other at the radio station, at gigs, if I'm visiting and eventually she asked aren't we both Afrikaans and I said yes, but don't tell anybody!

Boo: (laughs)

Lyla: "I've actually gotten to meet her family and they speak Afrikaans at home and sometimes she would Skype with them and I kept on hearing the Afrikaans expressions that I grew up with and just the way you are able to express yourself in your mother tongue. It used to embarrass me to speak Afrikaans, I don't know what it is that made me feel that way but, I think it goes much deeper for me, it goes back to not liking what I grew up with in terms of family values, the Afrikaans way of life, but then there just came a point when I started speaking to Yvette in Afrikaans. Before that, she used to speak in Afrikaans and I would reply in English and the same with my siblings. Two weeks ago my sister phoned me and I had a conversation with her in Afrikaans the whole way through, it was only when I put the phone down that I realized, holy fuck, I just had a whole conversation in Afrikaans. I don't even know how I remember all the words after not speaking much Afrikaans in the last five years. So now whether Yvette and I are at work, at the shops or at home – it's back to Afrikaans. It's nice to be reminded what it feels like to express yourself in your mother tongue. "

Boo: "That's powerful."

Lyla: "I don't feel that embarrassed anymore. Yvette always says to me – stop faking it – because at first when I started speaking Afrikaans again, I still spoke with an English accent. I sounded like a real soutie trying to speak Afrikaans again – I wouldn't do it in front of other people and I find myself in the last two weeks when I've been at the radio station, when I see her I go - hello hoe gaan dit, wat gan aan? – and people would turn around and be surprised that I'm speaking Afrikaans firstly and secondly we're chatting away in the language. It sort of happened subconsciously that I felt okay in my skin to speak Afrikaans."

155

Boo: "That is super powerful, the idea of feeling comfortable in your skin. And I'm sure that your friendship and the opportunity to express yourself in your mother tongue has made you feel really, really at home."

Lyla: "Another thing is, my dad who I haven't spoken to in eight years, I believe he knows that I changed my name because he is still close with my brother. I've wanted to call him, I've had this urge to call him in the last year, and you know, never mind all the shit that I'm thinking about, of how we're supposed to get past our differences and where to start the conversation – that was secondary. The biggest thing on my mind was, how do I say – hello pa dis [Afrikaans name] / hi dad it's [Afrikaans name] – because that feels wrong it doesn't feel like me. I feel like I'm gonna say – hi dad it's Lyla – and he is gonna say – who the fuck is Lyla?"

Boo: (laughs) "That's the title of this chapter – who the fuck is Lyla?"

Lyla: (laughs) "I couldn't get myself to pick up the phone and say hi to him in Afrikaans and call myself by my birth name because it felt like I would be going against everything I've stood for these last couple of years."

Boo: "So are you saying to me that on one hand the sense of being able to express yourself in your mother tongue gives you comfort, a feeling of nostalgia? Obviously when you were probably most exposed to Afrikaans would have been as a very small girl when your mom was around which was happy for you, really happy memories of your mom. So there's kind of that comfort, nostalgia, home thing about it but there's another side of you that you've worked so hard to kind of build your unique identity of somebody who you feel you can relate to and aspire to being and invest in - and she is not [refers to myself as Afrikaans name] - she's Lyla Illing. She's an identity of your creation, that you get to control – her look, her sound, her feel, her destiny."

Lyla: "Ja, as crazy as it sounds, if you call it what it is, it's two identities but it's not what I meant for it to be."

Boo: "Sure, sure."

Lyla: "It also just sort of happened, it's like I put [refers to myself as Afrikaans name] away because she was the person who held onto the abuse, who held onto people's opinions and who held onto feeling less. Like when I moved to Johannesburg I still pronounced a lot of English words with a very thick Afrikaans accent and people made fun of me for it, they meant no harm but I felt embarrassed. It was banter, it wasn't supposed to make me feel less worthy but I couldn't help but feel that way. So letting go of my old name and Afrikaans was like saying it doesn't matter where I came from, no one has to know that I grew up in Hluhluwe or Sodwana or that I was born in Richards Bay or that I've been in the Vaal, and you know I kind of just hid those parts away and I was just Lyla – Lyla who is in Johannesburg right now. It helped a lot that I lived with an English family when I was an au pair before working in radio. It definitely helped with the accent and just the use of the language, even though I'm not completely there yet. I want to find a way to be able to express myself as clearly in English as I used to in my mother tongue."

Boo: "Did your folks know they were raising a little rock star?"

Lyla: "I think my mom knew somewhere deep inside, you know? She only knew my for the ten years we had together and when I changed my name my siblings expressed that they felt like it was wrong because my parents gave it to me and I should have honored that. I feel like my mom would have embraced my decision to change my name. I don't feel like she would have taken it personally, but, I think the voices in my head from when I was a teenager, and having had an abusive stepmom, being verbally abused, you know, that becomes the voice in your head. I think hers is just one of the voices who told [refers to myself as Afrikaans name] that – you're never going to be anything, and when you're eighteen you're on your own and we don't care if you've got talent, if you want to go to college or university you'll make your own way. And you know, whatever the story was. At thirteen, fourteen, I was told that I would never make it and that I don't matter. I'm not the only person who has gone through it and you don't have to change your name to overcome it (the pain) but somewhere along the line… I don't know. People who really know me, there's a handful from high school who has gone through this with me – who got to know [refers to myself as Afrikaans name] and now know Lyla and they have completely embraced it and it's not a weird thing for them to call me Lyla now. I think at first it must have been a hell of a – what the fuck – moment. But having those friends who went through it with me makes me feel like, yes I'm still the deep-down-inside-me, it's still me, but things did change for me when I decided to be someone else. To have a different identity and to speak life into that. But as for [refers to myself as Afrikaans name] I think it was more of a… it's hard to pin point. It's about something that I wanted to forget. The name made me feel like it defined me."

Boo: "So clearly you feel there's a particular set of baggage around being labeled as Afrikaans? What do you feel that baggage is exactly? Is it tradition, is it ideology, is it identity – how would you define it?"

Lyla: "I think it comes more from my perception of how I think Afrikaans people are perceived because, you see, I think it comes from having grown up Afrikaans and then to living with an English family when I was an au pair. I felt like the English family were a lot more open-minded, very different culturally, even though we were all Caucasian, it was a cultural, a language thing. They were different. They were more worldly whereas where I grew up with a closed-minded family who brought me up to believe that people of color won't go to heaven, and well, they were very racist. And you know, nature versus nurture, to each their own. When I look back I feel like they just didn't know better so I can't just hold it against them but I can choose to not want to be associated with it. So for me it's a lot more personal than to say it's just about the language. It's about what I experienced with the group of Afrikaners that I was brought up with."

Boo: "Did you always feel different or did something happen to cause you to change your mind – why do you think you are different in that belief set?"

Lyla: "I always knew I wanted to change my name because I always wanted to be a rock star (laughs) whatever that means when you grow up, you know, because it's not as easy as you think it's going to be. We've also spoken about religion, and that I was exposed to having to believe that black people don't go to heaven, then after that I was exposed to full blown Christianity and I was singing in the church band, but you know, the only reason I was going to church was because they put me on a stage, and I'm honest enough to say that. But, I can appreciate why people hold onto religion because when I was going through a really tough time in my teens – it was something I held onto. I was able to say I believe I am going to be okay because God says so. I feel like I got through things because I told myself to believe. Who or what I believed in wasn't relevant; it was the fact that I believed I was going to be okay or get through it. What I'm getting to is, I was told to believe a lot of things growing up, even with my mom, as dear as she will always be to my heart. It's weird because she brought me up - of course she was trying to instill beliefs in me - but she didn't make it feel forced, like I had to believe what she believed. Whereas with my dad it was definitely forced, but either way I feel like I've been told to be a certain person and believe certain things and live by certain ideals for as long as I can remember. And I remember from a very young age, making up my own mind. I remember writing about how I see different situations or if I had a certain experience I would write about it. It wasn't absolutely crazy things. People think that I was this rebel when I was a teenager – I wasn't, I was a very big introvert. I was a really good girl. (laughs) People don't think that when they know me now, but, I remember being thirteen, fourteen and just writing about how I experienced certain things and my dad going through my things and telling me it is not okay to write. I don't understand where that comes from but I was discouraged to write and express myself."

Boo: "Do you think that was a desire to somehow contain you and your emotions or do you think it was about the contents of what you wrote, that it was distasteful to him somehow?"

Lyla: "I think it was a bit of both and if you ask me now what my thirteen-year-old-self wrote I won't be able to tell you because I can't remember, but it must have been something that didn't sit right with him. Maybe he thought he was protecting me against myself, because I know that I am on over thinker, so I don't know what the motives were but I know that I've always been discouraged to think for myself and it's something that I fought. Between the ages of ten and fifteen my stepmom was always trying to kick me out of the house. She had already had her own kids and they were grown up, and I can understand that she wanted her own time now and she never asked for my mom to die and to be stuck with [refers to myself as Afrikaans name]. She didn't want another kid. Unfortunately it was just bad luck for me and she would find ways and find reasons to fight with me even though I truly believe I'm an accommodating person. I didn't used to fight back or be a brat or break rules and I could never understand why they had a problem with me in the first place, because I'm actually just a very chill person. But there was a point where she was always saying that… it goes deep… but she was always just trying to kick me out of the house

158

and she'd always threaten me with leaving me at an orphanage. Like if you're not going to live the way we want you to then you can't be here. It happened a few times and she was also physically abusive and my dad knew it, and he would come to me when she wasn't around and apologize for it, but he still didn't fix the problem. He was an enabler. So when I was fifteen, she got physical again and she said to me that she wanted me out of the house and for the first time, I think that was the first time I actually really heard myself. Because I always just used to shut up and cry and let her say what she needed to say and I think it comes from her anger, I don't think it's a reflection of who I was – but it took me a very long time to realize that. But for the first time I said to her – well okay well maybe I will be better off at an orphanage, so cool, let me get my bag – I started packing my shit and she chucked it out on the floor and got black bags and said – that's how you'll leave my house, in black bags. My dad said to me, it's better for me to not be around her, but yet again he didn't address the problem and I've been out of the house ever since. I truly felt like, you know what, I'd rather fucking live on the street and try become some band's fucking roadie, I didn't give a shit how I was gonna eat or sleep. My life changed since that moment. It took me a long time to make peace with how shit happened and to feel like it wasn't my fault. It took me along time to feel like the abuse I suffered wasn't to do with me, you know, she had her own shit. Yvette is one of the people who I've told this story to. We got a little tipsy the other night and she wanted to stay up late and I had to work early the next morning. She was making a joke saying – you're failing, I'm going to go and get a black bag for you now – she was making a reference to my stepmom. I let it go but that ripped me apart because it totally just took me back to feeling like I'm … I am…"

Boo: "Disposable?"

Lyla: "Yes, and I am just in someone's way again. The next day I told her what she said was really fucked up but we were laughing about it. She apologized saying she didn't think it would hurt me and I was like, no, I was lying awake, it really hurt me. She felt like shit. But through talking about it and addressing it, now it's a standing joke and it's refreshing to laugh about it even though yes, deep down inside, the bad memories are still there – but it's a friendship that has allowed me to make light of situations and own them. And be like, yeah well, it happened, I've been told to put my shit in a black bag and leave, it happened, but look at where I am now. So leaving the language and my name behind – it was like leaving a whole life behind."

PART NINE

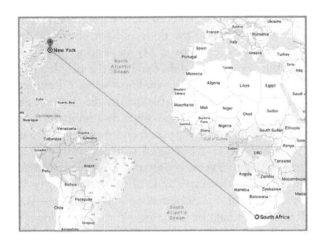

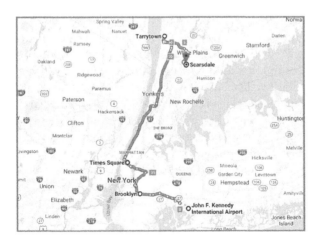

LIMINAL INDIVIDUAL

"In anthropology, liminality (from the Latin word līmen, meaning "a threshold")
is the quality of ambiguity or disorientation that occurs in the middle stage of
a rite of passage, when participants no longer hold their pre-ritual status
but have not yet begun the transition to the status they will hold when
the rite is complete."

Falling in love used to be a priority.

"Making it" used to be a priority.

After having to take the New York subway for the first time and breaking down in tears in Brooklyn after the confusion, I switched my social media apps off, switched my Tinder app off, so I could save my phone battery for Google Maps. It was at that moment that I realized; my priorities had all changed.

Why had I exchanged a career in radio for "just another" day job? One where I was playing with bubble guns, negotiating with little ones to pretty…pretty…please, piss or get off the pot? Having to deal with toddler tears (and sometimes my own at night.) Living in the richest suburb in America, Scarsdale, a stone-throw away from New York City, was a status shock over and above the culture shock I was already trying to embrace.

I kept on telling myself that New York chose me, it was the only thing that got me through the initial growing pains of my world having changed so dramatically.

When my New York job offer first came through, as much as I wanted it, the only thing that went through my mind was – "why the hell NOW? Now, that I have a great job, great friends, my own place and some stability? How am I supposed to leave the life I have made for myself, leave all my ex-boyfriends, and leave the start of a promising career behind in Johannesburg? It took me so long to find my feet. For the first time since high school I have a nickname, people calling me Lyla-Belle, people I look forward to spending my Friday nights with, a familiar face to bump into at the grocery store, the feeling of belonging to a community - something I have never had before. My name and face are on website banners, they say my name on the radio, and I have a stage to play my music on, a few people who listen."

But how the hell could I say no to New York? I had been craving change for some time, but wasn't sure if I should actually move abroad. I literally asked myself what I thought Willem would have done, and my guess was that he would have gotten on that plane – so, I held onto that.

Sometimes you meet people who help you find the courage you need, to take risks. But taking the leap to New York also showed me that sometimes putting yourself first, in order to take these risks to grow, you have to be an asshole. You have to break someone's heart. You have to put love on hold. You have to say goodbye to things you cherish. I wasn't sure I could be that person.

Although my life had meaning, although I loved working in radio, I was tired of reading about my bosses in magazines and seeing my friend's faces all over the media when I knew what went on behind the scenes. I got tired of living through my phone and pretending with the rest of my fellow B-listers that our lives were SO great and SO much fun, when we were all just getting by on paid-for Tweets, walking the red carpet in borrowed dresses, and attending all these "glitz and glamour" events, as a means to an end – at least, I was.

On my flight, I felt my heartbeat change as the time zones did, as I flew across the coastlines of Africa, and into Dubai, and over the Atlantic Ocean into New York. In those airborne moments, something inside me changed forever. I was flying into my future, completely uncertain about my end goal but completely confident that I was headed in the exact right direction.

During my orientation week I stayed on campus with hundreds of other au pairs. All of a sudden, I had friends from eleven different countries. I had my first slice of New York pizza. I had my first bagel. I took a moment to admire my first American sunset, alone. I took off my shoes and felt the grass between my toes, trying to fathom that I was on the other side of the world. I blinked and a few weeks passed.

As expected, I missed the excitement and fun of working in the media industry. With every diaper I changed and load of washing I washed, I shook my head thinking "I could be making radio right now."

But in the bigger picture, I was happy to step away from that "glitz and glam" way of life for a while – although I was part of wonderful teams and communities in the media industry – I wasn't fulfilled, I felt like I was on my way to being caught up in a façade. Being at every event, meeting every celebrated creative, being in every photo, providing publicity for other people's careers – it took over my life and I had less and less time to bring the music and stories that were in my own heart, to life.

I think that's the real reason I left - to find some space for my own ideas to sprout. I was immediately inspired when I arrived to New York, but the initial period of adjusting to my new environment stretched on longer than I could have anticipated, and although I arrived with a pocket-full of ideas, I had to get my hands dirty shuffling soil and laying solid foundations first before I could plant those ideas and water them. The wait was frustrating, I felt like an anchored sailboat, being shoved around against my will every time the water rose as if it took a breath. The ropes that were on either side holding me to the dock loosened and tightened as the wave of water pushed me around. I felt controlled by my new circumstances. I was afloat in a beautiful marina, but going nowhere, just being tucked around.

When not knowing how to buy a ticket for the NYC Subway, and not knowing which line to take and where to change trains, left me feeling like such an idiot, who was not used to anything, I reevaluated the choices I made and the people and things I chose to spend my time and mind on. I realized that there was more to life, and more of myself, left to discover. I had my signed copy of Jen Su's handbook "From Z-A-lister" in hand where I lay next to a New York swimming pool – but no part of me could relate to the things I wanted when I started out in the industry anymore. I didn't want to be an A-lister, I just wanted to tell stories through music and radio.

Once I put those "celebrity" goals to rest, I put the "finding love" ones to rest too – I wanted to get to know myself in ways I never had before. That became my tunnel vision.

The new set of priorities I started living by, no longer included finding "my other half" or someone to spend Saturday night and Sunday morning with - just so I didn't have to be alone. I realized that I would have to become selfish with my creativity and ideas, in order to not merely be a brain behind someone else's career again. It took me a while to get out of the mindset of wanting to find a radio station to intern for in New York – every part of me knew I would have been able to work my way up and become a great producer for a team here – but I kept realizing that I didn't want a repeat of what I had already accomplished in South Africa.

A boyfriend (or girlfriend) still sounded like fun, we all like having someone familiar by our side, but it was no longer a priority. I had to convince myself that just because I had always been in relationships, didn't make it wrong to not be in one for a while. New York's no-strings-attached culture sat well with me – I hardly took part in it, but when I did, the dating didn't take up so much of me, the way I let it in the past.

I was tired of reading the same "Why relationships don't last anymore" bullshit articles that talk about our spoiled for choice society in the modern world, who thrive on one-night-stands and commitment-free flings, and how it is so wrong of us to live that way.

No.

NO!

There is NO way that every person on this planet is meant to find the perfect partner, get married, have kids, have a stable income and live happily ever after, in their first attempt. There's space for us dreamers who are career chasers, paper chasers, wanderlust infected, us free spirits. Not everyone is meant to meet their soul mate at sixteen. I have met so many versions of the love of my life and I thank god that I have been lucky enough to experience so many different levels of love and lust.

My new life in America was just like I had seen it in the movies. American flags hanging from perfect three-story houses in the suburbs, huge black SUV's on the roads, and cute guys at the local fire station. Squirrels running over perfectly trimmed grass at the park. Everything was bigger and there was so much variety. In the city, New Yorkers were mostly rude and always in a rush. Some apartments I saw the insides of were so small. Buskers and the homeless roamed the subways. As lovely as the suburbs were, something about the picture-perfect white picket fence houses there, just didn't sit well with me.

I grew up with mud between my toes, ran around barefoot in hand-me-down clothes, I had always dreamt about "a better life" - and "the American dream" was most definitely not overrated or unwelcomed. But I hoped that I would always stay a little "rough around the edges."

Leaving the suburbs and heading into the city was like a weekly reality check I signed myself up for. It kept me in line, and in touch with myself. The city felt like a jungle and was as rough as it was gorgeous.

Now that I had figured out how the TV guide works here, how to drive on the other side of the road without wanting to throw up, how to tip waiters and how to finish the massive servings at restaurants, I still had a couple more things left to adjust to. Like trying to keep in touch with my friends and family, now that we were in different time zones. By the time I was ready to chat at night, most of my friends were sleeping, and by the time I fell asleep, I was being woken up by "good morning" texts.

I spent my first few days off - by myself at bars and in guitar stores in Times Square. After celebrating alone, in honor of my former colleagues, winning award after award at the Liberty Radio Awards in South Africa, I could not face another weekend of secretly feeling homesick. So, I found a little place in Brooklyn, known as the Madiba and went looking for something familiar - advised by Yvette.

Other than the pap-en-sous and old ANC banners on the walls, I found friendly faces and warm conversations. But I didn't find home. And the rude awakening that no one, apart from the owner, gave a shit that I am a South African at a "Proudly South African" restaurant in NY, reminded me that I should not be giving a shit about trying to find a comfort zone and old habits to hang on to here anyway.

NOT A DRIVE-THRU
(Poetry & Prose)

I invited all the girls I know but only the boys show
So I sit between two 40-something-year-olds
Both in the midst of a divorce
The type they told me to look out for
Little do they know that dirty old men is my preference
And they should be looking out for me
I am definitely drunk he says an hour after I tell him that I need to stop drinking
And we talk about work and make fun of rich people and laugh when he talks about writers being depressed as if it's not a given
We talk about things that don't really matter but not about him popping my New York cherry after the last two rounds of drinks we probably should not have had that other night
Then he says I am mature for my age
And I wonder if that is supposed to make me feel better
For knowing exactly how to hide that it fucked with my head when he did not call
The last time I had a night like that it was followed by three years of waking up to the same face
The guy fucked it up in the end but hey he had the balls to try
In his defense he did mention that it's complicated.
But I have made enough excuses for people who treat my mind and vagina like a drive-thru
The ones who judge me by the colors like a picture book like they forgot to read
Just because I am wet between my thighs and behind the ears oh they don't want me to waste my youthful years
On them
Well it's mine to waste
I'm only planning on 27 in any way
And they try to make up my mind by subtly polluting my freedom of choice with their memories of failed attempts at loving and being loved
They have done this a couple of times
They must be right
That is why the power of youth is back on my mind
And I walk myself to the subway this time
Focus on what I want to achieve this week
Spend all my time planning it out
I have no time left to execute those exact plans
Leave it till the last minute

It's more exciting that way
I once heard someone say

Then I remember how good it is to not have anyone to report to or have to micromanage on how to keep me happy
And somewhere between 14th and Park I make peace with the fact that I cock block myself every time I vomit my mind into a blog or a song
I don't like having a face I cannot show
So
I think I'd rather just be friends, in any way.

WHY I CHOOSE TO DATE ASSHOLES

It's been a long time since I have had the energy to deal with another self-proclaimed asshole, but I'm on holiday so I am recharged, and turns out you don't have to go all the way into the Everglades to find a Gator in Florida. Nope, there's a nest just outside the town of Kissimmee… and I arrived just in time for their next feed.

"What made you swipe right?" He asks as he carries our first round of Gin & Tonics from the bar to the seating booth. "And what are your first impressions?" he wants to know next.

He tries to hide behind that "just making conversation" face but I see right through the small talk, as I sense his need for validation and praise almost immediately. We are after all, the instant gratification generation. He thinks he is very funny, and entertaining for acting this confident, too. It's charming. I recognize this behavior.

I have dated a version of him before, I think to myself. As a matter of fact, I have spent the last couple of months trying to prevent myself from dating his type again. By "his type," I mean … the asshole type. But I am already attracted to him. His rough thick scales and the dangerous eyes of a predator, there's no doubt I am in his territory now.

Although I am conscious of what he is, it is against my nature to judge him, or feel intimidated by him. Being a "the glass is half full, not half empty" kind of girl, I decide to stroke Gator's leather-thick-skin-ego, and I wait for his bite, the snap, the sudden jump, which will be followed by my "catch me if you can" opportunity. Alligator skin is back in fashion, and I'm just about ready to parade around in it like a trophy.

I have an appetite for excitement, despite the anxiety I feel when I can't help but think about how hard it is for me to not get emotionally involved, the second Gator has my undivided attention. This time it's even harder than the times before, I mean, writer meets writer and for a change I don't get a confused stare back at me when I explain how I see myself and the world. But that is not enough for me to let my guard down. My walls are up but our warm and genuine connection slips through the cracks, and I allow myself to enjoy it for a few moments. I know he sees me, I know he is experiencing the same glimpses, but it doesn't take long for his inner asshole to resurface and before I know it I am made to feel like I have overstayed my welcome, once again. As the sun comes up, he looks at me puzzled as to why I am still in his hotel room.

On the other hand, I have no doubt that assholes have feelings too. No matter how much they try to deny it. But that is just what I believe, no evidence has been found just yet. Maybe that is why I choose to stick around? I am fascinated by how they seem capable of switching their emotions off whilst engaging in what appears to be genuine connection - something I am curious to find out how to do. It fucks with my head. I am very intrigued by this quality, as I sure as hell don't possess it when I feel a genuine connection. Maybe that is why I keep hanging around this same breed of Gators. Studying their behavior.

Why is it so hard for me to see the bad in people? Why do I get off on experiencing and accepting people for who they are, at the cost of my own sanity?

Here is my theory. Someone has to love the assholes, might as well be me, right? Even they need love, they actually need it more than the others. And even though I know how it ends, I choose to show my soul, show them something real in anyway. What they do with this new experience is their business once I drive off into the sunrise alone, in the Uber, back to my life filled with all this gross emotion and real connection. Yuck, right?

Apart from the obvious daddy issues, I think it's safe to say that the number one reason I date assholes is that, well, I find I have a lot in common with them.

Assholes tend to have a strong sense of identity and direction. They are smart, tactic, they make use of their freedom of choice. They question and challenge ideals, and most of the time they are brave enough to own the fact that they are indeed, assholes. I like people who can give it to me straight, even if I don't like what they have to say. It's like taking advice from a stranger. It's refreshing to see the world through someone's eyes who thinks the sun shines out their ass. I think it is important to be THAT selfish, for at least a fraction of your life.

Unfortunately I am way too in touch with my emotional side to say it's easy for me to carry on dating assholes. It's hard, and I can't do it to myself anymore. I know by now how these encounters end, the male characteristics I possess, hate not getting what I want when I want it in the end, so why do I continue to engage in these games? Is it the thrill of the kill? I don't know, but quite frankly I don't mind the temporary downer that comes with having to say goodbye to an asshole who I had a temporary genuine connection with. I'd choose that, over a relationship based on pretense and unrealistic expectations, so I fit into society, anytime. Hanging out with assholes keeps me on my toes. They are fun and they make interesting friends. Watching them operate gives me something to think about, but it's tiring.

I miss my comfort zone, I miss being in a stable relationship, but sadly, even the good guys find a way to disappoint me, eventually – and I, them.

So as I see myself, repeat history here in Florida, I am left to think, I am the one who pretends to be happy-go-lucky when in fact, my expectations are secretly unrealistically high. I am the one who insists on walking myself out, because I have already in the back of my mind put him down to just being another, predictable, asshole that I don't want to open my heart to.

I am the one who has her walls up so high, when I really enjoy genuine connection. But I can't say that out loud because that would come with expectations and commitment, that I don't think I am ready for either. At least that is what they will think I want. The truth is, I have no idea what I want. I am just a newborn New Yorker who sits behind her Mac, thinking her opinion means more than the beauty of merely accepting a situation for what it is. Pointing out everyone else's mistakes and crucifying them for leaving, when I never asked them to stay.

Perhaps the biggest asshole in my story has been me, this whole time.

IDENTITY CRISIS: ZULULAND-GIRL GOES UPTOWN-GIRL

A couple of weeks ago, I was a struggling musician living off the bones of my ass. Scraping together loose change for half a tank of gas, scooting my way from my radio job to my music gigs around Fourways and the West Rand on a motorbike Sasha gave me after mine got swiped.

Kitted out in a sizzling hot helmet from my friend Mendes, so I could finally give my ex-boyfriend his back! That being said, I was in the best position financially than I had ever been in before, but earning big bucks at twenty-four means very little when you've been supporting yourself from the age of fifteen, and still are.

So back to a couple of weeks ago, being a struggling musician…

Well…not that much has changed; I am still a struggling musician, living in the basement of somebody else's three story house, I just eat my fruit cut up now (like a lady), spend my free time Googling how much lip fillers will cost, and am driving a big black SUV - caramel Frappuccino with extra cream in hand - to the corner where I busk.

When I packed my bags for New York, I did not realize that I would be moving to the richest hood in America. Not only did I sign up for a culture shock, but a bittersweet status shock too. I went from having a strong sense of identity, to having an identity crisis, in what felt like overnight.

It would be too easy for me to ignorantly pretend that I hate the lifestyle here, just because I grew up with much less. Yes, people are different here and it's a complete contrast to how I grew up or what I'm used to, but if anything, it is refreshing to be surrounded by ambitious individuals who only want the best of what life has to offer.

But, being someone who prides herself on being "rough around the edges" and unconventional, I have no idea how to act or who to be here, some days.

As much as I want to fit in, I have never wanted to hold onto my Zululand roots this tightly, since I can remember. The tomboy kid who ate mangos off the pip, sticky hands and grimy feet from playing in the pineapple lands or in the bushes at DumaZulu Lodge (my second home growing up)... now Googles "how to cut a mango" because if I don't eat my fruit cut up, it might just be the worst thing that has happened in New York since the markets crashed in 2008.

On the other hand, it's been kinda fun doing things "properly" or the educated way (I guess). I am no longer referring to cutting fruit. I am talking about getting my shit together. Where better to find the inspiration to better yourself than here, in a town that thrives on "doing things the right way."

Who doesn't want to live out their days in a town where even the guys picking up the garbage are handsome hunks, worth a second-glance? No offense Pikitup...

The trouble is staying true to you, and not selling yourself short in the process, and that is easier said than done. It takes a lot of courage to say: "I want to better myself" or "I want to work on my English" in a town where most people were born into being and having the best, already.

So naturally I come to the conclusion that Willem is "out of my league" because I do not speak four languages like he does. But I have to remind myself that he doesn't play four instruments like I do. Yup, just added the harmonica to the list! On my way from 44th street to Grand Central after buying the instrument, I figure... this is New York... so I rip open the package and shove the harmonica on my mouth attempting to play Neil Young's "Heart Of Gold" for the first time. "One woman band!" "Play us the blues, girl!" "Play us a note, I haven't heard that instrument" people comment and interact during my walk. I might not have an actual stage to play on right now, but I love the crowd!

Selling yourself short is a self-inflicted sickness. The only cure I turn to is this phrase from Michaela: "The sincerity of your intention is the success of your action." Whenever I want to cringe at the idea of how much my surroundings are influencing my way of life and my evolving-identity, those words are a reminder of why I am here and what I stand for.

As if an identity crisis isn't enough to keep me occupied, being Lyla, I go and throw dating into the mix too.

... Dating is actually very close to nonexistent in New York. Well, so far that is my experience. You just meet SO many people all the time, that you hardly have time to meet up with any of them for a second date, even when you are mutually interested to.

And I thought that dating in Johannesburg was a mess...

But at some point I have to stop bashing the dating scene and own up to being "bad at dating" myself. I suck at this. Matching & meeting for blind dates after being in a string of long-term relationships, feels similar to applying to a job that I am WAY over qualified for. And even if he makes it to date number three, I am so vague about what my intentions are that he probably knows even less about where he stands with me, than I feel I do with him.

Love, work, miracles... We pray, or hustle for the things we want, and then question them or stare blankly ahead in denial when it's handed to us on a silver platter. Because: self-doubt.

Back to being a "struggling" musician... the more I hear that phrase the more I feel like there is no struggle in being a musician. If you are doing what you love, for the right reasons, the struggle is what you thrive off.

I was brought up in Hluhluwe; a small, sometimes shitty, rural town in South Africa, went racing through my early twenties in Johannesburg rubbing shoulders with the who's who... and now (to my surprise) living in America's wealthiest town. Yeah, I might be a "struggling" muso in the midst of an identity crisis, I'd be surprised if I wasn't! But I would never want to be anything other than exactly that. In Jim Carrey's words: "I think everybody should get rich and famous and do everything they ever dreamed of so they can see that it's not the answer."

PISS OR GET OFF THE POT

For the first time in years I had to buy my own ticket if I wanted to see a show. I gave up the free-VIP-media-passes-life when I quit radio and decided it was a fun idea to move to the opposite side of the world. I was starting to hate myself for it a little bit.

Every functioning cell in my brain told me not to buy that damn Blue October concert ticket, but against my own advice, I found myself in line in front of Irving Plaza, alone, about to see Neil's and my favorite band, live. We fell in love to their songs "Home" and "Fear" playing in his car, driving in circles on Roodepoort roads just to delay having to say goodbye and go our separate ways at the end of nights out when we were still secretly seeing each other.

I didn't speak to even one of the twelve-hundred souls at that show, I just cried from the first moment Justin Furstenfeld started singing, sobbed through their song "Hate Me" – hating myself for not having Neil next to me. Hating myself for being in New York.

I was drowning in my six-days-a-week work schedule, taking care of four kids – a job that I signed up for - no one forced me into that. It was so important to me, to do my job well - I always put it first. When I made the decision to come to the States as an au pair, I knew that it was going to be hard, busy, to juggle my work life with my personal creative goals, but for the first few months it was just too much. My personal life and creative goals were nonexistent.

I finally caught a break when I landed a regular gig at a venue in Times Square. My host family gave me time off to go and sing there every second week for a while. It changed my experience drastically. It was surreal to perform in front of an audience in a venue on the infamous 42nd street. It wasn't Madison Square Garden, but it was still New York City. A place to start.

I got the gig through a charity organization – The Set NYC who fundraises to fight for stronger laws against child and sex trafficking.

The hard months of adjusting to life in New York all started to feel worth it when I started playing shows. With a new jump in my step, I booked my first studio session at The Loft in Bronxville, and recorded an original song professionally for the first time – my song "Bodega Raffy."

"What was it like to record Christina Aguilera?" I asked Al, the studio owner and engineer, with my eyes as big as saucers. "She cried a lot because she was still finding her voice. She was doing all the scales in every take and her producers told her that it was great but that she had to stop doing it with every note she hit. She cried because she felt like she was failing." I gulped as I walked into the recording room to sing in the same space she did, Rihanna did, Britney did.

There was a shift in my reality, a shift in what I thought was possible. I started to believe in my music dreams again, the way I did at fifteen. Recording in these spaces didn't make me the new Britney – I didn't want it to. But I was appreciating the once in a lifetime type of moments I was experiencing. When I get to do big things in my career, I don't feel intimidated by them, I don't feel nervous, I feel like I belong there and that as special as it is, its just another day in my life. Another part of me, the fifteen-year-old-girl inside of me is in complete disbelief that I am no longer being held back in an abusive home where I was told I would never amount to anything. I try to find the balance between those two feelings to appreciate the moment but to also own it like I belong there.

I hated Yvette for always asking me "can't you just come home now?" because as much as I denied it, I really wanted to go home. She visited me in New York for two weeks and we traveled together in Florida. As I predicted, she found herself an American hunk before I did and returned to South Africa – married to a Floridian. We referred to him as "Lyla with a dick" because he is literally just another version of me. He moved to Johannesburg to make a life with her, and we joked that us three should work together in radio. He landed a show in no time and I started a podcast, interviewing New Yorkers and sending him the clips to play on the radio.

I felt good, having a few creative projects running in my time off from my au pair job, and went to see any and every music concert I was able to get to. Katy Perry, Ed Sheeran, James Blunt, Miley Cyrus, Erikah Badu, Jon Bellion, Lykke Li, The Gorillaz, Paramore, Mike Shinoda. As the months passed, more and more people visited New York from South Africa and I got to see many familiar faces – all green with envy that I call New York home. I started to see the wood for the trees - I started to value my opportunities despite my homesickness. I was still crying myself through concerts, alone, but I was okay with that. It was sort of a beautiful experience in its own right. Necessary. I decided to see it that way.

All the times I was pushed and pulled around in New York crowds, shouted at for walking too slowly on the wrong side of the sidewalk, got caught in the rain, got completely lost on this island, paper map and phone GPS in hand – all of those moments grew me a tough skin before I could even know so. Each time I had to return to the suburbs after spending time in the city, it felt too quiet, too in order, too predictable. I started having a hard time imagining living anywhere but

New York, or New York City – for that matter. I was mingling with New Yorkers and South African expats alike and saw myself clearly for the first time since I moved here, and with that came confidence.

The cool thing about introducing myself to people in New York, was that I didn't have to be Lyla who works in radio and now wants to make it in music, I was just Lyla who wants to make it in music. I didn't have to change people's view of me here like I had to in South Africa.

Shaun Peterson, a South African expat known for bringing the expats together for braais in New York, connected with me on Facebook and invited me to his next event. He told me to bring my guitar if I wanted. I rocked up at Brooklyn Pier 11, guitar in hand and Springbok rugby jersey on, where a hundred or so of us gathered. A couple of hours into the get together, he gathered us around for a group photo. He egged me on to take my guitar out and lead the group to sing our national anthem. By the time we were halfway through the anthem, I had goose bumps all over, I knew there and then that something special was happening. Having worked creating and producing live radio, I have gotten to know which few seconds of interviews would stand out above the rest of the minutes of conversation, which lines gripped the audience the most, which lines to take out and rerun or use as a promo. I understood the ingredients that went into creating moments of impact, moments that would stick with people for a while – and this was one of these moments, and it was mine.

During my train ride back to Scarsdale, I posted the video to Facebook after watching it over and over and over again. Back at home, still slightly tipsy, I passed out after the commute. I woke up to the story being featured across news sites in South Africa the next morning, my name and photo was being spread around far and wide. Some of the biggest radio stations featured the story too, and journalists took words from my Facebook posts and turned them into articles. The crazy part is, I would be lying if I said I didn't intend for exactly that to happen. I'd be lying if I said I didn't expect for it to blow up.

IN THE NEWS

Watch South African Expats in New York Belt Out SA's National Anthem

By Jenni Baxter
sapoeple.com

Watch this beautiful rendition of South Africa's national anthem – Nkosi Sikelel' iAfrika – as sung by a group of SA expats in New York this weekend.

Photo: Lyla Illing – "Leading the South African National Anthem at the SA New York braai. Man, very few things make me happier than moments like these. #MyPeople #Manhattan #Brooklyn"

Durban born, Joburg-bred singer, songwriter and former junior radio producer at Hot 919 FM, Lyla Illing – who can be seen in the video, on the guitar

– told SAPeople: "This weekend we had a braai in New York, a get together after the rugby [Springboks vs All Blacks rugby match] on Saturday."

After the End of Summer Event, Lyla wrote this wonderful message on Facebook to her friends and former colleagues from Joburg's Hottest Breakfast Show, which will resonate with many other South Africans living abroad:

"Braaivleis under the Brooklyn Bridge, and the Manhattan skyline in the background, ululating and lip syncing all around."

"This is us saying it: We love YOU, South Africa!"

"One thing I don't say enough: I miss you. My friends and my family, my radio people and my friends in music. I miss you."

"Every day is a battle without you, but every night here is like a dream. ❤ Thank you for standing by me. I feel it."

South African Expats in New York Sing SA's National Anthem
947

This past weekend South African-born (Joburg-bred) singer, songwriter and radio producer Lyla Illing hung out with a group of South African expats after the rugby to have a braai.

This was to celebrate an End of Summer event. This is enough to give you all the feels, but then you see Lyla (seen playing the guitar) and the group belt out Nkosi Sikelel' iAfrika - ALL THE FEELS!

Lyla then took to Facebook to send this message:

"This is us saying it: We love YOU, South Africa! One thing I don't say enough: I miss you. My friends and my family, my radio people and my friends in music. I miss you. Every day is a battle without you, but every night here is like a dream. Thank you for standing by me. I feel it."

WATCH THE VIDEO AND TRY NOT TO FEEL ALL THE PRIDE IN THE WORLD.

We miss you all, too and thank you for keeping the spirit of South Africa high all around the world.

If you love South African's living abroad, 947 loves you.

Check out Lyla Illing, all the way in New York.

South African expats belt out national anthem in New York
By Lee-Roy Wright
Jacaranda FM
This will make you feel so proud to be a South African.

Stop what you are doing and sing along.

Many South Africans have been through a tough week. Massive flooding and heavy storms have affected thousands across the country and we can all do with a little bit of positivity right now.

Lyla Illing posted a video showing herself and a number of South African expats in New York singing South Africa's national anthem, 'Nkosi Sikelel' iAfrika'.

The group got together after last weekend's nail-biting match between the Springboks and New Zealand. You can even see Lyla proudly wearing her Springbok jersey.

The unity, camaraderie and feel good vibe watching them singing and feeling proud to be South African is truly inspiring.

This is beautiful!

Breakfast with Martin Bester and Tumi Morake
"Feeling down today? Well, we'll leave you with this epic, feel-good video that will make feel proud to be South African!"

Lead SA
"I am an African not because I was born in Africa, but because Africa is born in me."

Watch South African expats in New York sing SA's National Anthem.

Lekkerblog.co.za
South Africans singing Nkosi Sikelel' iAfrika in New York will give you goosebumps! (Video)

PART TEN

THE UNITED STATES OF AMERICA

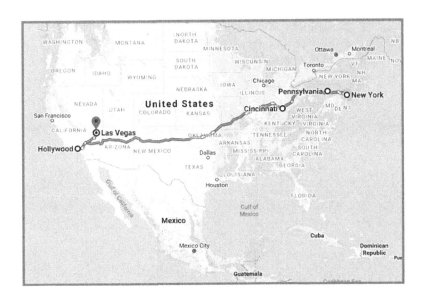

I AM NOT OKAY

Yvette: "Just let it happen, let them take care of you now that they know."

Lyla: "I can't! I don't know how to be vulnerable! I HATE when other people have to step in, I don't want them to know what I'm going through!"

I was screaming my feelings in desperation to Yvette in tears on a 3am phone call to South Africa after I had to tell my host family what had happened.

I had driven myself to hospital in their car earlier that night, and drove myself home 7 hours later, souvenirs in hand - a pair of yellow hospital socks, a blue – in case of vomit – bag on my lap that the nurse gave to me, and what was left of the little bit of trust I used to have in human beings.

When you go through something like this, it is like you go through it twice. Once when it is happening, and a second time when you have to talk about it. Which is why I don't. Which is why most of us, probably don't.

Yvette: "Lyla, say it out loud. You were raped. NYPD has started the investigation. You were in the ER. Say it out loud and hear it, so you can let your host family take care of you now. Don't do this alone."

I fell onto my basement-room floor trying so hard not to let the cries come out and seep all the way up through the three-story house into the corners of everyone else's rooms but I wasn't in control anymore. I was having the breakdown I had been putting down since the two days ago when he didn't take no for an answer.

Yvette was the only one I spoke to about it from the beginning, from when it happened, through calling NYPD, through going to the ER. Everyone had the flu at home including my host-mom. I was put in charge, driving the kids to school and was really running the house working 7am – 7pm with a lunch break in between. It was the worst possible timing for me to have a personal crisis, so I decided to put everyone's needs above my own and continued to work for two days without telling my employers or agency what was going on. The ER visit and rape-kit took much longer than I thought it would, my host-mom reached out at 2am to hear why I wasn't back home – it was out of character for me to stay out that late and she thought I might have had a car accident.

I returned home with the hospital paperwork in hand after 3am. I begged the doctor to write me a letter saying I was fit to go straight back to work. I handed it to my host-mom trying to avoid having to tell her what was going on, but there was no way around it, and she wanted to be there for me.

The hardest part was trying to explain why I didn't ask her and her husband for help in the first place. They felt like they failed me because I didn't turn to them, but how I acted had nothing to do with them and everything to do with my personal experience of being abandoned by my own dad. I was used to dealing with things on my own and preferred it that way at that stage.

Not only was it hard to rely on people around me for support, the shame that came with having to admit that I was assaulted was excruciatingly embarrassing to me. I felt like it was a reflection of me and somehow indicated an inability to stay out of a dangerous situation like that in the first place. The thing that broke my spirit was the fact that I trusted the person who did this to me, and that made me feel like I had poor judgment of character. How was I someone who got herself into a situation like that in her personal life and also someone who was trusted with the lives of four little ones in her work life? Nothing anyone said could help me see myself clearly at that stage. I was just beating myself up, I felt naked around everyone who knew, knowing that they would never look at me the same again.

Up until that day, I was Lyla who could deal with anything. I used to turn every painful ending into a victorious new start. I used to carry the weight of the world on my shoulders with ease – grateful to have experienced so much. I used to relentlessly claw my way out of the deepest darkest holes people pushed my soul off into. But that Lyla no longer existed, I had never felt so powerless before, and every little thing that ever went wrong in my life suddenly came back to me all at once at such a speed and intensity – that for the first time, my spirit was broken.

I said the four words I fought so hard to never have to say my whole life, out loud; "I am not okay." I couldn't believe my own ears – I always thought I was strong enough.

Without warning, I was suddenly just a shell of myself and was only sure of two things – I was quitting my job to return to South Africa, and starting therapy as soon as possible.

My employers didn't take my resignation very well, they were supportive and knew there was nothing they could say, but at the same time really wanted me to stay. Part of me wanted to stay but I was too broken.

I had eleven months left on my contract, but cut it short by six months, which left me with five months working for them in New York – enough time for them to find a replacement and for me to fight the case and say my goodbyes in New York.

I was going home, and nothing anyone said could change my mind. I couldn't find a single reason to stay in America. I could care less that I finally made headlines in the news just a month before that. I could care less that I finally knew how to navigate my way around New York without my GPS. I could care less that I had a trip booked for Vegas and California.

I was going home.

HAVE A LITTLE FAITH, KID

I said goodbye to 2017, folding laundry in my pajamas in front of the TV, watching the Times Square ball drop on NBC.

Some of my friends were in the crowd, bravely shivering their way through minus thirteen degrees Celsius into 2018, totally understanding that I declined their invitations, and other friends were no longer speaking to me because I stopped showing up to hang out after the assault.

I think it's safe to say that, when I quit the 20-something year olds' perfect radio dream job, that I lived and breathed, and loved - when I decided to throw a backpack over my shoulder and head for New York, I did so, not too sure if I was running towards something, or away from something. But I picked the scarier direction, and ran for my life through those boarding gates at OR Tambo, hoping for the best, but preparing for the worst. I always do.

I must have been in New York for about a month when I was in a subway on my way to explore another corner of the concrete jungle. A tear rolled down my cheek when it hit me, that I was in New York, and I did not know why. For what possible purpose? I did not know then and I still didn't know why, as I sat there folding laundry, waiting for 2017 to creep into 2018, one second at a time. I had three months left in New York before returning home to South Africa - Norman Vincent Peale once said: "Shoot for the moon. Even if you miss you'll land among the stars" but I had no zest left in me to make the most of what was left of my failed voyage to the big bright yellow ball of cheese in the sky. I was floating around the galaxy, New York – the moon. The moon I landed on for a split second only to be forcefully pulled back off of it again. What a sight to see, what a place to call home for a moment. What a destination to reach after a lifetime's traveling, dodging black holes and meteors to get to my destination successfully - but what was the point? I could hardly keep my feet grounded, and there was no air for me to breathe. I was ready to come back to earth - get on a plane to South Africa and call it a day already.

I wanted to experience America, but not this way. It was supposed to be like the movies, I was supposed to be scouted during my subway and Central Park busking ventures, but even playing shows at famous New York venues got me nowhere. I sang my heart out for nothing, got dressed up in my Swaziland stage gear for nothing – no talent scout in the audience promising to make me a star or die trying, no record deal to sign my life away to, no agents fighting over wanting to represent me. The excitement of moving to a new country had worn off. I was in the midst of an assault case. All the things I thought I was coming to find here, the career, the fame & fortune, the fulfillment and the love story, the fantastic WIFI and unlimited data plans, the functioning public transportation system and the world's best pizza slice… all the things that were supposed to make me happy here in New York, did not turn me into the "brand new happy person" I thought it would.

I thought I was coming to find myself in New York, but it turned out I already knew who I was. I had been in New York for nine months… and nothing about me had changed. I was still the same person who didn't know how to let anyone in, the same person who put others' needs above my own, the same person who was always waiting for the next thing to go wrong.

I thought, wow, I've played shows on the infamous 42nd street in Times Square – but guess what? I was still playing my same songs, singing about the same things, to the same types of people. Nothing had changed. What was the big deal about doing it in New York versus in Johannesburg, in anyway?

You could still find me at the bar after my shows getting to know the locals, making friends and being mistaken for throwing myself at every person I was making conversation with, by everyone who was watching. If they only knew how irrationally in love I still was with the same people I had been in love with over the years.

I tried moving on from the people I still had feelings for, I tried forgetting, I tried abstinence, tried a year of no serious dating, and I learned that no amount of alcohol could wash away feelings and memories I was not ready to put to rest yet…and that was okay.

As for the completion of my "single for a year" challenge which was closely followed by a reminder that there are men who have no regard for the word "no" …I was sad to say, I'd rather be alone now anyway.

I thought, wow, I live in the wealthiest town in America, Scarsdale, a stone's throw away from Manhattan - a lot of people's "end game" or "goal." Well, guess what? I still go look for the people who speak "my language" … the people who come from similar (shitty) backgrounds, the dreamers busking in parks, singing because they have the music in them, not because they are paper chasers. And sometimes I get mistaken for being homeless or a hooker but I can't help but to sit myself down on the sidewalk outside of Grand Central, on the corner of 42nd and Park, and just watch…the city at the end of the night. Just watch the city play out in front of me. Like it knew I had a ticket. Like it knew I was coming. Like it knows what I long for. Like it knows what I need to hear.

I used to sit there on the sidewalk, 42nd and Park, and remember that I am still who I was a week ago, a month ago, 5 years ago – whether that was a bad or good thing.

I used to sit there to remember "what" I am. Sit there and be reminded that for the last 10 years of my life I had been getting by, relying on the kindness of strangers – and I tried to be thankful for that instead of feeling resentful towards my father for not being a dad to me. As I stared the Chrysler building up and down, watched people stream in and out of the doors of Grand Central, I sat there thinking about the kindness of strangers more and more, the people who had been the parents to me I didn't have – even when I kicked and screamed against any idea of having parental figures in my life again. I was always saying I didn't need any of them – when I really did. And thank God they stepped in each time they did. I don't know who I would have turned out to be if I didn't have so many people looking out for me during my teenage years.

I used to sit there on 42nd and Park, trying to come to terms with the fact that I hadn't changed in the nine months I'd been in New York. When I flew into JFK in 2017, I really, really wanted New York to magically turn me into someone sparkly and happy, somebody who could stand on her own two feet for once, but I was just the same old victim, the same old girl being knocked down again and again.

With every sweater I drew out of the laundry basket and folded, I felt more and more afraid that I had forgotten the things that made me Lyla.

Sometimes I wondered if I came to New York, only to let my soul drown in its luxury? I wasn't getting my hands dirty trying to "make it" anymore. I walked past street performers in the subway no longer dropping a dollar in their guitar cases. "Nobody gives a fuck that you're just another hopeful soul singing Jeff Buckley Hallelujah" - I thought.

Did I become the bitch, the rude, disconnected, diva? I wasn't trying to make friends anymore.

Was I settling for security over connection? Because the relationships I had with people here weren't ever fulfilling, yet I stuck around all this time.

Did I decide to live in America just because it looked better on my social media and resume? Was I being absorbed into someone else's idea of what my life would play out to be, and the things that were supposed to drive me? Whatever the reason was for my move to New York, it was meaningless in anyway. I was set to fly back home to South Africa, and I was set to return home more damaged than I was when I left it – and I felt like I should have known the story would end this way.

New York wasn't what I hoped it would be, New York didn't heal my broken heart or make it easy on me that past year, but sitting there on the sidewalk in front of Grand Central, trying so hard not to love and admire this city that broke me, I realized that New York never promised to turn me into a sparkly happy person. And I couldn't get myself to be mad at it. I couldn't get myself to call New York out on its shit – and I think anyone who has been in this city long enough would tell you that it is this Concrete Jungle's flaws that makes it such a fucking masterpiece, so fucking hard to ever leave.

I had my reasons for calling 2017 the hardest year of my life, but I wouldn't have wanted to spend it anywhere else.

New York was harder than it seemed, and every next door I had to knock on, was harder for me to. New York chewed me up and spat me out, the city lights blinded me and the lonely hearts who swore "they had good intentions" left me a bigger mess than I was when I arrived here. New York ruined me and reminded me that I already know myself, very well. And maybe that's what I needed more than the instant gratification and "happily ever after."

With the clothes heaped neatly in the basket beside me as the ball dropped and Ryan Seacrest gave the signal that we could kiss 2018 hello… I thought for just a split second – what if I stayed? 2018. New York. Round 2. Maybe I'd throw the winning punch the second time round? But I shook my head, hugged my pillow, and slept that idea off, put it down to not being an option.

My weekly therapy started when the New Year did. I used to go into the city on my Wednesday-afternoons-off - I traded that for an hour of speaking about my feelings and crying into tissues.

One of the first things my therapist said was "you have to make peace with the fact that justice will probably not be served. I am here to help you heal emotionally. You have to work on making peace with what happened whether or not justice is served."

At first I took her advice lightly, but as the case progressed, I started to realize that she was right. No matter that they found his DNA on my stockings, no matter that he had been fired from his job on New Year's Eve for assaulting a second girl – caught on camera; he was on the run and the case was going nowhere.

My therapist told me I was making the whole experience worse for myself, by allowing it to hurt me so much that I had quit my job and decided to head back to South Africa – and essentially give up on a life in New York. She asked me a few times to explain why I felt I had to give New York up as a result of what had happened, and she repeatedly reminded me that I could still change my mind at any time. I kept telling her there was no way I could stay, and I kept telling her she was wrong.

But she was right about one thing - I couldn't actively fight the case if I left America, which was something I didn't know I could forgive myself for – having to look back at my twenty-five-year-old self ten years from now, knowing I didn't even try to fight for justice. Maybe that's what made me want to stay mostly, apart from the pizza, that is really as good as everyone told me it would be.

I made a list of everyone whose opinion mattered to me and called them with the question; "do I stay or do I go?" I dialed their numbers one after the other - my brother, my mentor Boo, my radio mentors, my life coach in New York Jen Glantz, my life coach in South Africa Dominique, the NYPD detective working on my case, and a lawyer who could give me advice on what my options were if I chose to stay.

Two people entered my life at just the right time – a South African actor who'd been doing his thing in Hollywood reached out to me over Facebook after stalking my YouTube. He called me and an hour and a half later we knew each other's angels and demons intimately. We fell into friendship instantly, he was the first person I really clicked with since my move to the states; we wanted to work together creatively from the first time we said hello and goodbye to each other – a good reason for me to stay. The other person who reached out was Leslie, my eldest sister – my stepmother's daughter I am not related to but had spent a few Christmas Eve's and other holidays with as a kid. At first it was extremely difficult to imagine having any sort of relationship with her, but she told me that her mom did the same things to her she did to me – because of that, we knew each other so well already. We decided to accept each other as sisters and be in each other's lives. I wanted to live with her in Uganda if I did end up leaving New York.

I had to sign up for some classes as per my visa requirements, and decided to study the Amish. "Fourteen miles is a long way from home" - a girl my age said in the documentary we were watching in class.

That shook me. I sat up and took notice – paid more attention than I initially intended to. I was asking the lecturer questions she couldn't answer, questions other students had never asked before. I stayed up Googling my questions that night – but there was so little information on their cult other than these few sentences that kept popping up.

"The Amish value rural life, manual labor, and humility, all under the auspices of living what they interpret to be God's word. Members who do not conform to these community expectations and who cannot be convinced to repent are excommunicated. In addition to excommunication, members may be shunned, a practice that limits social contacts to shame the wayward member into returning to the church."

Learning that families still set a place at the table during every meal for said absent shunned child after kicking them out of the house and community, sickened me. They want the child they have shunned to know that they have not only been kicked out of the house, but that their absence is acknowledged three times a day – I thought that was brutal emotional abuse.

With high hopes of finding some answers from the horse's mouth, I boarded the bus en route Amish Country for an educational tour at the end of the course I was enrolled in. Snow fell as we drove into Pennsylvania, it was my first experience of snow – I had something to smile about other than smirking at the name of the town we stopped in called "Intercourse."

The snow and laughs were welcomed distractions from an otherwise very emotional day, spiking a lot of anger and anxiety in my soul as the person who assaulted me was calling me from many different numbers, threatening and insulting me over voicemail and text that whole day.

Maybe that had something to do with the fact that I was highly pissed of at every Amish person I came into contact with during my trip. I had to stop myself from calling them out for all the ways they hold their children back with their ancient views and warped ways of living. Amish children are only allowed an education up to the 8th grade, they are not allowed to use technology or think for themselves. They are not allowed to pursue a career or express their individuality. Only three percent of Amish youths ever leave the cult, because if they leave home, they are shunned – no longer welcome in the family or community. The three percent who leave, are set up to fail. It is a disgusting system and I couldn't help but draw parallels between their cult and my childhood.

During the Q & A with an Amish-Mennonite I had the chance to ask one question. "What is the cult's views on music – is anyone allowed to play instruments or write songs?"

"The harmonica is accepted but no one is allowed to play the instrument or sing any of the religious songs individually, it has to be done in a group so as to prevent anyone from developing the ability to express their own individuality or feel superior to the rest of the group. Writing music is not allowed. We only sing religious songs that have been passed down to us by previous generations."

"I have a follow-up question, what happens to kids who are shunned, where do they go, is there an organization in place they can turn to?" I was getting worked up and she could hear it in my voice. She eventually broke down crying, pointing out how their way of life is heaven and hell. She told us there was no one in place to take care of the shunned youths, who are forced into the life of being a runaway – a life I know so well.

Not only was I disturbed to visit a community where they emotionally abuse their children, take away their right to higher education, instill fear in them to the point that they are too scared to go out into the outside world; I was also incredibly saddened that the members of their community are denied the experience of expressing oneself through the magic world that is music.

I found myself deeply burdened, disproportionately grateful that I was not born into this cult – and feeling that the freedom I have to express myself through music and words are not only talents but also a responsibility. A responsibility I have towards every child who has that right taken away from them simply because of their place of birth. It could just as easily have been me born into that cult, I always think that way.

Visiting their community is something that will never leave me. It woke a part of me I didn't know was there. Despite what I was going through with the assault and all the other my-dad-doesn't-want-me-baggage I was carrying around, I knew it could still be worse. Being brought face to face with the Amish, made me want to fight for my music and words in bigger ways than before. Things were put into perspective for me. Fuck wanting to land a record deal overnight. Fuck wanting to play a show at Madison Square Garden overnight. Fuck wanting to get radio play overnight. The freedom to write and express through music, the freedom to experience the power of music between my own four walls – that is what I am grateful for. It is not about writing the perfect pop single, it never was for me, and I knew then, that it would never be - music is more than that. No matter how my career turns out, it is the moments of honesty I experience whilst creating that's going to be my best memories I want to look back on one day, not how many times my song was played on the radio. I was just a different person when I left Amish county that day, I've just experienced the process of creating, writing, composing in a different way since then.

Back in New York, I sat across the booking agent who I played shows for in Times Square, and he gave me his phone to call the girl who was a victim of the same man who assaulted me. I had stopped playing shows without saying why but the booking agent put two and two together when the offender was fired from his job for assaulting the second girl he also booked shows for at that venue. The booking agent didn't know me very well, but he told me something told him I'd be making a mistake if I left New York. He asked if he could pray for me, so amidst the noise in the diner we were in somewhere between 7th and 8th avenue, we bowed our heads, closed our eyes, and he asked Jesus to guide me. I appreciated it, and wanted it to be true.

I went to meet Jen Glantz for a life coaching session a block away after that. "Can you ask for your job back? Stay in New York." I couldn't wrap my head around the idea.

When I reached out to all these people for advice, some part of me hoped they'd give me a pat on the back, say well done for trying, and tell me it was time to come home – but none of the conversations went that way.

Staying started to look like the only thing that made sense. All these people told me I was stronger than I thought, and I decided to believe them.

I asked my au pair agency for a transfer, I wanted to look for a family whose schedule wasn't as demanding as my current hosts. If I was going to stay, I was going to need a lot of time to work on myself – and Scarsdale just wasn't the place for that. Anxiety-ridden, I interviewed twenty-seven families until I had it narrowed down to a South African couple in California, and a small family in Manhattan. Both only had one baby, and offered me a light and flexible schedule. I loved them both, and the thought of living with other South Africans seemed comforting, but when I Skyped with the Manhattan family – I just knew in my heart that it was right. I once read a postcard that said "Nothing can stop New York City" and my life felt a little bit like that, at that moment. New York was asking me to stay – in bold and beautiful ways. I was made an offer I couldn't turn down – I had a family who felt like long-lost friends, the opportunity to live a block away from the World Trade Center, working some hours at night only. The word "no" didn't even come up as an option in my mind. It was clear - New York wasn't done with me yet.

I was set to move to Tribeca in two months time. After signing my new contract, I felt in charge of my life again, a feeling that I wasn't familiar with anymore.

I knew it was going to be hard on my Scarsdale host family to hear that I was staying in America but not with them, but I had a new sense of self-love so strong that I knew I could never again in my life make any decision to benefit anyone else's happiness over my own – something that has never come naturally to me.

I wanted to hold onto the high that came with making a decision independently, it was the breath of fresh I'd been gasping for after having so little control over my privacy, my emotions, my rights during and in the aftermath of the assault.

Gathering those last traces of hope together in a bundle and choosing to stay in New York, felt a little bit like I was emptying my pockets, lifting up my mattress, turning the freezer upside down, throwing every handbag out onto the floor scraping my last loose change together – and I just, just had enough money for a one way ticket. Two dollars, seventy-five cents – the cost of one subway ride – and even though that one ticket could get me as far as Coney Island, or the Brooklyn Bridge, Central Park or Times Square - I had to choose my final destination carefully. That's how my life felt – like I was going to run out of life soon and had just enough hope left in my stomach to take one last chance with, make one last move with. I had so little left of myself, and using my last bit of energy to fly across the globe, return back home and run out of life – there, seemed too easy, predictable, not the way I wanted to go out. I thought; if I was going to run out of life, if I was going to fall apart, die anyway, I'd rather do that here in Manhattan, go down fighting, die in the line of duty, die on the job, die trying to do what I love doing, die trying to find a single shard of peace, happiness – here. Here, where every interaction feels like a movie scene. Here where I know each street corner and building already, because of TV. Here where I casually pass Madison Square Garden every time I ride the subway to get myself downtown. This place that gave birth to every music star that has ever been God to me. The concrete jungle - I thought I'd rather die "no one" between its four walls than back home. And besides, there were still a half a handful of – not quite friends, but rather, almost-familiar faces - I was hopeful to make some Manhattan memories with. The South African I met at The Irish Bank restaurant, and the guy making bubbles in Central Park who showed me around good busking spots for myself there. The FOX news camera guy whose help I wanted with a music video, and the other guy who sold me my first guitar and gave me his number.

Then there was the guy I found most curious – Tyler who was dating a girl who was dating a girl, too – I liked all three of them. The steps he took always seemed heavy, like he was slamming his feet into the ground but involuntarily. Like it was the weight of the world on his shoulders, his burdens, his grudges towards anyone who had ever done him wrong, weighing him down and making him do it - making him plant every next foot he put down, so hard into the ground. But he always smiled and he once let me take a drag of his cigarette. I thought he made good cocktails, got my humor. And his two girls were cute and fun to be around. I said I'd teach him to play the guitar, so he bought one with one click – the same one I saved up for my whole life.

I knew no one on a personal level and none of them really knew me – but it was something to start with. The kind of setting, plot and characters that made for an entertaining sitcom playing out in my head as I tried to imagine what life would be like once I left Scarsdale for Manhattan in two months time.

I'M NOT COMING HOME
(Lyrics)

No trains come
And no trains go
I see the tracks light up
But none of them stop
They're just passing through

I keep my suitcase packed and
My passport in my pocket too
I just need enough cash

For a one-way ticket back

Fourteen miles could be a long way from home
If you were born on the wrong side of the world
But fourteen miles don't feel so far anymore
Now I'm out here on my own, so I'm not coming home

They keep my place at the table set
And they're waiting for a call
But I have no regrets
And I don't feel bad at all

Fourteen miles could be a long way from home
If you were born on the wrong side of the world
But fourteen miles don't feel so far anymore
Now I'm out here on my own, so I'm not coming home
I'm not coming home

DO YOU KNOW WHERE YOU ARE?
(Inner conversation)

(Arriving at the Scarsdale train station)

I know you travel this road everyday, but when last did you stop to look? Do you know where you are? Will you remember this moment as clearly as you do your list of personal favorite memories captured in your mind? Even the ones you don't tell anybody about, the ones that keep you up at night? Will you remember this moment?

Why aren't you captivated by it?

When last did you go out alone, when last did you free your mind from unrealistic expectations? When last did you acknowledge the shadow walking beside you or are you too tangled up in the frustrations of taking one step forward and two steps back?

Don't be so caught up on the things that went wrong.

(Arriving at Grand Central Terminal)

Hmm… who else has walked these hallways in Grand Central - Eighteen-year-old Ed Sheeran who was just a song writer trying to make it like me? Or maybe some of my ex-lovers who are scattered over the globe now?

(Looking at the clock in the center of the terminal)

I am sure they have walked here where I walk. They've seen what I am seeing now, yet our time ran out and we have nothing left in common apart from walking the hallways of Grand Central at some point in our separate journeys. I once heard that the only reason that time exists is so that everything doesn't happen at once, but sometimes, I need it to.

So I get another coffee to get pumped up and I proudly say to the barista "I'm down to three a day now!" I hear myself talk like an alcoholic who is trying to kick the habit.

I have no appetite for alcohol anymore and sadly it has nothing to do with the price of liquor here. **(Laughs)**

I watch the exhausted New Yorkers try to take a nap on the subway. It must look to them as though I'm just a tourist, doing this for fun, but I am tired, too.

I've come a long way to be here on this downtown, four train. And I listen to my brother's music. I give in to another Manhattan meltdown. I feel my chest warm up as I try to … hold … my breath.

But, I exhale. And a tear runs down my cheek again. **(Starts crying.)**

I look the other way.

I don't really know my brother but clearly he has felt the things I feel too, judging by the music he writes.

(Excited) I'm above ground again! And that first sight of city lights hit my soul like the sun rays of a warm South African sunrise used to. Then I hear Doc's voice in my head again, the words he said in that radio lecture comes back to me, almost instinctively, like a warning going off in my mind every time that I'm here – "don't let the city lights distract you." But tonight, I might have to let them.

(Arriving at the Staten Island Ferry)

I've been told that there are no free rides in life – I have found a few.

Maybe the memory I have of friends who bought my mom a car when she was sick has changed my mind about that saying. Or the countless friends who gave me a place to sleep when I was fifteen and my dad told me I couldn't come home – and I haven't been home in nine years, like he asked.

(Looking at Manhattan from aboard the Staten Island Ferry)

Have you ever seen anything this beautiful? Do you know where you are?

Lose track of time. So much can happen in time if you let it. If you can be patient, if you can wait.

Sixteen years ago I saw the towers fall on an SABC2 news broadcast and sixteen years later I am in New York for the 2017 Tribute in Lights. Sixteen years ago I never would have thought that this was my future, but look what time does.

Do you get it?

Now I'm back somewhere underground, waiting alone, at some ungodly hour again for something – sometimes you have to.

(Looking at the NYC subway map)

Do you know where you are?

I've missed the train home, I have to wait for the next one, so I pick up one of those big New York City pretzels from a food truck right outside Grand Central and sit myself down on the sidewalk, my back against the wall, and I watch "New York."

Like I'm in a movie theater, I watch "New York."

"New York" happening, right in front of me, like it knew I was coming, like it knew I had a ticket.

I wonder when the dejavu will stop. Something tells me I've been here in a previous life before so my guess is that the visions won't stop anytime soon.

The wall my back is against is cold but I wouldn't want to be anywhere else in the world right now as empty as this feels. **(Cries.)**

I know I will look back and long to be sitting on this sidewalk, here in this moment again, by myself just taking in what's happening around me.

So much on my mind, but not a care in the world.

As alone as I am and as hard as this is, I know where I am; I'm on the corner of 42nd and Park and I know where I am.

For the first time in my life I know where I am.

Then the beggar opening the door for me back into the terminal, his voice echoes: "Does anyone have a quarter? Does anyone have a quarter? Does anyone have a quarter?" And I realize that could be me.

(Looks up at the celestial ceiling in Grand Central)

I feel the troubled look in his eyes and I can relate as I try to decipher these higher-caliber problems in my mind. I almost envy him. I remember being a runaway at fifteen - the times I had to use all my mental energy on trying to find the next place to sleep, and finding the next supermarket to shoplift food from. I had no time to miss the people who left me. I had no time to question it, try and make sense of it all.

Now, it's all that I do.

339 SUNRISES

I missed 77 sunrises since I moved to Scarsdale – slept through them.

And then I blinked and the number was a gigantic 339. I was counting.

I had almost been in New York for a whole year, but had no sunrises to show for it.

Being awake and around for the sunrise, used to be a given, it didn't used to be an effort when I worked in radio. I was up at 4am each morning, by studio at 5am and had my team on air by 6.

Perhaps this explains my huge disappointment with missing that many sunrises.

It became a little less hard for me to wake up early once I secured the new job that was to start April 2018 in Manhattan. I had something to look forward to, and I was about to take my first trip to the other side of the U.S. too. I had a one-way ticket to Las Vegas with my name on it, sitting in my email inbox. I bought this ticket on Black Friday a few days before I was assaulted. As the February date of travel kept creeping closer, I tried convincing myself to still go on the trip even though I was forever changed, afraid to travel alone after what I had just gone through. I managed to scrape together my guts and book the rest of the trip, despite the fact that I was having panic attacks frequently. It happened for the first time when I walked into a Target looking for my usual face wash – I couldn't find it between the shelves and suddenly everything around me was a blur, I needed to sit down and breathe it over. My therapist monitored the situation during our weekly Wednesday meetings, and I was clear that I didn't want medication. I wanted to try and work through it on my own.

When I booked the trip before the assault took place, I pictured myself, guitar in hand on the Las Vegas strip, serenading couples exiting little chapels. I imagined myself hanging my selfie-stick around a branch in the Grand Canyon, making impromptu videos and interviewing fellow travelers for my YouTube channel. But the girl who got onto that plane heading to Las Vegas in February, was not the same girl who booked the ticket back in November. I was looking over my shoulder. I had every detail of my trip planned out, obsessively so. A backpack filled only with hiking clothes and no cute dresses. I had no intention of interacting with anyone, no intention to dress up and catch the perfect stranger's eye.

When I got off the train at 125th street to take the bus to the La Guardia airport, I missed the bus because I did not have the correct pass. I was hoping to get on the next bus but when I was ready to pay for my pass at the ticket vending machine, I froze and forgot my own ATM card's security pin. I called Yvette in a panic because my pin has to do with her home address numbers. At that stage I could not even remember her address, and I also never told her before that I had used her address as a reminder for my pin. She must have thought I had lost my mind when she picked up the phone and I started screaming with a shaky voice "what's your address? What's your address, I need it NOW!"

After missing the bus twice, I opted for taking an Uber instead. My trip hadn't even started and I was ready to say okay, this is a disaster, I am turning around and going home. But the driver asked me about my accent and started giving me tips on where to watch 4th of July fireworks in 2018, so I got distracted enough to put those thoughts of telling him to take me back to Scarsdale to rest and walked through the doors of the airport, trying very hard to walk toward those boarding gates as if I wanted to. I walked myself onto that plane, shaking but excited.

I had a connecting flight through Cincinnati airport in Ohio; I sat there with none other but Willem on my mind. The thought of him entered my mind uninvited, he was the last person I wanted to be thinking of – but airports just did that to me, brought him back to me. The last time we spoke he tried to get kinky with me over text after telling me he liked the song I wrote about him - he must have seen it on Facebook. I asked him why we couldn't be together. He said it was because we were on opposite sides of the world but I didn't believe him. "If you want to see me, why don't you just get on a plane? You seem to be very good at it." I fired. He has been in almost every country of the world and was waiting for a plane in an Abu Dhabi airport while we had that exact conversation.

Walking toward the boarding gate, Las Vegas ticket nervously clenched in my right hand - it is possible my anxiety-ridden mind was looking for an escape, something else to focus on rather than the trip ahead of me I was panicking over.

Maybe that's why I thought of him, or maybe I just always do.

DOES SHE LOOK YOU IN THE EYE?
(Poetry & Prose)

I've been looking, I've been looking for a feeling
So I travel back & forth in time
I'm not believing
The things my eyes are seeing
Across new oceans
Across new border lines
You've been searching, you've been searching for the meaning
Across new oceans
Across new border lines
Another country
Another culture
You learn another language
But when will you learn to speak your mind?
Boy I can tell you
Now I understand the way you choose to live your life
But tell me,
Who are you with tonight?
And does she look you in the eye when she loves you?
Does she look you in the eye when she's above you?
Does she look you in the eye when you tell her,
About the things that keep you up at night?
About the things that save your soul?
I didn't think so.

GIN AND TONIC'S AT SOMEONE ELSE'S BLACKJACK TABLE

After touching down at McCarran airport, I arrived in Las Vegas that night with my backpack filled with only hiking clothes, only to be told my hiking trip in the Grand Canyon had been cancelled due to snowfall – I had no idea what I was going to do for the next three days. I walked past the limousines lining the airport parking lot straight onto the bus, and got myself completely lost in sin city. Eventually I got off at a McDonalds – I thought at least I'd be safe there until I called an Uber – what I should have done at the airport in the first place. I was in a bad neighborhood by the looks of things, finally my driver pulled up and took me to the strip, I got off at Planet Hollywood in the center of all the action, and for a moment I tried to imagine myself enjoying the rest of the night despite everything that had already gone wrong. I wandered around the casinos feeling like a complete weirdo – who the hell does Vegas alone? What was I thinking? I wanted to hit myself over the head, or shove my head in the Bellagio fountain and never come up again. I walked past groups of people having the time of their lives, feeling completely out of place.

I decided to be brave and see if I could find anyone to hang out with – I posted in the Facebook group "South Africans in the United States" to see if anyone else was around, and I downloaded meet up apps and then Tinder eventually. The first guy I met up with, asked me straight up to have sex there and then, and when I laughed it off he excused himself to "go to the men's room" … and never came back.

In the moment I thought it was hilarious, I really couldn't stop laughing about it. Not upset, but not optimistic, I decided Vegas might not be my best bet and got on a bus to Los Angeles overnight. As fate would have it, I was seated next to a homeless guy my age, drinking wine out of a five-liter water bottle and asking me to hold his hand. I got up to change seats, and was wondering at that point if my mind was playing tricks on me – how could everything possibly be going so wrong?

I finally met two decent human beings upon arriving at the bus station in Los Angeles at 5am that next morning - Yoyce Jones and his sister. We decided to share a cab to Union Station where we went our separate ways after grabbing a coffee and chatting each other's ears off – meeting them put me in a significantly better mindset and I started to feel like a person again (and a little less crazy too.) Yoyce gave me one of his old metro cards to use and I boarded the red line towards Santa Monica – I got to the beach just in time for my very first American sunrise, ten months into my stay, but better late than never.

The best part was, only having to share the beach, the pier and views of the Ferris wheel with the early morning joggers. It was quiet and peaceful until about 10am, but I didn't mind the company. It turned out that my life coach Jen Glantz was in Venice Beach – a stone throw away. We met up for a quick hello. I blabbered on about my last crazy twenty-four hours of my life but couldn't help thinking that I wouldn't blame her if she didn't believe a word I was saying – that's how bad the story was!

She gave me a pat on the back for doing something out of my comfort zone, and a few tips on what to get up to in the neighborhood but I wasn't thinking clearly. I was functioning on no sleep at all and decided to head to Hollywood. I got back on the Metro red line and arrived at the Walk of Fame an hour later. I didn't realize how little I care for sightseeing, museums and tours until I found myself bored in Vegas and LA – a catastrophe, totally unexpected. It was like a repeat of how I felt about New York – like I wanted to experience the location but with a different purpose. I wanted my career to bring me face to face with these dream destinations. I was supposed to play big shows and make music for people here – that's how I thought my first visits to New York, to LA would have been, but my life had taken a different course and I had a hard time accepting reality. I tried to appreciate the experience anyway.

I went back to Las Vegas for two days, since I had to fly from McCarran airport back to New York. I knew there was no way I could walk around the party capital of the world in what was supposed to be my Grand Canyon hiking clothes. I had to throw some clothes out of my backpack into the trash to make space, and went shopping – the first (and perhaps only) sensible thing I had done that whole trip. I bought the shiniest dress I could find, one that glittered with gold, and I vowed to stay in it for the next two days of my existence – it was the only way to fit it and look like I was having fun. I jumped into the shower and took a well-deserved power nap – the first time I'd been in a bed since I left Scarsdale two days prior.

After having drinks with Tarryn - a South African girl who reached out to meet up, I went on to spend half the night at a fancy hotel getting frisky with a tall dark and handsome, leaving glitter all over his bed, and spent the other half of the night back at the very suspicious hostel I was booked in at, downtown.

I woke up the next morning, unharmed, not robbed – I was pretty impressed or perhaps the right word is surprised. I had until 4pm to go and see sights I didn't care to see – before I needed to head to the airport for my flight back to New York.

No way in hell, I got a message from Tyler telling me he was in Vegas too – we met up not long after. His girlfriend was attending a conference and he had the day free. When he asked how my trip had been so far, I didn't tell him the same horror version I volunteered to Jen the day before. I just said it was really great so far and tried to pretend like I totally had it all together. I walked him to his room to put his bags down and on the elevator ride back he insisted that I had been scarce and demanded to know why. I knew him well enough to feel comfortable saying it out loud to him. "I've had to open a case of rape against someone who worked at the music venue I used to perform at." Way to kick off a catch up session in Vegas, but him and I were kind of always just like that. We just said whatever troubles were on our minds and then drank until we remembered things to laugh about again – and this time was no different.

He kept the gin and tonics coming while losing every round at Blackjack, it was very entertaining to witness. The hours went past faster than I wanted them to, I was finally having fun in Vegas and couldn't believe I had to leave Tyler and catch a plane soon. We took a much-needed break from the drinking, and walked over to the food court. He grabbed us some sandwiches from Egg Slut. There I stood in my glittering dress, my blonde hair a mess, and a backpack over my shoulder, chewing on a piece of bread and before I could stop it the words came out. "Tyler, kiss me."

He paused, and kissed me.

We looked at each puzzled and laughed.

"I'm sorry." I spat out as quickly as possible. "I'm sort of a mess."

We got into a cab and played inappropriate music loudly, I can't even remember where we headed, but we continued drinking when we got there. The kiss could have ruined the fun, but I was glad that it was long forgotten and almost like it never happened. "What happens in Vegas…" right?

I really didn't want to leave him - we were just having so much fun. I don't recall the drive to the airport, but somehow recall Sheryl Crow "Leaving Las Vegas" playing as I ran up to the boarding gates. I thought what a coincidence that the song was playing – but maybe it was playing only in my intoxicated head for only my own ears to hear. I guess to this day, I will never really know.

It was back to Scarsdale, all my airport-hopping-adventures were long over but the memory of Willem was still haunting me. Torturing me. As if I still saw him everywhere I looked just like when I was at that Cincinnati airport. I couldn't get a hold on my thoughts. I couldn't stop myself from still feeling him, as if he was right next to me. It wasn't healthy and I needed for whatever it was that was happening inside me, to be over.

60 SECONDS
(Poetry & Prose)

Sidestepping snow, begging on the corner of Lincoln and Crossway, please, please give me 60 seconds. I need to get him out of my head for just one minute. One minute was all I hoped for when I started running toward that place in the distance, where I saw the sun was setting. And I planted my tired feet so hard into that tarred road, I left holes in it behind me.

The empty trees lining the street on both sides rocked back & forth in the same icy wind that rushed up through my nostrils and into my head. For the first time in months I had a breath of fresh air in my body and I did NOT, want to breathe it out.

The yellow line in front of me. The only spark of color in this black and white world I painted for myself since he left.

And his world? Oh! His goddamned world is filled with colors. And white lines on the table in front of him, and they help him to forget about me as they rush up through his nostrils and into his head. But he will never say so.

My heart is black and the snow lies white, and the yellow line in front of me, it jumps around on the road, my eyesight blurry with that breath of fresh air still tingling around my untouched body. I do NOT, want to breathe it out. I refuse to let the last breath I take, be one that's filled with the thought of him, filled with the thought of what's not mine anymore.

Filled with his goddamned curse on my soul. And I ran.

I held my breath and I ran.

I ran the same way I did toward that boarding gate at McCarran airport that night, after she calmly said "you're late and they probably won't let you on that plane back to New York, dear."

I ran for gold in my gold Las Vegas dress and I left glitter on escalators and hallways as far as I sprinted toward that airplane, my body functioning solely on the Gin & Tonic in my bloodstream, I ran onto that airplane like I ran down Lincoln street tonight to forget him for 60 seconds, and I did.

BREAKING SOMEONE'S HEART, GOT THE T-SHIRT

Last night I had to break a little girl's heart.

And I broke it, the same way so many humans have broken mine – by leaving.

I knew "the talk" was coming. I knew the year I was given to spend in her world, was coming to an end in two short weeks and that it was time for me to tell her this.

I walked into her life knowing this day would come, I taught her how to hit notes on the piano I knew I wouldn't be around to hear her play in harmony one day. I had ample time to prepare for the devastating end, but when she sobbed into her drenched pillow the same way I have sobbed into mine when others have left me, when I had to look her in the eye - her red swollen eyes - and face up to this inhumane mess of emotions I am leaving her with, I realized that all the time in the world could never have prepared me for this. I was never ready to break her heart the way I had to last night.

I am so used to being on the other side of this equation, that I hadn't given much thought to what it would feel like being the bad guy this time.

I am used to being the one left screaming into a wet pillow, left by someone I love, left with a broken heart. But this time I was the heartless one.

She let me hold her hand while I was telling her why I had to leave her, and then I heard myself say it – "I am not leaving because I don't love you anymore, I am leaving because I am needed elsewhere, now that I have fulfilled the role I had to play in your life." (Or in adult language, now that my one year contract had come to an end.)

I heard myself say it.

I heard myself, as I said those words. The words I hand picked to explain this situation to a 6-year old. And I think the 6-year old girl in me was listening too. Those words echoed in the back of my mind while I was lying awake trying to make peace with this situation I did not know how to walk out of without feeling like a complete asshole and jerk.

As those words bounced around the walls of my restless mind last night, they started to make sense to me in my own journey too.

I started thinking about my daily prayer I say, where I ask for help to make peace with the people who have left me. The tinder-dates who ghost me, my dad who left me to pursue his path after my mother died, the path he was always meant to walk, these paths that don't include me. And I ask for comfort, trying to understand that I should not take it personally but rather cheer them on to fulfill their destiny as I am fulfilling mine.

For the first time since I started saying this prayer I finally felt it. I finally understood it. I can finally say, that I understand with every piece of me that not every person is meant to stay in our lives forever. I get it, now that I realize I can't stay in hers forever, and give up my future for the sake of what she thinks she needs in order to survive - my presence. And I know she is going to be SO fine without me.

The advantage her and I have, is the opportunity to communicate openly about this transition and prepare for it. Our willingness to stay in touch for as long as she needs me to. For me to call her until she gets bored of hearing from me and gets distracted with her arts and crafts and hangs up the phone. And I will smile when that day comes, knowing she has closure.

We have that advantage.

Not many endings come prepackaged with this luxury of closure.

And I am angry. I am angry that death comes sweeping in out of nowhere, and leaves us without closure. I am angry that boys and girls treat us like shit when they do not possess the skill of how to deal with endings appropriately. Not all of us have this luxury, not all of us have this skill. Not every person who has to leave your life in the pursuit of their own happiness – which they are so entitled to – will take the time to make sure that you are going to be alright, the second they disappear out of the world you took the time to carve a place out for them to live in.

I am angry. I am angry to realize how hard it was for me to break her heart last night, when so many humans have broken mine without batting an eyelid. Without so much as a "sorry I made you sad tonight."

I am angry.

But in my anger, I realize that, the way someone chooses to deal with having to leave you, is something we do not have control over.

If there is one thing I do hope I can help myself to understand today, it is that I have to know with all my heart, that not every person is meant to stay in my life forever. And I hope I can wish every person well, who has had to leave me. And to know that it is not because I was unworthy. I hope I can wish those people well, the way I hoped this little girl could find it in her heart to forgive me for breaking it last night, so I could move forward in my journey.

PART ELEVEN

MANHATTAN

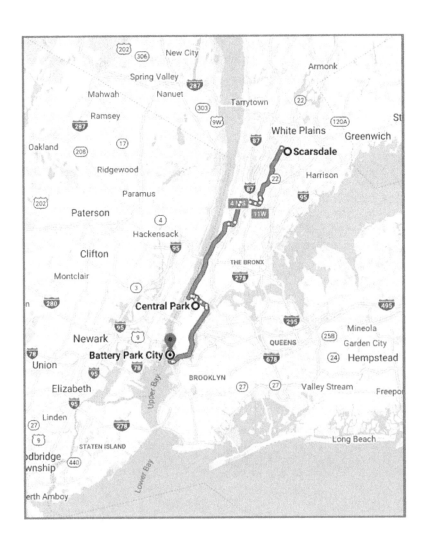

YOU WANT ME TO DO *WHAT* ON INTERNATIONAL TELEVISION?

With one week left in Scarsdale before my big move to Manhattan, it seemed that my bad luck had finally run out. Apart from cracking the neck on my guitar by accident during a photo shoot on the Brooklyn Bridge, everything else was looking up. I played two charity shows – one in Times Square for Global Connectivity's event "You are not alone" where I sung R.E.M.'s "Everybody Hurts" and saw someone in the audience cry to my singing for the first time. The second was for WestCop - the agency who helped me through the aftermath of the assault and offered me weekly therapy ever since. It was National Crime Victims' Rights Week and WestCop was hosting their annual art show for sexual violence survivors. Sharing the stage, and performing for fellow survivors was an experience that healed me more than I could have ever anticipated. There were tears. Sad ones, angry ones, healing ones, happy ones. My therapist and her team did what they promised to do when they showed up beside my hospital bed that horrible night. They promised to give me hope, try to restore my dignity, and they did.

The Hollywood actor who I became friends with a couple months prior, decided to take a trip to New York. He drove from Florida to me – a seventeen-hour drive – because he had a vision of us making a video singing in his car. It sounded crazy but my heart told me that him and I were cut from the same cloth, so I decided to trust him. I told him to pick me up at Grand Central. I got into his car, two coffees in hand, and felt like I was best friends with this stranger I just met in person for the first time a couple of minutes ago.

The creative chemistry was undeniable, we drove around New York talking and singing for three hours. We stopped at the place he was staying, both dying to pee. "Does it have a rooftop?" I had no interest in seeing the city I live in from yet another rooftop, I was just trying to buy more time with him. "I've felt Mandela's energy while I've been up here, it just sort of showed up and I channeled it, tried to learn from it," he explained. I felt like him and I were the same person. "Do you want to take a picture of the view?" He asked. I laughed – "no, I live here. I don't need a picture. *You* take a picture."

As we said our first goodbye, I knew there and then I was going to love him for a long time, not in the way I love other men. He felt like family.

After I edited our video, we put it online and the support we received was overwhelming. In no time, the media in South Africa picked up our story and

199

quoted us talking about each other in Facebook posts. They were painting a love story picture and I couldn't be more on board, although it was hard to tell what he was thinking. He was calling me every hour freaking out about how well our video was doing, speaking life into me. After some long conversations he told me to run a bath and that God is going to take care of me, he felt I needed to hear that. I wasn't sure what I was dealing with, and if I was supposed to feel comforted, lovey-dovey, or spooked... like it was too good to be true.

He meant well, and as weird as some of our interactions were, I felt like I had met my match. I didn't understand it, but we were on the same wavelength, for a brief moment at least.

"Are you sure he's not gay?" Almost everyone asked me.

First of all, his sexual orientation didn't matter to me, and second of all, he told me he got that question a lot. I wasn't bothered by any of it – even if he batted for the other team, I still would have felt the exact same way about him. But he started calling less, and I moved to Manhattan and was distracted with settling in – at some point I decided to let it be and just appreciate it for what it was. I chose to put any sparks to rest and carry on with my life as he with did his.

I moved out of the basement room with next-to-no natural light, which I lived in for a year, into an apartment with windows as walls. And every afternoon, the sun danced its way down the Jersey City skyline that was across the Hudson river, laid out in front of me, and as it brought the days of the world to their end, in breathtaking and colorful ways, night after night, it brought the feelings of self-guilt in me to an end, too. No, the sun was not mad at me for missing its first moments of the morning day after day for a year, as if it didn't even exist until I opened my eyes to meet the day. Despite my ignorance towards it, it still religiously filled my daily 5-8pm's with its beautiful show while setting in the sky, as if I deserved it. It did not care about my loyalty, it did not care if I deserved its beauty or not, it just showed up for me, as if I was the only one it was putting this show on for, as if its only goal for the day was to see my face light up with a smile when I admired it through peaceful eyes, as I felt and accepted the ways in which it was changing me.

And I felt a little more at peace about the ones I treat in the same way that the sun treats me. People often tell me it's wrong to love so unconditionally. Day in and day out, they try to fill my mind with their ideas of how, and how not to love. Who to allow, and who not to allow into my life, into my heart. What something does and doesn't mean. Who I should forgive, or stay mad at. And I just don't, I don't. It's just not that "black and white" to me. I stay wide open. If the sun never denies me its light, its warmth, no matter how many times I've taken it for granted – who am I not to follow its example and love so unconditionally?

Adjusting to my new life in Battery Park City was hard, but for weird reasons. All of a sudden I had time, a lot of it. Time to write love letters to the sun – at first I felt like I was supposed to feel bad for not working around the clock. I felt guilty all the time and couldn't believe my almost non-existent work schedule. I also had a hard time sleeping, because I was used to sleeping in a basement room with a tiny window hardly allowing any light in. In my new room, one of my walls was a window – the entire thing. I could see the Statue of Liberty from it. The Jersey City lights from across the Hudson River shone so brightly all through the night – I had trouble closing my eyes and not staring at them. But the luxury was secondary. I felt at home, like I had so much in common with my hosts culturally – something I didn't make a priority previously, something I didn't realize affected me as much as it did, in hindsight. I was overwhelmed by my new circumstances. The new start changed me, healed me. I cried all the time because I was so happy, and realized for some time now I had forgotten what that felt like.

To "worsen" my already terribly awesome, God-given miracle situation, I had another shock to the system when I got the news that my application to sing the National Anthem of South Africa for the Springboks was successful. They were facing Wales at RFK stadium in Washington D.C and the match was to be broadcast internationally.

I had been rehearsing the anthem daily for months in blind faith since I sent the application in, in October 2017 – but nothing could have prepared me for that "yes" I got in my email inbox. I was sure of only one thing – I had no idea how I was going to pull the whole thing off.

NEW YORKER

Dido sums it up perfectly in her song "Life For Rent" when she sings about a woman who doesn't learn to buy and "nothing I have is really mine." A very big part of how I choose to live my life is true to those words.

Now that I was living in Tribeca, every guy who tried to date me had something to say about the fact that "I was living the 1% life" based on where and how I was living, so much so that I got sick of it. I thought they were unintelligent for coming to the conclusion that I am living a "1% lifestyle" based on location and luxury – instead of realizing it was my mindset that resulted in me living a "1% lifestyle" - if they really wanted to call it that, in anyway. It was just a turn off and I played dumb as soon as those same old words came out their mouths.

What's the point in trying to explain "nothing I have is really mine" to someone who is just trying to get me out of my panties and then ghost me afterwards, anyway?

I tried to be less uptight – I carried on going out on dates, but I wasn't as fun as I used to be. I wasn't as free and easy going. After the assault, I was never sure who I could trust, who I was safe around, and even though I wanted to be with someone, even though I really liked a few people I met, my sense of intimacy was long gone. For someone whose love language is physical touch, this was painful. As if someone just flipped a switch that changed me since that day, and I didn't know where that switch was or how to flip it back on again. Some dates were fine, fun, good, and others left me depressed and in a mess all over again. For no particular reason at all, I sometimes had panic attacks after being with guys I'd known for a long time and had no problems being with in the past. One night I came back home crying on the lawn outside my apartment building, hating myself, wishing I'd die. I had to reach out to my therapist because I wasn't sure I could trust myself to not do something stupid – and that is unlike me, talking about how intense my depression was to her was unlike me. A sign that I really needed help.

Well, help came in it's own form when I met Willem 2.0 – another Frenchie, a look alike, I swear even more gorgeous than Willem himself. I knew when I met this guy, that, I wanted him just because of who he reminded me of – I felt a little bad for it. He was so much fun, moved at the same speed of light Willem did, giving me no time to worry about having to be brave, just going in for the kill straight off the bat when he knew I was into him. I loved being with him, we were like magnets, everything came naturally and we talked about dating exclusively – but that was all it was, talking.

He wanted me to show up whenever it suited him best, but couldn't return the favor. Over the months I let it fizzle on hoping it would just fizzle out, but it was hard hearing from him out of the blue every time.

I told Tyler about Willem 2.0. "He says my personality is dominant, Tyler."

"It's because all French men have pussies, Lyla. They are fem by nature so of course you're going to come across in that way to him."

Tyler knew just how to crack me up. I of course told him he was wrong. It wasn't like I was asking for advice or anything. We often shared our dating stories. His girlfriend left him for the other girl, so we both had a lot to laugh and go on about. I finally got him to play some chords on his guitar, even made him sing Guns & Roses with me one time we tried to get a practice in, but our jam-sessions usually turned into just drinking, he did whatever else he needed to do to numb the pain. Sometimes I left his apartment, worried that he wasn't going to be okay. I found myself worried often, the next day, but I never told him so.

I had to deal with me. I had to find my identity all over again now that I had moved to Manhattan. Who I was and who I was becoming were so far from each other, the growing pains were ever-present, and all the changing sometimes broke my heart further, messed with my mind.

The only thing that finally put my troubles to rest, the only decision I could make that would finally bring me some peace, was to decide that I didn't have to live past twenty-five if I didn't want to. I wasn't sad about it. I was actually relieved giving myself what felt like freedom of choice. My life was unbelievable, I was so happy, every bone in my body was, and I was afraid my life would never be as good, as peaceful as it was there and then. I was scared it wouldn't last. So I told myself that I could throw in the towel if any of it changed – I gave myself permission, because I felt like I had been through enough, I felt like I had won already, and whatever amount of days that were ahead was just borrowed time. In a way, that decision helped me to really squeeze every ounce of life out of the last couple of months I had of being twenty-five. Death had its eyes interlocked with mine everyday for months, calling my goddamned name, and that made me enjoy the sun on my skin, the wind in my hair, as if it was the last time, every time – in a happy way. I don't know what more to say about that period of my life.

I found purpose, a reason for existing, in using my radio skills again. I threw myself into interviewing the locals for a segment (The New York Minute) I was doing that aired on Dustin Miller's radio show in South Africa, first on Eden Am radio and then Radio Today. I went on to publish the eleven episodes on Apple Podcasts.

Below is one of the conversations that stuck with me, and reminded me who I was when I couldn't remember.

THE NEW YORK MINUTE

Interview with Kishan – *Being a bubble busker, and homeless in New York City*
Location: *Central Park*

Lyla: "We are in Central Park today, you can hear Ralph there on the saxophone, one of the many buskers in this vibrant park in the middle of Manhattan, and today I'm speaking to a very special busker, Kishan, also known as "The Bubble Guy" here in Central park and I'm going to chat to him today to hear what it's like being a busker, in the city. Kishan, I haven't seen you in three months. I walk into Central Park, the mall this morning, and all of a sudden people just start to circle around you and me, what was up with that?"

Kishan: (laughs) "Most of those people that we spoke to, they actually all know me and they were just poking fun at me. Those guys are break dancers and every time they see me talking to a girl, they come running over."

Lyla: "I love seeing that, I love seeing you guys interact. Wherever we were walking, we went past the food stands and we were talking to guys selling nuts and they were just giving me free samples and saying hi to you by name, we're walking down these avenues and I just hear them calling out – hi Kishan, hi Kishan – people with cameras in their hands. Seems like you have been around for quite a while?"

Kishan: "I have, I've been actively involved in Central Park, in this specific location for almost eight years, and we're all kind of family out here. We all have to kind of look out for each other's support. Sometimes someone needs to run an errand or go to the bathroom and they would ask me to keep an eye on their business or watch their table while they are gone and vice versa."

Lyla: "So there's a certain level of trust and community?"

Kishan: "Absolutely."

Lyla: "So, you caught my attention because…"

Kishan: "I'm good looking?"

Lyla: (laughs) "yes apart from the obvious… you caught my attention because you make huge bubbles. Literally bubbles big enough for people to get inside of.

I just see people circling you with cash in their hands wanting to snap away, so you're basically a busker making huge bubbles here in Central Park."

Kishan: "Yes, I never thought about being a busker, I didn't even know what a busker was until I got into the whole bubble business and then at some point I learned that I was a street performer. I never saw myself as a street performer and then probably a year or two later I realized I'm actually in fact a busker, and I had an English man define the term busker for me. (Laughs) So yes I do these giant bubbles and when the weather is behaving I put people inside bubbles."

Lyla: "What was the English man's definition of busker, do you remember?"

Kishan: "A person who performs in public in exchange for money, I believe it was."

Lyla: "And did you instantly know that you love doing this and that you were going to spend eight years doing this already?"

Kishan: "No but I kind of knew I was going to love it for a long time before I fully got involved. I was helping a friend to expand his bubble business, and just by observing people's reactions in the audience, I said to him – hey Steve, I'm gonna come out here and I'm gonna make bigger bubbles than you – and he said bring it on. And that is where my journey kind of started in the bubble business.

Lyla: "And now you're the big guy in the business?"

Kishan: "Well when I do something I try to go all in and of all the guys who have been doing it, I'm the only guy who really poured everything into it, give it my all, to the point that I am so attached to it I have trouble getting away from it or take any time off."

Lyla: "And wait, you've been on Glee, right?"

Kishan: "I was on Glee, a few years back. They actually found me here and asked me if I'd like to be in their TV show."

Lyla: "Had you watched Glee before they approached you?"

Kishan: "I never even knew what Glee was or that it existed, it was only after we did the filming that I decided to find out what this Glee was all about, and that's when I found out that Glee is actually a very popular TV show."

Lyla: "Yeah, even in South Africa people really enjoy the show. Crazy how life turns out right? You don't always know that your passion is going to turn into your career. If I can highlight something that I really love about your work, I have kept an eye on buskers in New York City and specifically in Central Park and I have tried my hand at busking as well. It's tough to get somebody to put a dollar down in your bucket! I think it takes a level of rapport, you have to build it up to get them to put that dollar down but what I've seen you do, is you give people the opportunity to be part of your project or your performance, like when you put them in the bubble, and instantly it makes them feel as though they're part of what you're doing, and I think that just makes them want to put down the money, right?"

Kishan: "Yes, one thing I learned a long time ago is people really always remember how you made them feel. People, especially in public, they approach you in a very apprehensive way and you have to do something to put them at ease, so if you see my little set up, I don't have any signage that tells people to donate or give me money, it's very inviting they are welcome to join, and that just makes people want to open their pocket books and give you money. You know I was having this conversation earlier this morning actually – really it's in giving that you receive. So if all you're trying to do is get, get, get, it just backfires it doesn't work."

Lyla: "It doesn't come from the right place."

Kishan: "It actually pushes people away."

Lyla: "When I've spoken to New Yorkers, the general idea they have of buskers, are that a lot of buskers are homeless or this is their only job, this is the only way they have an income, but I've found that so many people do this because they love it or they're making a little extra cash. Do you feel that people often mistake buskers for being homeless?"

Kishan: "Yes, that is something I learned along the way. I think I was actually one of those people as well before I became a busker. I would be on my way to work and I'd see a busker in the subway or somewhere, some place on a street corner, and somewhere deep in my mind I would just assume that that person was homeless, trying to make a few dollars. But, that's not necessarily the case. Real musicians actually who don't want to get caught up in the music industry or having to sign their life away to some meaningless contract actually work on the streets especially in New York, and they make a very good living out of it. I have friends who cut their own CD's and promote their own music and they live in amazing apartments in amazing neighborhoods in New York and they travel around the world, they get hired for gigs and they're nothing anywhere near homeless. Interestingly, I started doing bubbles when I was homeless."

Lyla: "Tell me more about that?"

Kishan: "Prior to being homeless I used to be a chef, I worked in New York City restaurants for about fifteen years or so, but I just always felt there was more to life that just going to work fifty, sixty hours a week and paying bills and sleeping and getting up and going back to work. There was a yearning outside of that whole conventional way of living. So, then one day I just quit everything. I gave everything up and I decided to move to the streets, which was really helpful because it took away all the unnecessary invented responsibilities like rent and trying to keep up with the Jones's so to speak and it really kind of freed up my mind and my time to really look at things. It was one day while I was being homeless in Central Park that I saw this guy making bubbles and that's where I got the idea and I took it from there. "

Lyla: "So you had a job, a good job, had a place to stay, you've got family in the city too, right?"

Kishan: "Yeah my entire family lives here in New York."

Lyla: "And you just said – I'm gonna go homeless for a bit, see what it's like, challenge my own mentality, challenge these ideas and ideals. What did you family and your friends think about this, did certain people start avoiding you?"

Kishan: "Well, no. I feel like being homeless doesn't mean that you don't pay attention to your hygiene for example. I had a gym membership - I was still working out just like everybody else who lives in a house. I was still hitting the showers twice a day. I was still eating at restaurants because I still had money."

Lyla: "And you had a girlfriend?"

Kishan: "Actually, I met her – she's the reason I'm not homeless anymore, because, after meeting her I felt it was disrespectful to her to be sleeping on the street and then visiting her a couple of nights a week, so I just moved back indoors."

Lyla: "How long were you on the streets for?"

Kishan: "I lived homeless for three years."

Lyla: "And what were some of the highs and very, very lows – for somebody who would maybe want to challenge these ideals also and try this out for themselves?"

Kishan: "Well for me personally, the best thing was the time freedom. It allowed me to spend a lot of time in bookstores reading, because I felt like reading was one of the ways to get knowledgeable about this whole journey of life. I never really had any lows, because I did everything in stride. The only problem with being homeless was, I couldn't get quality sleep, because every few hours, something would happen, somebody would walk by or do something to interrupt you. I've never been to a shelter - that would have defeated the whole purpose of moving outdoors. I didn't want to be part of that system. I wanted to earn my own money and pay my own way."

Lyla: "And I think you've created some very special relationships from what I can see, and this seems like quite the community here in Central Park. I'm sure everybody has their little arguments about territory, about busking corners and such?"

Kishan: "Yes. Everyone tends to get territorial and I mean everyone. The hot dog guys have a bidding system that they go through every year so that the highest bidder gets the best spots. The artists that sell their paints, they get here early. Recently we actually had a physical fight between two artists – they were selling the same material for different prices and they got into an argument that turned into a fight. The break-dancers, they get territorial over who was here first, and who grew up here and who was born here. In my personal life, the bubble business, I've helped a lot of guys get into the business as a way of earning money and they also got territorial. In the grand scheme of things it's the wrong approach because I always say there's enough room for all of us, and as long as the wind is blowing you can make bubbles wherever there is air. But you know, if you get caught up in that "me, me, me" mentality and if you think that guy over there making bubbles is stealing your oxygen then, it backfires. You don't ever want to compete, you want to be creative. Once you start thinking competitively, you lose your ability to think creatively.

Lyla: "We're sitting here in the mall in Central Park, and you actually have your set up right at the edge, what is this waterfall? They call this the center of Central Park, isn't it?"

206

Kishan: "Yes, the Bethesda fountain."

Lyla: "And that's where people can find you most days?"

Kishan: "As long as the weather is good, if you see a giant bubble floating by, chances are, it's me."

EASY
(Poetry & Prose)

I walked out the door with no destination in mind
Like I used to before they started telling me I need a plan for every   breath
alive
And I noticed a door I'd been passing by
Decided to open and enter this time
Followed a staircase
To a quiet place
Where souls were writing poetry

And I found myself
Between two shelves
And a dead-end, up in front of me
I stood there saddened
Confused by the urge I have within to write
That I ignore
Because I don't want to be a book - on a shelf.
Between thousands. Unread.

But then I drew out a book of poetry called "Easy."
I wanted to read something I couldn't relate to.
And on the last page of the book - Page 59
I read a prayer saying thanks
For the gift to write and express
Whether or not it gets read.

DOMINANT
(Poetry & Prose)

Last week, I was called out for coming across as 'dominant' - after a first date, based on 'a feeling he got from my attitude'

So I told him ...

"Listen here buddy...I once took the C subway train to Coney Island when I was supposed to take the 2 train up to Grand Central. And I rode for 25 minutes in that wrong direction, before checking the map, because, well, after 2 months of living in New York, I was sure I knew where I was going.

And a year ago when I quit my day job to move across the globe, I handed in my resignation 2 weeks before my Visa was granted and before my new contract was even official.

And in New York, you get two types of people. Pedestrians who stop and wait when there's a red light, and those who walk in anyway. I am that second person. And I run-walk in the direction of that red light and challenge yellow taxis whilst taking a bite of my dollar slice pizza, off the paper plate in my hand and I turn left and walk 7 blocks up 8th Avenue, when I was supposed to have turned right to be walking down on 8th Avenue, not up. And I walked 14 minutes in that wrong direction, before checking the map, because, well, after a year of living in New York, I was sure I knew where I was going.

And I start conversations because I have a lot to say.

And I think buddy, you're mistaking my confidence for dominance."

And he said, "Yes, I think I did. I am fascinated, can you tell me more?"

And I said ... "well I prefer guys like you, who ask questions, and seek to understand women, instead of being intimidated by a little personality."

And we kissed and we kissed and we kissed.

MANHATTAN MAN
(Poetry & Prose)

He did another line
I looked the other way and turned the music up
He looked at me with admiration when I declined
As if saying "no" to blow, was some kind of achievement
I've felt the urge but never entertained it
And I think it's an easy way out, a sign of weakness
An easy way to drown out the noise
And numb all the feelings

I crave peace and a moment of sanity, a moment where my soul doesn't hurt and the voices don't scream
But I don't want it like that, not by those means

I turned the music up
And thought back to a week ago
"Just imagine you're standing in front of a handful of people when you walk into the stadium, pretend that the crowd and camera aren't there," they advised me as I prepared to go sing the anthem.

But I said no. "I want to feel everything. I want to see everyone. I want to absorb the insanity, feel my heart beat - hard - in my chest. I want to freak out, and shake, and cry and vomit from the anxiety. I want to feel everything."

He did another line
I looked the other way and turned the music up
We all have our vices
Our bad habits
God knows I have mine
Self-destruction
Procrastination
Overeating and then eating nothing at all
Always working on another project, God knows for what
Just to feel worthy, like I've achieved something
So who am I to point fingers, and this is New York, after all. Everyone is doing coke.
Still, I want to judge.

Instead I give myself a pat on the back for attempting to be social on a Saturday night
I gave him a pat on the back for acing the playlist again
We did a toast to celebrate our year of friendship
Slow waltzed in his living room to Bloodhound Gang
The Ballad of Chasey Lain
And we're in love, but not with each other
And we're both pretty happy about that, I think.
Still, it's hard to fathom
Why, him and I?
On such a beautiful, warm Saturday New York night, such a waste.
Alone, together
Oh, we'd both much rather be with somebody else
But they left us behind
We're not spoiled for choice
Although, the company is still good
And I think we'll both take what we can get

Have you ever ignored another world?
Ignorant to the person next to you's reality?
Cos him and I …
I think we talk past each other sometimes
I hear him, but I don't think he hears me
And he tells me that I'm gorgeous
But I don't really care what he has to say
I'm tired of reading into everything
And I don't want to be called dominant again, if I do

So I say nothing

And I let it go
He poured another round of ginger ales with vodka and lemon juice
He looked at a picture of her
"She would have been 21 today"
He says as if she died
She isn't dead, but to him, sometimes

I leaned into the window, glimpsing at the Central Park scenery across the street
I was watching the yellow cabs race and all the traffic lights change from green to red, and back to green
And I wondered where his white line was taking him
Because he didn't look much happier after he snorted it, anyway.

I THINK YOU KNOW YOU LOVE SOMEONE
(Poetry & Prose)

And I think you know you're in love with someone, really really in love with someone, when you start to compare the feelings you have for them, to the feelings that you have for New York.
Don't you think?

Because New York has left you breathless so many times, in the worst, and most wonderful kinds of ways.
It's the city that pushes you off cliffs and then catches you, teaching you what it feels like to jump, not without, but despite, fears.

It is the city that has built you up just to break you down, given you everything you have ever dreamt of and then filled your head with voices that threaten to, one day, take it all away from you, but you ignore them.

The voices drag your soul out and the people disappoint you and even when you have the best of what life has to offer, and you know how many deaths you've had to die to be here, tonight, in New York, you're still not sure it's ever enough, that you've ever done enough.

And these days? These days you're not so sure you know the person staring back at you when you look up at the reflection in the coffee house window, but you stay.
You stay, because honestly, the thought of leaving New York doesn't even cross your mind.
No, the headlights from the yellow cabs racing toward- and past you - in their different directions, they leave you blinded, but just blind enough to blur out all

the bad intentions of this place as if it's not even there, all you see is the glitter and the gold, and there is so much of it, too.

Goodbye is not an option, no.

Even when this place lets you down, you still feel like the luckiest girl in the city.

You smile because the lights lining the avenues, religiously switch on and shine to light the way for you when the moon rises in the evening sky.

And the music pouring out the door of the corner café is playing for your ears only, as if it knew you needed a drum beat to skip along to on your walk that was never motivated by any specific destination in mind.

And no matter which corner of this island you land up in, you are always home, and you are always okay.

If you told me there was a world where I would fall in love with a man the same way I fell in love with this city, on these same terms, I don't think I would have believed you, and even now, it's hard for me to admit, too.

Hard for me to imagine saying to him, "this is what it feels like to be loved by you." And I don't think he even knows half of it, half of what I feel, but it's not my place to tell him, is it?

Just like, New York doesn't need me to tell it that it's loved by me.

Who am I to think that it waits around for a declaration from me, no. It buzzes and breathes and functions anyway. It's beautiful and brilliant and it's mine for as long as I want it, it doesn't wait for me to say so.

Yes, I think you know you're in love with someone, really really in love with someone, when you can compare the feelings you have for them, to the feelings that you have for New York.

And even though he sometimes doesn't follow through, it still feels like he had every intention of loving you, the same way you had every intention of being a couple of blocks further north that night, but you just didn't make it there, you just didn't go.

You were dressed for the occasion, guitar in hand, but got stuck around the round table at your friend Tyler's place, wine glass in hand somewhere uptown again, the way you have so many times before.

By some drastic turn of events you didn't make it to the venue further north, to play your song to the crowd that night.

There are two empty bottles on the counter as the clock strikes 12 and this time you wake up the next morning and it's not in your own bed, no, you're still at his place, but he was never next to you or on top of you, and you are happy about that, too.

He sends you out the door, Aspirin and Fiji water in hand, and you know that's about as real as a friendship in this city gets.

So on a Tuesday morning, with no need for the walk of shame - to your own surprise and delight - you're sitting on a Central Park bench with your back against a plaque engraved with some words on it, your back against its purpose, its words to remind you that you are right for being a dreamer.

You sit there and you try to look the other way when the leaves dare to turn from green to yellow and orange again - they're hoping you're not looking; they're hoping you don't notice their colorful warnings that scream "the New York summer is coming to an end, my dear."

They're hoping you don't notice, because they are not so sure you will be able to deal with their reality.
And as the leaves fall onto the cement sidewalks, the wind brushes them along, and through the crackling and crumpling noises, you hear them whisper at you - the memories of the months you spent without the sun, and they make sure to remind you how hard that was for you.

God. You know you love New York, when you are willing to stay another winter, survive the bitter cold burning through your nostrils, lose the feelings in your toes - stay, just so you can have another New York summer when the snow melts away once again, a long long time from now.

Because when it does, all will be right in the world again. And you know you will find it in your heart to forgive the sun for not shining bright enough when you so desperately needed it to.
So, I think you know you're in love with someone, really really in love with someone, when you start to compare the feelings you have for them, to the feelings that you have for New York. And, if one day, you take a moment to think about how New York has treated you, in its bad ways and in its good, know that - that's what it feels like to be loved by you.

CALLS FROM UGANDA
(Poetry & Prose)

After declining the call from Uganda through sleepy 2am eyes, I managed to arrange the letters on the screen into three words – "is it urgent?"

"YES!"

And somewhere between my eyes meeting the Jersey City skyline lights through my bedroom window, and the three rings before my sister picked up the phone, I made peace with the news I knew she was about to deliver - my dad had died.

And I felt relieved that it had finally happened and that I no longer had to wait for the call. And I felt like I could finally hurt him back and not attend his funeral, the same way he did not attend my mom's, and left me to cry at an open grave at the age of ten.

And I felt at peace with the three times I tried to reach out to him to make peace, which he ignored. And now that he no longer breathes, the 11 years we've been estranged for, finally felt like a fact, and not like another one of my issues I pretend doesn't exist.

Like the fact that I have to do intense stretching every day in order to move around without an ache in my back after a motorbike accident a year ago. "I don't have back problems" I tell myself as I excuse myself from the conversation to go and stretch in the Starbucks restroom.

And the fact that something always feels missing in my life, no matter how happy I am, no matter how great my achievements, no matter how much I write, no matter how great that bike ride felt over the Brooklyn Bridge last night, I still call Yvette and tell her everyday that something is "still" missing from my life and every day she tells me "you need medication" and everyday I tell her, "I don't suffer from depression."

And the fact that I tell myself "I have no friends here" while I ignore texts and calls from people who are reaching out, and I judge people for the way they choose to deal with their problems in New York – by throwing money at it, throwing coke at it, throwing sex at it – and I act like I have never dealt with my problems in counterproductive ways and I excuse myself from his Central Park apartment so I can go and sit in my room and stuff my face with another cup of caffeine with depressing music playing on repeat as I scroll through old texts from ex-lovers.

And somewhere between my eyes meeting the Jersey City skyline lights through my bedroom window, and the three rings before my sister picked up the phone, I made peace with the news I knew she was about to deliver - my dad had died and now I will hate myself less for still having love for him in my heart even though he abandoned me. I made peace with the fact that my back should not be feeling like this. I made peace with the fact that living in my head too much and being an over-thinker will always be a heavy burden to carry but one I am thankful to have. I made peace with the fact that I do have friends here, and I ought to be less judgmental and I need to make an effort from my side too. And I promised myself to respond to every message in my inbox when the morning comes. And I did.

The phone stopped ringing as she picked up the call.

"I want to have a dress made for you with African print material, here in Uganda and I'll send it to New York!" She explained with excitement.

I burst out with laughter - "oh! I thought dad died."

"LYLA; THE VOICE OF A NATION"
(Headline & article, People Magazine South Africa)

The Greatest Anthem In The Greatest Country
Written by Robert Clunie May 28, 2018

A TEST date on the second of June against the Welsh peeved many a Springbok supporter the very minute SA Rugby made such an announcement. It precedes a massive series against the English on home soil a mere seven days later and a kick-off in Washington DC means that scores of fans will long be in La-La Land come its onset. But while the one-off spectacle will undoubtedly fatten up local rugby's coffers, there is an additional sliver of feel-good to come from it: it'll provide the spotlight for one of SA's most gifted voices to shine.

The name Lyla Illing may not resonate with many people in South Africa as yet, but big things are to come from the Hluhluwe-born songstress. Her tale is somewhat of a rags-to-riches epic, one where a stubborn political and economic upbringing so nearly curtailed her road to success, but a little dogged resolve will undoubtedly see this young woman from a rural Afrikaans household accomplish greatness without the typical stilted attitude a few artists adopt.

"I grew up in an Afrikaans household and spoke Zulu better than English!" Lyla says of her childhood. "I never felt like I fit in; it was extremely difficult growing up in a community who had a hard time adjusting to democracy when apartheid ended. As a kid, you see everyone as equal – sadly the elders in my family did not."

214

Nevertheless, Lyla was able to shape her own perception despite the oft-inflexible positions of those around her; various iterations of our national anthems were a particular contentious topic. "I remember my mom being extremely upset when Die Stem was changed to Nkosi Sikelel' iAfrika – but I remember my sense of pride when the new anthem was sung during rugby matches. Somehow I always managed to make up my own mind about my views and how I chose to see the world."

Lyla was very close to her mother, though, and it was through her that a burgeoning musical talent blossomed, although she sadly succumbed to breast cancer when Lyla was 10. "My mom was a choir director and pianist at the school I attended. I started singing because she did. I remember singing to her in the car on the way to school in the mornings – we couldn't afford a car radio but I didn't realise we were 'down and out' because she always made everything seem fun."

Lyla had to relocate to Pretoria after her mother's death and, unfortunately, her father's support was not as forthcoming – he'd rather have her study business economics over music. As a consequence she moved out at just 15. High school students are obviously in no position to fend for themselves, but it was a move she simply had to make. Therefore Lyla had to rely on the kindness of strangers for room and board – she'd often travel from place to place with nothing but a suitcase and a guitar.

She also worked as a waitress to put herself through Matric, but luck had it so that her employers funded her radio production studies after she left school. What followed was live shows in bars and clubs and, finally, auditions for televised talent shows. For some time after she also worked as a producer for reputable radio personalities like Darren Scott and Jeremy Mansfield. Success was palpable and Lyla figured if a career as a singer failed she'd have something to fall back on.

At 23 she left South Africa for New York to start a new life. "When I moved to New York in April 2017 it was my first time traveling abroad; I am the typical example of a girl who never stood a chance. I had to work really hard to create a future for myself and I've had to make some compromises along the way, but it has made me work so much harder.

I networked relentlessly in the radio and TV industry in SA and have funded my own recording sessions in NY studios. No matter how hard I tried, playing shows twice a week at venues in Johannesburg, I just couldn't get myself to stand out. So I took a chance on NY. It has punched me in the face a couple of times but I really love this city. I landed a weekly gig in Times Square, but stopped performing in November after a sexual assault by one of the venue's staff members. When I managed to pick myself back up, I busked in Central Park and carried on creating video content, collaborating with other singers."

While the move has had its challenges, on the whole it's been an interesting and rewarding journey. "It's quite the upgrade living in Battery Park, Lower Manhattan with a beautiful view of the Hudson River and the Statue of Liberty. I am a 'cultural exchange visitor' in America, which means I have a family who sponsors my stay abroad. I help them out with their little one and in return they fund my travel and studies. I hardly travel or 'party it up' here. In my free time I produce an online podcast – also airing on Eden AM radio in SA called The New York Minute and am working with a mentor on having my book Relying on the Kindness of Strangers published."

How does this all relate to a rugby match? Well, it just so happens that an expat braai was held under the Brooklyn Bridge not too long ago where Lyla and her trusty guitar led our national anthem. As with so many things nowadays, a few smartphone cameras were promptly set to their record function and in no time at all the video went viral. A few radio stations in South Africa granted her rendition a handsome amount of airtime and since then heaps of praise and admiration has come her way.

"I am blessed to have creative people in my circle. I am blessed to be able to call the people who inspired my career my friends and mentors now. They are excited when I do something big and the coverage just comes naturally – I don't have to 'sell' the story or 'trade favors' for coverage. I want my career to reflect the relationships I've built instead of getting attention for my looks. I wanted to make sure I knew who I was before some agency swept in and told me who to be."

"I am proud to have come this far and I think I am finally ready to go and knock on some record label doors." Lyla's superb execution of Nkosi Sikelel' iAfrika saw an old friend and radio colleague of hers John Walland send forth a copy of an article of the anthem on to SA Rugby. The sport's governing body afforded her the opportunity to record a professional audition clip and, upon its review, placed her on a list of other hopefuls who'd wish to sing it at a major match.

The Wales-Springboks match was announced sometime later after which a duplicate was sent to USA Rugby. Her singing talent and locale would greatly work in her favour. "Whilst all my friends bought tickets for the match, I refused to secure a seat next to them. Instead, I rehearsed the anthem daily, in blind faith, so that I would get the gig. And an e-mail came through weeks later informing me that I would have the honour of singing our anthem in DC!

Singing the anthem means more to me than the stadium I get to sing in and more than the TV coverage. Landing this gig is me celebrating the freedom to choose who I want to become one day. I know in my heart that my mom would have come around to democracy if she was alive to see the example I am setting, and could see who I grew up to be."

SINGING THE ANTHEM IN PT SHORTS FOR NELSON MANDELA

And there I stood in white PT shorts and in player 25's jersey, belting out the national anthem on a world stage. I don't know whose shock was more overwhelming; that of the rugby management team standing 10 meters across from me, staring at me in utter shock, the shock that my friends & family watching on TV back home had to be feeling, or that of my own.

The 'disabled' toilet cubicle I got dressed in minutes before, looked somewhat like the scene of a miscarriage. My dress lying crumpled up on the floor with a pair of scissors next to it – my idea; dead. My vision of how I wanted to look on international television whilst representing my country; will forever be just that – a vision and not a reality. These realizations rushed through my mind one after the other but there was no time for mourning. A staff member from USA Rugby stared at me like a deer in headlights with my dress in her hands. I was standing in my underwear and high heels when we both realized that the zipper broke, for good, 6 minutes before show time. I felt the radio producer in me come out. "Quick, go and get me an outfit in the Springboks locker room!" And she ran. When we managed to get the tight jersey over my head, I looked at the miscarriage on the bathroom floor one last time in complete disbelief, took a breath, put on a smile, and walked out onto the field in my stride, as if a casual outfit (hugging my curves in all the wrong places) was my outfit of choice.

I took my place on the field, looked into the crowd and made eye contact with as many people as I could, acknowledging them, smiling at them. "Do you want to sing the anthem a capella?" The sound guy asked when he put the microphone in my hand, knowing that he is asking the impossible of me to sing in time with the backtrack without the help of a monitor. "No, I can do it, cue the backtrack." I responded with confidence.

As we all waited for our teams to run out onto the field, I felt the light rain falling on my face. I looked up at the heavens knowing that, where I come from, rain is a sign of enlightenment, so I said my prayer just loud enough for myself to hear it. 'God bless Africa. May her glory be lifted high. Hear our petitions. God, we ask that you protect us, your children. Intervene and end all conflicts. Protect us, protect our nation, our nation South Africa." I felt emotional and fought back the tears of joy, knowing the big moment was seconds away.

Then I thought about Madiba a lot, and I thought about my sister in Uganda whose heart I knew was going to be breaking when she didn't see me in the dress we worked so hard on. The next thing, I got pulled straight back to reality when a hand grabbed the jersey I was wearing, tugged and pulled it down over the shorts "there, that looks better!" I saw her mouth say, with a look of annoyance. I could not hear anything with the earplugs I had in my ears. "Thank you for your help!" I exclaimed, but she didn't give me a smile in return. Just the look of a disappointed parent. I smiled anyway. The yellow earplugs I was given by a music teacher as a "plan B" the day before, blocked 90% of my hearing out so that I could try and hear the anthem backtrack and not the sound of my own voice bouncing around the stadium. I wasn't given a monitor, and the Welsh anthem singers refused using their backtrack, as a result to not being provided with monitors.

The next moment, it wasn't so quiet anymore, I could hear the crowd screaming despite my earplugs, and one by one, the Springbok players ran out onto the field past me. That was the proudest moment of my life, I felt content in every way. I felt my heart beat in my head and throat and took deep breaths, expanding my tummy, not caring how chubby I was going to look in the tight jersey designed to be worn by an athletic man with a flat chest and no love handles. In that moment, I reassured myself that, my voice is bigger than my body, my spirit means more than my appearance.

"Please rise for the National Anthem of South Africa. Performed by South African born, New York based singer-songwriter, Lyla Illing!" I heard over the sound system.

I had asked the same USA Rugby staff member to stand in front of me and clap along to the beat of the anthem, because I could not hear myself or the backtrack very well during the rehearsals earlier. For the next 1 minute and 20 seconds, my eyes were glued to her hands meeting beat after beat.

When the anthem backtrack started playing, I just felt like it was no longer about me. I was singing for the players whose first time it was to play in green and gold. I was singing for South Africans who flew in from all corners of America to be there and celebrate their roots. I was singing for Madiba.

In that moment, I didn't feel scared, or nervous, or upset, or not good enough, or fat in what I was wearing. I felt brave, and fearless, confident, untouchable and so, so proud.

These priceless moments have cost me many things. And although no price tag could be put on an opportunity as massive as that of standing in front of the world, representing my country in song – despite my strong sense of identity, I couldn't help but contemplate my value, every step of the way.

I think back to March when I received the news.

"You've got the gig, just get yourself here and back, do your own media, book your own hotel and make sure you look good." Oh and… "here are two tickets for the match in return, and a pass to wait in the shared staff room before the performance, help yourself to the bottled water." Reality check… I was a nobody, and I was treated like one ahead of the performance, and that was okay with me.

All I heard was "You've got the gig." That was all that mattered to me. I didn't allow my emotions and the knock to my self-worth to get in the way of how proud I was, of making my dream a reality.

So now, when people ask me how it was, how it felt… they are expecting me to tell them about the thousands of dollars I was paid and how I was limousined around like a celebrity. If you know me, you would know that none of the above-mentioned materialistic things mean anything to me, but since everyone is asking, I will tell you. And I think it is important that I do.

From the moment I received the news that I would have the honor of singing the national anthem of South Africa for our Springboks in DC, I promised myself that I would grab this opportunity hands on and make this happen no matter how much this was going to cost me, no matter the rocky road I saw laid out ahead of me.

So I put my life on hold for the next 6 weeks, to prepare for this life-changing moment. I had no idea how I was going to pull this off with no agent, no manager to represent me, no family around to keep me grounded. And sapeople.com hit the nail on the head when their headline ahead of my performance read "from a braai to the stadium." They were of course referring to the video of me leading the anthem at an expat braai in New York the year before. I was lying in bed awake night after night trying to comprehend how I was going to sing in a 46,000-seater stadium on international television, when the biggest crowd I played to a week before leaving South Africa was a hundred or so people.

But I had no doubts in my mind that I could do this, and do it well. So I kept moving forward and rehearsed in my bedroom and in front of strangers at random tourist attractions in New York. The hardest part wasn't preparing vocally, or emotionally. The hardest part was, preparing for this, alone. Planning my own transportation, dress, hair and makeup appointments, in the capitol of America, in a place I wasn't based in, and am not familiar with.

But I thanked God every day for making my dream come true, and that the powers that be were prepared to take a chance on me. And I did, I contemplated my value every step of the way. It was an extremely confusing feeling, when presented with the opportunity to perform on a world stage, but not being granted the support to match such an honorable & demanding task. Not having family or a team of my own around to help me on the day of the performance.

But the day came and it went, and I promised myself I would treat it like I would, any other 24 hours.

Fast forward to 3 hours after the match had taken place.

"I am so tired of something always going wrong, I try so fucking hard" – I cried to Yvette over the phone after throwing up in a public bathroom at Union Station, DC, before putting myself on a midnight bus back to New York. The anxiety of the 12 interviews I did 3 days before the match, and getting myself to DC, hair and makeup done, getting to the stadium, standing in line like everybody else to get my ticket, having no monitor, and having my dress zipper break moments before going on live television – the anxiety eventually caught up with me when I finally had a moment alone, waiting for the bus at Union Station, and I threw up, and mourned the loss of a moment I imagined, looking like a lady in a beautiful dress - a moment that I could never get back.

It felt like a bad hangover, and I had no energy left in me to feel angry at the magazine for the deal they made with me – promising me an exclusive article in issue 22, and failing to have it printed, after threatening me with dropping the story if I was to speak to any other magazines or do any other media in the month-long build up to the event. "We had a little oopsie" I was told on the day the magazine hit the shelves without my article in it, a mere 5 days ahead of my performance. They then promised to have my story published in issue 23, but that did not happen either. I had to settle for an online write-up I could have published myself.

As a result, I ended up staying up every night, booking and doing 2am and 5am interviews (to accommodate South African time) in order to make up for the publicity the magazine failed to provide me with. But I did it. 12 interviews in 4 days and I aced each one of them.

My God. And there I stood in white PT shorts and player 25's jersey, belting out the national anthem on a world stage. Praised by a crowd, 30,000-strong. Comments on social media of "how cute she looked dressed like one of the players" and "she pulled a Madiba, and wore the teams' colors!"

Viral videos of my performance and peace in my heart that I made my country proud.

My audience on social media was all the confirmation I needed, that I did it. I pulled it off. I jumped all the hurdles. Kinda like how a Springbok hops as it runs from danger.

I got to the place I call home in Manhattan at 4am the next morning.
And I got in my bed alone.
No ceremonious family welcome.
No pat on the shoulder. No kiss on the cheek from a late night lover.
No manager holding my hair and making sure I'm hydrated.
No thank you email from the organizers.
No big deal.
From a world stage. To my reality.
Me. Myself. And I.
And I would pay it all, again - the cost of making my country proud.
These priceless moments, have cost me many things.

WALL STREET SERENDIPITY

I was too heartbroken to look at that gorgeous African print dress from Uganda I was meant to wear for my anthem performance. I had it buried deep into my cupboard where I couldn't see it until I got a call from Iresh one day, a South African in New York who works with the charity, Ubuntu Pathways.

Iresh invited me to perform at their Heritage Day fundraiser, hosted on a Wall Street rooftop. I said yes a thousand times, pulled the dress out from under the pile and took it to my tailor in Brooklyn to get it fixed up. What more appropriate event to wear the dress to, than a Heritage Day celebration.

Yvette's husband happened to be in New York the night of my performance, so I gave him my room to crash in and was happy to have a wingman at the show.

About a hundred-and-twenty people attended the event, it was a big deal to me – getting to perform on a New York City rooftop. I had all the fun in the world performing familiar South African hits to the homesick crowd, and slipped in a few of my own songs too, one in particular – the one about Willem. It mentions a few details relating to him, but none I ever thought anyone would pick up on, none I thought were clear enough for anyone to ever put two and two together with.

I had no idea that I was playing to someone in the crowd who knew Willem very well, and figured out exactly that the song was about him simply by hearing a

221

few of the details. This person never came up to me to ask about it, and everyone had their phones out filming me, I didn't think anything of it. I was just enjoying singing lyrics that I wrote there on Wall Street, about Wall Street a year prior, lyrics I held so dear to my heart.

When I got home I finally had a chance to check my phone. It was him! Willem texted me. He sent me a screenshot of myself singing on the Wall Street rooftop. The person who put two and two together sent him a video of me performing Bodega Raffy and he sent me a screenshot of their conversation about how they were figuring the whole thing out and linked it to him. I wanted to pass out.

I told him I never thought it would get to him and that I hoped he didn't take it personally that I still perform the song after all this time – I just love the song, so.

I didn't know what else to say.

My high came crashing down when Yvette "jokingly" asked me if I was sharing a bed with her husband back at the apartment. I was so offended that she thought I would ever do that to her. "I was sleeping on the couch so he could have my room!" I shouted at her. My best friend thought so poorly of me?

She repeatedly told me she didn't mean it but it hurt me so much that I felt like I couldn't have her in my life anymore. Maybe she didn't mean it, and maybe she just caught me at a bad time, but I told her to give me space. When she didn't, when she cried my ear off over the phone I laughed, not because I didn't care that she was hurting, it was just a shock to my body that somebody was fighting so hard to stay in my life – I wasn't used to it. But there was nothing she could say, I couldn't be her friend anymore and I couldn't get myself to feel bad about it, then.

I lost my best friend that night, we entered a six-month period of not talking to each other anymore, but I went to bed finding comfort in something else - the feeling of sureness I had in my stomach; the fact that I was performing a song to a small crowd on a random night in New York, what were the chances of someone in the crowd knowing Willem well enough to realize the song I was singing was about him? And send him a video of it? I felt like my creative process came full circle for the first time, and that healed me. The fact that the universe pulled all the strings to have my words travel to Willem across the globe through someone who was a stranger to me – it made me feel validated. Like I always knew my feelings for him were real, and his for me. Just having it happen the way it did – it was validation of my feelings, my reality, my creativeness, validation for my soul. I'd think twice about questioning myself, doubting myself in love or art ever again after that experience.

That morning I woke up for the first time, at peace with the Willem-saga, ready to move the fuck on from it.

TWENTY-FIVE - DEAD OR ALIVE
(Poetry & Prose)

Something died here today.

There's not much of a smell hanging in the air but I open the window anyway. Only a crack. Only ten centimeters. That is as far as it is engineered to open. Because I'm twelve stories high with a two by three meter window-wall. Of course they know better than giving me the option of opening it wider than ten centimeters and doing something stupid. Assholes.

Something died here today.

Is it the guitar in the corner? The one I dropped during a photo shoot on the Brooklyn Bridge and damaged? Cracked at the neck, held together by it's six loyal strings. I haven't had the heart to throw it out.

That's not it.

Something died here today.

I'll call Neil. It has been about a month since I told him to stop calling. A month since I felt like I am ACTUALLY over him, two years after our romantic relationship ended. But it's kind of like we kept all the other stuff alive when the romance died. The friendship & inside jokes. Maybe they finally died too. I'll call Neil, just to make sure. Maybe that's it.

"Neil, I don't know how to be twenty five. I'm exhausted. I'm ahead of my time. I rushed ahead. I am old. I am eighty in my mind. Somewhere along the way, I missed twenty-five. And now I just can't catch up. So I think I'm done. I think I am ready to go. I've made peace with it. I think it's going to end for me soon, it's just a feeling I have, and I am okay with that."

"Lyla, you allowed yourself to be twenty two, for about fifteen minutes.

And then twenty-three, perhaps a week.

Twenty-four, you seemed to have rethought, because, my darling, you seemed to have lived nearly a year of it.

And twenty-five, the past year I've looked at your posts, sometimes with a smile, sometimes with regret, sometimes - even with a bit of jealousy, but you let yourself do something you had never done before, you allowed yourself to LIVE.

And I know you are not the type who settles down. And you move along before someone has the opportunity to abandon you again. You run. You leave, just in case. Just when someone gets to know you, suddenly, you're a memory."

Something died here today.
Something in me.

The old soul inside of me.
Burdened with its' over thinking, and its calculations, and its sensible reasoning based on what the vicious past taught me.

The old soul inside of me,
I think it died a while ago.
And even though,
With my eighty year old self in a coffin six feet below,
Even though I no longer have the wisdom to make sense of it all, the way I used to,
I prefer twenty-five.
The ABSOLUTE FUCKING chaos, of twenty-five.
I choose it.

I HAVE BEEN LOVED
(Poetry & Prose)

I have been loved
So why is it that the word marriage isn't in my vocabulary.
White dresses and manicured nails are not what my dreams are made of.
No, that is not what keeps me up at night.
But I do dream about a happily ever after with you. If only you knew how to make me happy.

Commitment isn't in my vocabulary.
I have given every ounce of my soul to a man who washed my love away with every sip of liquor he could find on the top shelf of an empty grocery cabinet.
Cup after cup, until my face became blurry and my cries were drowned out, cup after cup, until I became background noise like the radio playing in the other room.
He smiles through it all, because he knows what he's done.

So is this part of the plan, too?
My darling, the fact that, you don't look like you
Don't be afraid. I still know it's you
Even in a dark room, you know I would know you

There's so much you don't know
So much you choose not to see
You were loved
You were a man to me
And put your daughters before me like my father never could
You are strong, I wish you knew that.

So is this part of the plan, too?
The expressions on your face and the bags under your eyes now
You don't look like you

I told you
You are better with me

But I have stopped trying to make you believe that
And left you with your cups of liquor
The only company you keep
The only happiness you seek
As requested, my love.

I told you
You are better with me

You were better with me
But now I see
I am better without you
And you knew that all along
You made the bigger sacrifice between us two

Now I see, I have been loved.

PART TWELVE

NEW YORK AND NEW JERSEY

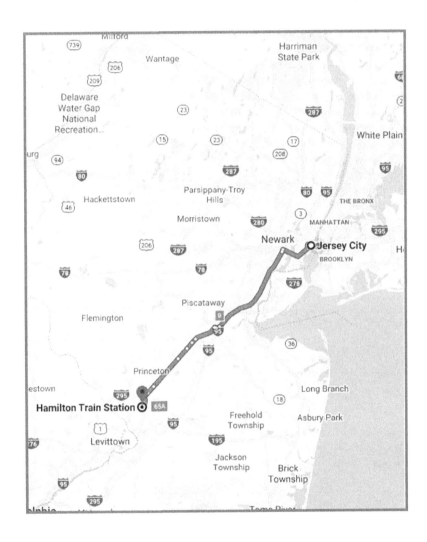

MY SOLO 26TH

I was singing wholeheartedly into the remote control to Neil Young's "Heart of Gold" but couldn't help but have Amy on my mind with every bad dance move escaping my body as I laughed away at my reflection in the window. (Contrary to popular belief – not everyone from Africa is blessed with twerking-talents!) The one glass of champagne I swallowed - in excitement to get my "party for one" started - must have added to my slow-waltz-singing adventure, with only the Jersey City skyline staring back at me from across the Hudson, the only witness to the whole affair. Not another person in sight to celebrate my big twenty-six with, exactly how I wanted it to be. Here is why.

Ten years ago, I spent my birthday alone, or rather - in the company of strangers - for the first time. It was my not-so-sweet, sweet sixteen. I woke up on an air mattress in a friend of a friend's TV room in a town called Klerksdorp, a place I'd never been in before, and stared at my phone that entire day waiting for my dad to call and wish me happy birthday. He didn't call. A couple months prior, I left home after suffering abuse from his wife, but somewhere deep inside of me I thought he would still show up for - at the very least – my birthday, I thought he would call, and today marks ten years that he hasn't.

As a result, every birthday since sixteen, I've made it my mission to have as many people as possible at the table for my celebration.

As many people as possible on the club guest list – including the girl I don't really get on with. As many people as possible at my pizza party - including two of my ex-boyfriends I'd really rather not see. As many people as possible – just to make up for the void that I refused to make eye contact with – my late mom and careless dad's absence.

As my 26th was fast approaching, I had my notepad out and started jotting names down, emptying cupboard drawers digging to find business cards of people I met only once and never spoke to again, but planned to invite, too. Scrolling through my phone for names of boys and girls I sort of hang out with in New York, but sort of don't. I finished reading through a few conversations I ended abruptly between myself and my (very, very long) "list" of future ex-boyfriends, (my "long" list is exactly two names long) and asked myself if it was time I revisited some of those "options" with my birthday fast approaching. Who wants to be alone on their birthday, right? Well, I actually thought that sounded like a refreshing experience – so that's exactly what I did.

I ordered myself a room full of balloons, swiped my card at Victoria's Secret, took out the old fairy lights, put my favorite movie on (Eat Pray Love) and mumbled my favorite lines along over the handfuls of popcorn I stuffed my mouth with. When I woke up, I devoured a very unhealthy breakfast by myself while taking in the gorgeous views out my window, watching the New York ferries chase each other around in circles, alone, that morning. And you know what, I felt really happy.

What if I didn't need a pile of gifts, a line of people buying me shots, or the grand big NYC-limo-ride party I had planned out in my head? What if I didn't need any of that this year, to prove that I am loved, to prove I'm not alone? I didn't. I didn't need any of that. Loving and treating myself well was the most fulfilling birthday experience. Not measuring my worth on the birthday call I didn't get from my dad. Not measuring my worth on the amount of people that showed up for my party so I could feel like I was loved and important.

Today I am a year younger than Amy was when she died. I will tell you on any day of the week that I am not afraid of dying young - and I'd mean it too – but I do wish she stayed a little longer, I wish she was a little more afraid of dying, and my mind might be changing about my "lack of fear" regarding the day I die, too.

Because twenty-six? Twenty-six is nothing in the greater scheme of things. Twenty-six is the flower sprouting, not even blooming yet.

Twenty-six is the kind of mess you know you are going to look back on and think "wow, I fucked up a lot, I don't even remember how I got there and did those things, the good and the bad. Wow, that was all me? What was I so hard on myself for?"

Because at twenty-six, I've worked in male dominated industries, promotion after promotion but still underpaid. And I've traded my career for high paying exchange programs where my fate lay in the paint-stained-hands of toddlers whose parents hired me and fired me purely based on the mood of a four year old deciding to like, or not like me on that particular day.

At twenty-six I've found joy in serenading a cleaner in Central Park with my guitar on a cold November night, and I've thrown up without a hand to hold after singing the National Anthem in white P.T. shorts on international television after a wardrobe malfunction.

I'm twenty six and all I remember about my dad is the marks on his body from the bullets he took from his time serving the Special Forces, the bedtime stories about Terrie (the tame lion they kept as a pet in their army camp) and the jumps he took with his parachute. The only thing he was good at, was talking about himself and the good old army days.

I remember the box with photos he keeps of back then.

No photo of him standing proudly next to me at my matric farewell, or on the day I got my driver's license. Those weren't moments he valued like he did his army days.

And some nights I go over his Facebook profile just to look at the narrow-minded posts he shares so I can remind myself that I'm better off without his birthday call anyway.

I'm twenty-six and think that it's a fucking miracle that I function. I'm proud of that.

I'm twenty six and have had to make peace with the fact that some of my peers in South Africa assume that my teenage years bubbled over with white privilege, when I went to bed hungry and abused too. The hardest part was I couldn't be mad at them for assuming I was privileged when I wasn't. And when they got to know me, they nicknamed me Sibongile out of love and finding out we were not so different after all, and that is so fucking special to me. And we exchanged stories of how we were pushed away and made fun of by the people closest to us for dating interracially, and how we overcame that, too.

I'm twenty six and have learned that not every "best friend" is the "best" for your wellbeing, and that it's hard to end relationships that no longer serve you, but that you'd be a coward not to. I've learned that you can have a high school friend you only say hi to every couple of months, and the two of you keep losing each other's phone numbers because you're both constantly traveling, but when you manage to reconnect again, everything is as it was, you guys are still as tight as ever, and now I know that for every person who feels the need to manipulate you into loving them, there is another, who sets you free out of the love they have for you.

I'm twenty-six and still not sure what religion I grew up with, after a lot of research it is starting to look like it might border on a cult similar to the Jehovah's Witnesses. I don't have a mom to answer these questions, and questions the doctor asks me, like "were you vaccinated as a baby?" Or when my astrologer asks, "at what time were you born?" - I don't know.

I'm twenty-six and can't fathom that there was a time I was taught to believe people of color don't go to heaven, and American music is from the devil, and that my first introduction to Alanis Morisette was in Benjy Mudie's Vinyl Shop when I was twenty three.

I'm twenty six and I've just come out liberated at the other end of my very first New York summer, I feel like the coolest kid, until I'm sipping on my G&T at Grand Banks with a guy called Ray and he talks about his second house in the Hamptons and the other four locations he vacationed at this summer and I'm brought right back down to earth when I know this is the coolest my life has ever been, but that I'm still the most boring girl in Manhattan to him, compared to the other American girls he dates.

I'm twenty-six and I've learned that the only handful of phrases you need to keep any conversation in New York going is "yeah, oh my God, really, exactly, I know."

That being said, I've learned that "busy" doesn't always mean "disinterested" and "in a rush" does not always mean "shallow," but I've also learned that people always have the choice to make time for you, and that they would if they wanted to.

I'm twenty-six and I have a stack of hate mail in my social media inboxes, being told not to wear that again, or that my performance was flat, just not good enough. Messages telling me I'm not doing enough for African countries with the platform I've been given. Messages from people I used to call friends, threatening to sue me for using my own photograph, and people telling me that my last post was inappropriate and shows lack of character. I'm twenty-six and I welcome all of it. And the more they tell me "you're wild," the more I think "not wild enough."

Because twenty-six is the type of chaotic tornado you know you are going to look back on years later and realize how brave, strong and exceptional you were back then already, back then when taking credit for being all those things was a thought that made your stomach turn.

And at twenty-six everyone is trying to tell you what to do next and is dying to push their unsolicited advice down your throat, as if following your own heart, listening to your inner voice wasn't hard enough to figure out how to do already.

"Rebellious, wrong, too eager, play it safe, it's a waste, doubt it, maybe I'm not good enough" – that is the sound of the little voice you're fighting against in your mind at twenty-six as you're helplessly kicking and screaming, punching your way through the weeks barely making it to the other side of every twenty-four hours in one piece, but you do. And you need to take credit for that. You need to tell people exactly where they can put their unsolicited advice, and not feel bad for it.

And I knew it when I heard myself think it in the TV room where I was dancing by myself that night, knew that – it was a moment I was going to remember for the rest of my life: celebrating twenty-six by myself, completely content.

It wasn't a night to remember because of the balloons floating around the apartment and the overpriced champagne that had it feeling like a dope-ass-rich-kid-Tribeca party, no. I knew I was going to remember the moment, because I felt something in me change between those four walls that night.

Every memory made, every chance taken, every note I missed, every relationship I misjudged – I just knew that, when I will look back at "26 in NYC" one day – no matter where I'll find myself in the future – I know I will look back at it all, even the mistakes, and remember it for the good it brought out in me, for the lessons it taught, for the smiles and tears of joy it brought. And Amy, Amy doesn't get to have that happen one day. She doesn't get to look back and say, "I was a mess at twenty-six, but wow, what a woman, what a talent, what a soul. I'm proud of myself." She doesn't get to have that moment as an older version of herself when her shit storm was meant to have calmed down.

And I might not be in and out of rehab, or falling apart in public, but I have thought it, thought to myself "What a mess, I am not good enough, I'll never catch up to my peers."

I think if an older version of Amy could look back at her "twenty-six" right now, she would be proud and happy about it all. So in honor of that, I decided to be proud and happy about my "twenty-six" right now, and not wait to realize it only years from now, or wait for someone else to give me a pat on the back for it.

And because of my messy childhood, I've lived so many lives, lived in three countries, attended seven schools by the time I matriculated, moved into some twenty-odd towns, lived in over thirty houses - looked back at it all and thought, "what a disaster" - only to realize that people are dying to live that way. Quitting their jobs and selling their houses to be on the road and explore. And I find myself grateful for the lack of security I've experienced all these years, the lack of ties that bind.

I'm twenty-six and have been called by a different name - was laughed at for changing it, and there was this boy I really loved at some stage I thought I was going to marry. I've cried over assholes for unnecessarily long periods of time and pushed away people who didn't deserve it, changed my career because "I felt like it," and say way too many things out loud that gets me into trouble, and not looked at right. And I never get it right these days. I never did. But I still choose it, all the mistakes, all the disasters, and every single heartbreak. Because the only thing worse than being a complete fucking mess at twenty-six, is NOT being one. Being denied the freedom to be exactly that. Because I often think about the fact that I could have been a girl in India, married off to someone they chose for me at seventeen. THAT could have been my life and only reference of love.

I could have been born an Amish girl in Pennsylvania, and they would have shunned me if I picked up an instrument or had dared to be vain enough to sing alone, dared to write a song and express myself. It would never have been allowed.

And don't get me wrong, I wasn't born into the freedom I have today, no. The ones who brought me into this world polluted my mind and put me through a childhood I am still recovering from, and even though I have been celebrating my birthday "alone" in the company of strangers for ten years now – it is an experience I am thankful for.

Because you know what my dad gave me? You know what he gave me when he left? Freedom. The freedom to learn from strangers. See how they live and function, and learn from them. And I've learned more from them than I ever would have from him.

The freedom to take chances, and fail without him lurking over my shoulder waiting to whisper: "I told you so."

The freedom to lose and find myself. Find and lose God and find him again in all his different forms.

The freedom to pick my own boyfriend, God, I picked ten. And I thank God for all the levels of love and lust I've experienced, and all the different versions of my soul mate I've gotten to call mine for a moment, before being shoved off to the side like damaged goods. I'm cool with that, too.

The freedom I felt to work as a waitress so I could further my education when I was denied one by my own father. The freedom to pick a career that makes my heart skip a beat. The freedom to get to know myself.

What he did was shitty, but I spend so little time thinking about it, because I believe that life fucks us all, one way or another. It's what we do to find freedom that matters, the boundaries we push and choosing to love wholeheartedly in anyway.

And I could have been a girl in India, or an Amish girl in Pennsylvania. Never knowing the freedom that is trial and error, trying and failing, dreaming and fucking up royally.

So "twenty-six, alone in NYC?"

"Twenty-six in NYC" is a responsibility. A chance. A number that screams "you SHOULD be afraid of dying LYLA, because you got lucky, girl."

"Twenty-six in NYC" is a rose-gold ticket with my name on it. My passport to fail until I get it right, and unapologetically enjoy the fuck out of that process whilst falling with my face into that cupcake, giggling as I swipe the vanilla frosting off my own nose.

Because I know things aren't always perfect, but at least I'm fucking free. Here's to you, Amy, and here's to twenty-six.

THE CHOSEN PEOPLE

Interview by Michael Shemwell, Shunned Podcast Episode 34

Introduction:

Michael: Welcome to the Shunned podcast, where we expose religions that use shunning as a tool to control people. This episode is going to be a little different in format - our guest today is a very talented musician so she's given me two songs to share and we're going to put these in the episode, I really think you'll like them and I think they're very meaningful. I'll play the first song and then we'll get into the interview. After the interview we'll end on what actually may be one of the more powerful songs I've ever heard that relates to shunning and how we try to blend in and re-create our life afterward and the feelings that come along with that.

Today we meet Lyla Illing from South Africa now living in New York City. I'm not gonna try to pronounce the name of the cult in the Afrikaans language that she was involved with. Early on in the show she will do that when she introduces herself. It translates to "The Chosen People." As one might imagine in a land where apartheid held strong for so long, the cult was definitely racist. Lyla was only involved for a short time as a kid and you'll see why, but it created dynamics that impact her to this day and set her on a path to try to help Amish youth here in America. Now what you need to know about Lyla, is that she's a prolific songwriter and performer. The song that I'm gonna play for you first is one that she wrote to help those who are leaving the Amish called "Not Coming Home." The way she uses this to help the Amish is that the proceeds from the sale of the song on iTunes are donated to the Amish Heritage Foundation - a group spearheaded by Torah Bontrager who has also been on the Shunned podcast.

Lyla: My name is Lyla, I'm twenty-six years old. I was part of the cult "Die Uitverkore Volk" - translated to English - "The Chosen People" and I am shunned.

Michael: That is an interesting name for a cult. I think I've heard about Afrikaans before because Jehovah's Witnesses were super proud of having literature in just about every language in the world. How did you come to be in "The Chosen People" religion?

Lyla: I was born into it, my family was already part of it so I spent the first ten years of my life as part of that community. My mom passed away when I was ten. I was forced to move since my parents were divorced so I went to live with my dad. So my escape just happened naturally. I still don't speak to my mom's side of the family now that I'm older. But looking back it was a blessing that I got out of it the way I did.

Michael: Got it. Can you describe it? What did the religion or cult teach you? I know you may not even really remember - your being just ten when you left - but do you remember anything, any snapshots of your life from being inside the cult?

Lyla: Yeah I think the main thing was that being white automatically meant that we were superior to other races. So it was very racist and Afrikaans was mostly spoken. Anything other than being white and speaking Afrikaans was looked down upon. The unknown was very scary and was automatically wrong. We weren't allowed to listen to American music, we were told it was from the devil, but for some reason country music was fine maybe cause… they enjoyed it?

Michael: (laughs) That's how the Jehovah's Witnesses are too a lot of times. My parents are the same way. Country music for some reason is okay I guess cos it's all white, I don't know.

Lyla: Oh man, it is funny to think back on what they decided was okay and wasn't okay, there were no reasons given. It just was what it was.

Michael: Yeah it's very arbitrary. A lot of cults will dominate your life and obviously you had a lot of restrictions as far as the music you listen to, things like the language, the people that you associated with but was this a very active cult, did you have to go to a lot of meetings or study a lot of books or anything like that?

Lyla: So I also wanted to mention that we didn't celebrate Christmas. The town that we lived in is a pretty small town and the kids in my family were the only kids in our school to be in this cult. Once a year, people from across South Africa traveled to spend a week together - a religious week where a lot of preaching took place. But at home we'd gather as a family on Sundays at somebody's house to listen to prerecorded tapes that the preacher recorded. We would sing the religious songs and all that.

Michael: It sounds interesting, what was the racist component to it? In the states at least - South Africa sometimes can be synonymous with apartheid. Does the cult only exist in South Africa or is it larger thing?

Lyla: I tried to do some research in the last year especially. I felt like I didn't deal with this for a long time. So last year it kept coming up for me. I tried to look into it, I asked my older siblings if they could tell me more about what we grew up with. A lot of us don't exactly know all the details so I don't know if it's practiced in other parts of the world and sometimes it sounds very much like it was almost like the Jehovah's Witnesses. It was almost the same but not quite. As far as the racism goes, because in South Africa, that was the current climate it enabled people in that specific religion that we practiced, they felt like, because the racism was accepted for a long time in South Africa it gave them more power and made them feel like they were right. My mom was a teacher - and I'll always say she was an amazing person - I just think because of her circumstances and because she didn't know any better... I grew up with a mom who refused to teach people of color. She was like "I will resign from my job if a person of color is let into the school." I mean it's hard looking back, it's hard to believe I grew up with people who were that racist. It was a choice I had to make for myself, to not be like that and rather see everybody as equals.

Michael: Your dad wasn't from that cult, correct?

Lyla: So when him and my mom were married, he was. They were divorced before she passed away. When I went to go and live with him, he identified as Christian, but it was apparent that he still hung on to certain things from the cult.

Michael: Yeah that's interesting how people claim to be Christian, but Jesus didn't seem to be the kind of guy who is discriminatory toward anybody. In fact it was the religious leaders the Pharisees who were discriminating against people or who were keeping the Scriptures and stuff to themselves so that they could be a higher class. Jesus wasn't that way, he went to the masses.

234

Lyla: It definitely seems as though people make up their own minds and their own rules to benefit them.

Michael: I'm sure that being in a country where racism was a part of the every day, then it's just easier for those things to exist and thrive.

Lyla: Some people haven't moved on, some have. As I mention, I have older siblings, I remember as a kid if they'd listen to any American song, the elders would be like "oh my God, these kids are on drugs, they're Satanists," you know. It would be a big thing, a big fight. Now that we're older, luckily with our circumstances after our mom passed away, we were forced to see more of the world and different people and I think we have all adjusted in our own ways. But it was still hard for my siblings (eight years older than I am) to let a few things go at first. Me being a lot younger, by the time I got into college I started dating interracially and that was extremely hard for them. They didn't speak to me for a couple of years. But we got through that and they are happy for me to do whatever I want to do now, but at first it was a big challenge.

Michael: Yeah, it takes people time to adjust perspective. You know, here in the United States there's still racism. When you look at a lot of the areas where it is the most stereotypically racist areas, they are predominantly white areas and you have people who are afraid of the unknown which is kind of what you talked about. People sometimes live in a certain amount of ignorance and that ignorance keeps them stuck. Until they can have different experiences and until they can get out of the bubble that they live in, it's very difficult for people to move on and to get healthier perspectives on things. So I am glad that your siblings have come around on that because it is hard – if you're told your entire life that something is bad, it is difficult to just flip a switch and move on. I know for myself, just our first Christmas, we had left the Witnesses in September and when December rolled around and it was time for our first Christmas, my wife Jenny was ready to celebrate and I wasn't. It's hard, I believed it was wrong and evil my whole life so it was hard for me to let go of those feelings. It takes people time to make adjustments. I know Christmas was something you mentioned you didn't celebrate when you were in the cult, what was the problem with Christmas?

Lyla: As kids we were always just told it was demonizing Jesus' birth (we called Jesus, Jaweh or Jashua). They believed people were just trying to make money with Christmas gifts. I can't remember if there was more to it. I was so close with my cousins as kids, now I only have one cousin who will sometimes respond to my texts if I check in. They are still completely living that life and I'm told their

235

parents arranged their marriages for them. I've never met their children.

Michael: Is shunning part of the doctrine of that particular religion or is it just what people do because they are afraid of you because you are being different?

Lyla: I think it's both. Because of the way I left when my mom died, they always had a hope that I would come back. The process for me as a kid, it wasn't like they told me at ten that if I left to go and live with my dad I couldn't come back. That wasn't the case, but now that I'm older, I chose different things, completely different to how they live their lives, so there definitely is a line that I will never be accepted the way I am. When my parents were about to get a divorce there was controversy around that. My mom feared that she would be shunned if she went through with the divorce. I think it's because she had cancer that they didn't cut us off completely.

Michael: At least they didn't leave you guys completely high and dry when she was sick, sounds like there's still a lot of pressure and negativity surrounding that.

Lyla: Yeah, I know they call me a lost sheep and "poor her we pray for her that she finds her way back." There's definitely that condescending thing of "you're not the same as us anymore."

Michael: Oh yeah, it's so arrogant to look down on other people because they're not living the *one* way you feel is the right way. It's funny how we can get wrapped up in what we think is truth if anyone doesn't go along with that. It's one thing to feel differently but it's another to treat people like garbage. When you moved in with your dad, at ten, it's kind of like "life 2.0" like you've got this new start. So how did things change for you when you went from living in the cult environment to living with your dad?

Lyla: Initially it was hard coming from a small town, having been in a private school where only white people were allowed, to living in a city, being put in a really big school with people from all walks of life. My dad... that side of the story comes with it's own physical and mental abuse. But other than that it was hard to adjust to a new school. I didn't speak to anyone. I think I had anxiety that was left unaddressed. It was difficult to settle into the world.

Michael: It's a big change for a ten year old to lose your mom and then to end up in a different type of environment. I was in the third grade when my parents moved and I had to go to a new school in the middle of a school year. Walking into that new class for the first time was absolutely terrifying.

236

Lyla: I did that *seven* times. My dad made me change schools seven times. It was a mess. He was in the military, and he remarried. We'd go to church as Christians but he hung on to a certain part of the cult. I was always the only kid amongst my friends who was not allowed to go to the cinema for instance. If I wanted to skateboard I was told it's only for boys. I feel like he was trying to protect me but he didn't know what he was doing. It was abusive.

Michael: Yeah, that amount of control is not love. It is just control. It's interesting that he was still isolating you on some level. That is definitely a hallmark of any type of a cult. You mentioned there was abuse, was any of that centered around his Christianity or his rules with the control?

Lyla: I don't know so much that the abuse was tied in around religious views. He was more just power hungry, wanted control over any and everything. Music was a big deal. They didn't like me expressing myself through writing, or listening to certain things. If I did something wrong they'd always threaten "we're going to burn all your Avril Lavigne CD's, it's influencing you badly." They were very extreme.

Michael: Anytime you're threatening to burn something of a kid, it seems a bit much (both laughing) …like there has got to be a better way.

Lyla: My stepmom had her own issues and continued to be abusive so when I left home at fifteen it was a combination of "you need to be how we want you to be or you have to leave" and also me being like "I'd rather leave."

Michael: There definitely comes that point when you're in such a controlled environment. Heck, any of us who have left a cult, you always come to that point where you feel you don't want to be a part of all that anymore, you'd rather leave. It's a big moment. How did it feel? What were the circumstances around leaving home at fifteen? At least in the states that's so young. I don't know how it was there?

Lyla: It's young even for South Africa. I feel kids in the states are a lot more mature, they're allowed to do things independently and that's not how I grew up at all, so it was a lot. I basically left home with one suitcase and lived with friends for the next two, three years of my life. Sometimes just for a weekend, sometimes for three months at a time depending on who would house me. It was crazy. I always hoped my dad would show up saying, "let's try this again." I thought he would be the adult in the situation, but he didn't do that.

Michael: And I'm sure on some level you just wanted him to prove that he wanted you.

Lyla: I still do. It doesn't go away.

Michael: Everybody wants to be wanted especially by your own parents. We would all in that situation have that dream that your dad is going to come and say "I was wrong, I really miss you and I want you back in our lives" and instead you just have to survive. You're a survivor of all of that. How did you make it through that time, I assume everyone wasn't always thrilled that Lyla was coming to live with them as you were bouncing around. That takes some hustle. How did you do that?

Lyla: It's a lot. What helped at first was that I was in a boarding school because we lived very far from school. So at first I stayed in the hostel during the week and just visited friends over weekends. I thought it was going to blow over but then it didn't. My dad stopped paying for my school and boarding. Luckily I had really great people in my life who helped. I started working as a waiter over weekends at sixteen to pay for school, and then I met a guy I really liked and we lived together for my last two years of high school.

Michael: In your mom's cult, your dad's brand of Christianity – what were you taught about people on the outside? Were you taught to distrust them or that they were okay? I'm just wondering because as Witnesses we were taught to distrust everybody on the outside. But the people on the outside, we found to be far more accepting and wonderful than the people on the inside. Was it similar for you?

Lyla: I can definitely relate to that. I was always told that no matter what society is doing and no matter how the world is changing "you don't have to be a part of *that*." That's what my dad always taught me. "You don't have to be part of *them*."

Michael: And then *they* were far better people than the people you were supposed to be able to count on who were supposed to love you and be your parents. So where did you go from there? You go through these few years of living with random people on the weekend, or boarding school or your boyfriend, how did that play out for you, how did you transition?

Lyla: After school I moved across the country to live with my estranged sister for a few months, she found some independence and helped me to try and get on my feet. I took an au pair job, which is kind of like a nanny job where you live with a family and help them take care of their kid. They really took care of me, put me

238

on their medical aid and paid for my studies, so I managed to get a degree in radio production. From there I could stand on my own two feet and live on my own for a bit before moving to the states. I did pretty well in my career in radio.

Michael: Got to ask, what did you do in radio in Africa?

Lyla: I was an on air producer for a primetime breakfast show, I loved it. I did that for three years, which on its own, was still hard for me to believe I was good enough compared to anybody else after so much emotional abuse. I'm sure a lot of people can relate.

Michael: Oh man, absolutely. That whole "not good enough" is a theme that runs through anyone who leaves a cult. There's a level of imposters syndrome that comes with that, and you feel like you're not cut out to do what you're doing.

Lyla: I am always so grateful to people who opened their homes to me, but as a result to how I had to live, I still feel like I never want to overstay my welcome anywhere, now in my adult life. Even when someone is welcoming I still wonder if they are just accommodating because they know I have no parents. That's not the way *they* are thinking but I always think that way.

Michael: I get it. Wow. That's an interesting point. Nobody wants to be pitied. You don't always want to be known for this one aspect of your life. You have so much more to you than that one thing. What prompted the move from South Africa to the United States?

Lyla: I think that because of the way I grew up I noticed I learned so much from interacting with different people from all walks of life, so I enrolled in a cultural exchange program between South Africa and the United States. I get to live with an American family and see how they live. Once you allow yourself to think outside of the boxes people made you live in when you were in the cult – once you see a bit more of the world, for me I wanted to see more and more so that I can be more open. I also loved working in radio but I wanted to try doing more music so that's really why I moved. And I felt that having this back story had to mean something. Deep in my heart I feel I want to be a voice for the shunned community and runaways. When I visited Amish country here in America I realized that so much of what I was seeing felt similar to what I grew up with and that was the first time I really started questioning what I grew up with. I always knew it was different and not exactly right, and now I *know* it was *definitely* not right. So with the music, I feel like I can sing about it, try and work through it.

Michael: Yes, it's a beautiful way to express yourself. I have to ask, how did you end up in Amish country, how did you get that experience?

Lyla: I had to take some classes as per my visa requirements, and visiting the Amish was an option as an education class and tour. At first I didn't realize how deeply I'd end up being invested in this. For everyone else it was just a touristy outing and some sightseeing. But for me it was an "ah-ha moment" and the point at which I started to question the religion I grew up with. I had to learn more about the Amish, I had to speak to the community more in depth.

Michael: Were you allowed to sit in with Amish families or talk to them, how did that work?

Lyla: There was a lady who was our tour guide, she was shunned by the Amish but part of the Mennonites now. She took us to the farmhouse she grew up in and we had a chance to ask questions. My question was, "what happens to the kids who want to leave and have nowhere to go" She said she has helped kids who didn't have anywhere to go although she had to do it in secret since it would be frowned upon in the community but it was very hard for her to look away. I realized I had to be more involved.

Michael: Have you managed to speak to any kids who are runaways?

Lyla: I have not, I know the Amish Heritage Foundation are on top of that and I have made myself available as a volunteer so they will hopefully call on me once a halfway home is set up and I'd like to help and be there for the kids even if they just need a friend or someone to help introduce them to the outside world. Apparently because there is more and more information available online these days, that has helped greatly in terms of encouraging kids to leave. Hopefully I will be more involved in the coming years.

Michael: I find it amusing, just knowing you from being Facebook friends, you said you moved here because you wanted to be more urban and do more with music and you live in New York City which is about as good as it gets, and you're such a prolific songwriter. It just shows something about you, from the time you left your parents home at fifteen. Whether it was hustling for a place to live, getting into programs coming to the states or taking on this urban goal or goal of writing music, I hope you can appreciate the hustle, the drive about yourself. If you're putting your mind to doing something for the Amish Youth or anyone who is suffering, obviously you can do this because you have already made so much happen than your circumstances would have allowed.

Lyla: Thank you, I appreciate those words. I think that's a big challenge for all of us who go through the process of trying to make it on our own. It is possible, it is not easy but it is possible.

Michael: When you are a person who is a survivor, sometimes you don't give yourself credit, or take a compliment, or see the positive, because you have always been hustling, you've always been fighting. So I hope you can take the time at some point to honor that, to look inward to the things that you bring to the table and to really appreciate that, because we all have those things and it's really hard when you grow up in a cult environment or a really controlled environment where you're so stifled. Just focused on surviving. It's really hard to attach to the positive qualities and the things you have to offer. So I just want to command you for what you have done because it's pretty awesome.

Lyla: I appreciate being able to talk to you about this. It's something that doesn't always come up when you are around people who don't know your whole story.

Michael: Is there any ways your past life still influences the way you live now?

Lyla: Yes, as a result I don't want anything to do with religion, although I respect other people's religions. Faith and religion for me is two different things so I feel a little bit blunt towards that. I think I'm also a bit more rebellious without meaning to be. I don't want to get in anyone's way but I don't want to listen to anyone either because I think that they will want me to do things because it benefits them more than me, or support the way they see the world. So as a result I don't stay long in peoples lives because I feel like I don't want to compromise *me* again, for anyone. That's not always healthy but … (laughs)

Michael: No that's interesting. I can see how that could be. I have to think on that one. Once you get into one of these environments and you've seen how you can be compromised by being around certain people for a while. I'm sure over time you'll develop more trust in people and probably more importantly – trust in yourself and know that you'll know when it's time to call it quits on anything that's unhealthy. But all that comes from experience and perspective and time. That's one of the things that have not been brought up on the podcast but I'd imagine that right now there's a lot of people listening looking inward at themselves and their own relationships thinking "oh yeah, I do that too sometimes."

Lyla: Yes, it's a big process to deal with, being scared it's going to happen again.

Michael: I totally understand that. Where are you now in your journey, what are you up to as Lyla?

Lyla: I am grateful that my siblings got to a place where they can be supportive towards me no matter what. That has been life changing, this past year has just been life changing because they are there for me more. Other than that I am trying to embrace the freedom that comes from not really having any family apart from them. The freedom that comes with that. I don't feel afraid to do things artistically, I can say whatever I need to say without having to worry that "oh, my parents aren't going to approve." It's a kind of freedom I am trying to be grateful for as hard as it is. I'd like to think if I didn't strand up for myself back then, I wouldn't be as happy as I am today. So being alone and happy is better than being unhappy and having this family around you trying to control you.

Michael: (laughs) yeah, absolutely. There is no lonelier place in the world than being with people who practice conditional love. The last time my wife and I were ever at any function of Jehovah's Witnesses was at a massive international convention with forty thousand people there, and I've never felt more alone in my life than sitting with forty thousand Jehovah's Witnesses knowing that, I know better now, and I don't believe this stuff and these people don't really care about me. And if I speak my truth only once – it's over. So I think it's beautiful that you said you'd rather be alone and free. And you know that you're not really alone. I know there are people you've experienced that are good and will try to help out, and now you have this community of ... heck ... you have a community of ex Jehovah's Witnesses and other formal cult members who are cheering you on. We all want to see each other do well.

Lyla: Yes I am trying to think of myself as being less "alone" and more that I am *choosing* this freedom.

Michael: If you could say anything to those who have turned their backs on you for all their different reasons, what would you say?

Lyla: I'd tell them that they shouldn't be afraid of what they don't know and what they don't understand. Respectfully, I would tell them that there's so much information out there, they should educate themselves. They owe it to themselves to get to know people from all walks of life and see they're not superior to them but that we are all the same.

Michael: Yeah, I think the solution to ignorance is information.

Lyla: I'd like to believe that if my mom was still alive, that she would have evolved. As a kid you will always see your mom as a saint and in my heart I remember her as an amazing person, but what I grew up with and who I am now – that's two different people.

Michael: Is there anything you have learned that stands out for you since you've left the cult?

Lyla: I think what I'm the most proud of is that I embrace people from all walks of life. Not only in the cult but also in South Africa, there are people who haven't moved on, on both sides of the racial divide. So as a young person I choose to spread as much love as possible and hope that people will catch on.

Michael: Anytime there's an "us versus them" it's such an ugly thing. You see it politically, you see it in religion, racially and ethnically. Every time you start having this "us versus them" it's just a race to the bottom and nobody will win. What do you enjoy about your new life since you left all that behind at fifteen?

Lyla: I think it would have been a lot harder for me to leave South Africa for a cool journey like coming to America. If I had strong family ties, if I was webbed into the family it would have been hard for me to travel.

Michael: What dreams do you have personally? Do you want a family or more relationships?

Lyla: It is still hard to think about having my own family one day. I think I just want to be involved in more charities and keep on traveling. To embrace the unknown - maybe *that's* the dream. (laughs)

Outro:

Michael: I'd like to thank Lyla for the interview, for being such a great person to work with. She has a good heart, you can see it in what she does. We're going to end this episode on what is a fairly emotional song, one that gets to me personally, one that I think a lot of you are going to be able to relate to as you try to fit in after leaving a cult. The song is called "Below the Surface." The name couldn't be more fitting. As we end all episodes, love others, do no harm, and go be happy."

I'M GOING TO CALL 911, BUT DON'T WORRY ABOUT ME

"…I knew it was inevitable that I would forget these declarations and reasons for people coming and going in my life, as soon as my time on earth started - but I was hopeful that I would recall it all again when I was ready to. Recall the reasons, recall the meanings, and recall that it was what I chose.

And then I did. On my twenty-sixth birthday in New York City, I remembered it all, clearly. I remembered what I chose around that boardroom table in that big white, bright room before my journey on earth started.

Up until that moment on my twenty-sixth birthday, I did not understand the fearless force that drove me to continue moving forward, despite the losses, despite the abuse I suffered, despite the loneliness, despite the unfair hand of cards life dealt me. But when I suddenly remembered that I chose for it all to be this way - I celebrated the freedom I created for myself, I celebrated the freedom I found. I celebrated coming back into consciousness, as I felt myself realize that I knew and understood exactly where I was.

From that moment on, I understood why it was always easy to be delusionally, and disproportionately grateful for everything that has gone right, as well as "wrong" in my life. Some part of me always understood that I needed to go through it, to be where I am today - at my desk, in my room, on the twelfth floor of an apartment building in lower Manhattan, at 1pm on a Wednesday, having the freedom to tell the story of how I found the way back to my conscious-self.

At least, that's my theory.

What I'd like to believe.

The only thing that helps me sleep at night."

A tear rolled down my cheek as I shut my Mac, overwhelmed at my realization, but at peace. Like I erased my own death wish and I could breathe again without counting every last hour, every last minute, every last second the way I had been for months, not subconsciously, but fully aware.

When you've come to terms, stood hand in hand with your own mortality, something inside you is changed forever, or at least, for how ever long you are willing to consciously hold onto this newly born version of yourself.

My angel of death was no longer lurking around. I started painting out of nowhere – I did a good job at it too. I wasn't Picasso or anything, but I was as amazed as everyone around me that picking up a paintbrush and painting the hell out of the Jersey City skyline came so naturally to me, as if I had been studying art for a couple of years, at least.

I love working on my creative projects, composing music, interviewing guests for podcasts, the video editing, so much so, that pulling all nighters aren't hard for me – it's fun to me, fulfilling to me. But as much as I love working, I never switch off, I don't know how to – there is always something new I feel the need to work on, something else I have to be doing. I don't know how to empty my mind and quiet it when too many voices and deadlines and idea charts burn through my neural pathways and keep me up at night.

Dipping the brush in viridian blue-green, and plastering it on the canvas – that taught me how to go quiet. That taught me how to just be – without thinking about my to-do list somewhere in the back of my mind, without thinking about that boy and whether or not I should text back, and without feeling anxious, sad, or anything at all – just quiet. Part of me stood still - as if I put my soul on hold as the Colgate clock's arms on the horizon circled themselves around their center - past twelve and past twelve again day in and day out. I hardly looked up from my pallet. I painted many nights away until winter was just here one day, and the trees were naked, all of a sudden. Like the change of season happened in a split second – because I wasn't keeping track of life outside my own four walls, I was enjoying my own company, and the process of witnessing an empty canvas become its own story – I even loved the bad ones, the ones that looked like I let a four year old loose with my supplies. It was one of the happiest times in my life, I even started running again – went for a jog every other day until my body hurt more and more from it. At first I thought I was just unfit, but then the leg spasms started - burning through my muscles, I felt like I was being ripped to shreds from the inside out.

I thought it would just go away.

I was hunching around the apartment, deteriorating everyday until the pain was constant and I had trouble dressing myself without wanting to pass out. I could hardly lift my arms up to brush my hair.

Two weeks of daily treatments didn't help - finally I was referred to a pain doctor who performed an epidural on me. I was at the doctor's office alone but had my sister on loudspeaker. There must have been a language barrier between the doctor and I, English not being my first language - I didn't understand all the medical terms. I thought he was only going to use local anesthesia just numbing a small part of my body, but it seemed more like general anesthesia because I still had my sister on loudspeaker when suddenly – I went completely quiet on my end of the line - I lost consciousness. I cried when they brought me back around – confused. I sat in the recovery room alone crying waiting for the effects to wear off before walking myself four blocks home.

I felt like the pain was getting better after the epidural but a few days later I tried getting up from my bed to pee around midnight – the spasms took over my body and pulled me onto the floor I couldn't get up for an hour. My face salty-wet from sweating and crying. I managed to get up after crawling around like an insect that was turned on its back and couldn't get back onto its own feet. I was crying so hard that no sound was coming out my mouth anymore, just desperate gasps as I begged the empty air around me for some sort of mercy.

It took me about another hour to put together a bag - I knew I was heading in only one direction from here – the ER. I called my health insurance company multiple times asking them to explain to me what to do and asking them if I was covered for this sort of emergency. The man on the other end of the line told me "yes" repeatedly – and that I should call 911.

"Call 911? Me, call 911 in America? Isn't calling 911 for big emergencies?" I thought.

In the movies they call 911 when there's an intruder, or a car accident, a fire, or a building falling. I couldn't wrap my head around dialing those numbers for my spasms, although I was in desperate need for medical attention – I had a slipped disc.

When my pain only got worse, I woke my hosts up at 5am to let them know I was going to call for an ambulance but that they shouldn't be worried about me. I had my bag backed and I was going to be fine all on my own. I explained, "you really don't need to come with me" I said unable to talk without crying and pulling a face trying not to show my pain.

My host-mom picked up the phone and dialed 911, and didn't leave my side that entire day - Googled and vetted each doctor who touched me, made me take off work for two weeks against my kicking and screaming that "I can still work."

She took care of me and put my needs first when I didn't know how to. I was drugged out on prescribed pain medication, sleeping through most of the days, had no feeling in my right leg. I felt frustrated and angry at my body for giving up on me like that, and then I felt angry at my dad for not being there to take care of me. It always comes back to him – like some sick habit I can't let go of. He was supposed to be my person.

When I regained my strength and managed to get back to life as I knew it – I had a new appreciation for my body - not having any pain anymore, being able to walk, work, tie my shoes, comb my hair without crying. I imagined it as if someone's vision was taken away for a month, and then given back to them again. I could imagine how much I would appreciate my world I take for granted if my sight was taken away and then given back to me - that's what it felt like to bounce back from the back problems too. Most of me was optimistic, had a lust for life, but that voice in my head kept whispering "doesn't it hurt?" reminding me of my dad's absence in my moment of need – again. And how I tried to be brave and not let anyone take care of me because if my own dad doesn't give a shit to take care of me, why would anyone else?

OUT OF PLACE, ON PURPOSE

"Can I buy you a drink?"

"Oh, hi, I'm Lyla, and thanks but I'm good." I smiled.

"Yes I know who you are. You don't remember me from the Springbok match you sang the anthem at?"

It was more of a disappointed statement than a question. I could see in his eyes that he wanted to shake his head at me with a pitied look but he just ignored me after that.

Eventually I remembered his face and the very heartfelt message he sent me over Facebook to wish me good luck before I sang the anthem, I briefly recall clinking our beer bottles to cheers when we bumped into each other at the after party too.

I felt so disappointed in myself for not remembering at first, but everyone I met around the anthem performance, and everyone who interacted with me on social media around that time – it was a lot, it was just a blur to me.

A bunch of us South Africans were gathered in an Indian restaurant waiting to welcome Springbok prop "Beast" (Tendai Mtawarira) to New York - I had probably already met half of the people who were there, before – but couldn't piece together their names and our previous interactions. They knew me better than I knew them – that was surprisingly hard for me to deal with because I felt the responsibility to remember each and every one of them – out of respect and gratitude for their support, but my memory was failing me and I felt small because of it, like I had nothing to say to so many of the people who were trying to talk to me only to be disappointed that I didn't remember meeting them before. I literally felt like I was involuntarily slapping people in the face one by one, I tried to hide out as far as possible in a corner, but my outfit made it hard for me to not be noticed.

When my sister saw me before I left for the states, she gifted me a Springbok replica jersey and a Springbok jacket – I wore both that night. I was the only one wearing Springbok clothing, at a Springbok event – I was a little puzzled, but more embarrassed for sticking out like a sore thumb.

Beast loved it though, he complimented me on my green and gold and after that I tried to laugh it off, feeling comforted by the fact that he appreciated my efforts to wear his uniform. "Lyla sang the anthem for you guys at the Washington, D.C. match, you know?" my friend Shaun butted in, bragging to Beast so I didn't have to. "Wow, I insist you serenade me tonight!" Beast smiled at me. For the first time that night, I felt in place and not nervous at all – rubbing shoulders with big personalities was what I did for a living in Johannesburg. I spoke to him as if I was interviewing him, getting him to tell me all the things going on in his life that he is passionate about, and I listened, making mental notes in my mind for follow up questions – I didn't mean for it to happen that way, it's just how I function. He went on about all his projects and kept teasing me to sing for him, I said "maybe after a few more gin & tonics!" and excused myself.

The event organizer along with the owner of the venue, cheered me on to take Beast up on his request. "I'll do it, give me a few minutes." I smiled and walked out of the restaurant, trying to decide if I should turn back or keep walking all the way to the subway and just never come back. I was not so sure the people at the event cared to hear me sing for Beast, some part of me kept telling me they'd think I'm a loser always looking for attention if I went through with it. I felt like the girl who knew how to steal the spotlight, but had no idea how to be anybody's friend.

Outside I stood with my back against the wall, and the cars were rumbling a stone's throw away from me at the four-way stop. Brooklyn was buzzing and I needed one moment of quiet. "Think Lyla, think Lyla, think" I kept egging myself on. If I could serenade one of my favorite Springbok players of all time, would I? "Yes, no matter what, I would." I answered myself back. But what the hell would I sing to him, what would make an impression, be memorable?

"Oh my god" I thought. I'd watched the latest Beauty and the Beast movie starring Emma Watson just the other day. With it being a classic, and with the similarity in name, it was just cheesy enough to hopefully get the crowd to see I was trying to put the spotlight on Beast, and not just myself. "I should sing that. I should sing that!" I chanted to myself. I pulled up the karaoke instrumental on YouTube and rehearsed the song twice to strangers passing by on the sidewalk, looking at me, probably wondering if I was high. I got a few cheers and claps from across the street though, and it helped to psych me up to go back into the restaurant.

When the time came, Shaun pulled out a chair for Beast to sit on, the music in the restaurant was turned down, and the stage was mine. I had the crowd's attention the second they realized what I was singing, and realizing why I chose that song in particular – they burst out laughing with approval. I tried to make them feel part of the song by telling them I needed their help to chant "Beast" when I was wrapping up the song – the same way crowds chant his name in rugby stadiums when he kills a tackle or scores a try, we all chanted "Beeeaaaaasssssssst!!!'

Every person was so awesome, smiling at me the entire song through, while I smiled at them – each one of them, phone in hand, recording the whole thing. I knew exactly what was going to happen once the video hit the internet, but I tried not to think of it, I tried to take a mental screenshot of the moment – not because of what I knew it was going to do for my career, but applauding myself for walking back into that restaurant when every part of me wanted to get on a subway train home instead. I wanted to make a mental note of what happens when I push myself out of my comfort zone, I wanted to remember what it felt like to be brave, so that I would be brave, the next time I was in doubt, too.

I met somebody I liked that night - I hadn't had instant chemistry with anyone in that way for a while. He asked me to stay and spend the night with him as he had to return to Florida the following day, but as much as I wanted to enjoy the night with him, I knew it was almost morning in South Africa – with daylight savings time in action, they were seven hours ahead of us, which meant that I was going to be contacted by reporters any minute, no matter that it was 11pm for me. I kissed the cute guy goodbye, and got in an Uber home. Nothing was sweeter than his phone call that followed, pleading with me to turn back and see him – but I kept on driving, hard as it was to.

I stayed up till 2am that morning sending the press release I'd put together to the media, I figured there'd be one or two mentions about it in the news when I woke up later that morning.

When I managed to fight my eyes open and roll myself out of bed, I started throwing a bag together for the Thanksgiving trip to New Jersey I was about to go on with my host family. Forgetting about the night before for a moment, I made a pot of coffee, took in the morning for a moment, leaning against my window-wall smiling hello to the New York ferries rushing back and forth over the Hudson.

"Buzz, buzz, buzz." My phone lit up. "I should probably check my email," I snapped in a panic, suddenly recalling the events of the night before, and clicking that it wasn't just a dream I dreamt.

I'd been trying to get featured on South Africa's News24 for the past year – the county's largest website and online news provider reaching millions of users both nationally and internationally. I finally got my break! I could hardly believe my eyes. As the day continued, there were hardly any South African news outlets I wasn't being featured on – the publicity was much bigger than I had anticipated, and I couldn't help crying when SA Rugby – a magazine I grew up reading with my dad – featured the story too.

Some of the outlets got the details a little mixed up. Beast was invited to a basketball game by LeBron James during his trip to the states – somehow someone wrote that I invited Beast and LeBron James to the event we were at in Brooklyn. My attempts at trying to reach the news outlets to set the story straight failed, most likely because I was just another email in their inboxes – I had no direct line with some of the outlets who covered my story, no manager or agent to get the job done for me. My day was a whirlwind, for hours my phone kept lighting up with notifications and messages and calls, and then everything went real quiet when it was midnight in South Africa, 5pm for me in New York. I had to meet my host-dad at Penn Station where we'd get on a train to Hamilton. He asked me to grab a bottle of his wine and a bottle opener from home. At Penn Station he grabbed two plastic cups at the pizza shop – I didn't realize we were going to split the bottle on the hour-long train ride into New Jersey. I could do with a drink, and I had something to toast to! Upon entering the train, I sat in the same row as him but didn't sit down next to him. "The train gets pretty packed, you might have to move up." He was right. The train was so full that some people didn't even have a seat. I moved up to sit next to him. I didn't mean anything by not sitting next to him in the first place, it's just that the year before, when I boarded the train with my Scarsdale host-dad, he said goodbye to me and went to go and sit in a different car even though we were headed in the same direction. I didn't take it personally – he probably thought he was giving me space *I* needed, I never really thought about it until that moment, it was really all the same to me – but it would explain why I subconsciously stayed out of my Manhattan host family's personal space by default, probably more so than I realized, or had meant to.

My host-dad and I toasted to the week that was, exchanged a few jokes and stories. I had trouble with an expression; I forgot the English word for it and kept repeating it in Afrikaans until I remembered. "Superficial! That's the word I was looking for" I exclaimed. He tried repeating the Afrikaans translation "oppervlakkig." I joked that it would sound good in that Barbra Streisand song … "dum du da da, dum du da, dum du da, da dum … oppervlakking" I hymned it and we burst out laughing.

The word "superficial" stayed with me that entire weekend, mostly because I knew I'd been keeping almost everyone in my life at arms length, hardly ever showing my whole self anymore, I was scared that word described me more than I was willing to admit to myself. I felt like I'd become a watered-down version of myself, not because anyone asked me to, but because I tried so hard to always say the right thing, please everyone, be whatever or whoever they needed me to be – and I was the only one to blame for it. I took a hard long look at myself every minute of that weekend, the internal dialect was harsh, but I smiled through it on the outside like I always do.

Every next dinner table I was welcomed at, every next home I was invited to for the Thanksgiving celebrations, made the lump in my throat heavier and harder. I had big success in South Africa with the Beast story, but I was still the same smiling-but-sad-inside girl - in someone else's home, with someone else's family, at someone else's table – celebrating the holidays. The story of my life.

It's always difficult seeing a family that actually functions, people who make time for each other, people who pray together – when I know I never had any of that with mine. I never make a big deal out of it, but that emptiness is always with me, hiding below the surface. Hidden away behind what I choose to show. And not dealing with it made me feel superficial to myself.

I had to come to terms with, realize, that I was no longer "teenager Lyla" who depended on strangers to take care of me. I was long past that. I wasn't a burden to anyone. I was actually standing on my own two feet, and just another guest at the table – not a girl who needed a handout or who was a victim. It took me until twenty-six to stop seeing myself in that way, to realize the work I had put in, paid off, and that I'd been successfully navigating my life for quite some time now and had to stop seeing myself as the teenage runaway that I used to be, and start seeing myself for the independent young woman I was turning into.

The void I have because of my mom and dad's absence, and the gratitude I feel towards those who treat me so kindly, treat me like family – that "void" and "gratitude" can never balance each other out, no matter how hard I've tried forcing it to. They are two different things. Two different feelings I feel simultaneously. After much thought, I realized that I had never looked at it that way before – and there was something comforting about acknowledging both feelings, instead of trying to replace the one with the other.

Kind of like how I can't say my mom's death doesn't hurt, just because the ten years I had with her when she was alive, brought me joy. The joy doesn't replace the hurt, the hurt doesn't replace the joy – those feelings are both there, and both valid of acknowledgement.

My new approach towards my emotions was hard to wrap my head around. I got on a train back to New York a day before the rest of the family. I needed to see what I started, through. I was a little uneasy, felt a little unstable because even after my emotional breakthrough, I was still stuck with the fact that my name started trending in the news worldwide because of the Beast story - first in other African countries, then in New Zealand, then in the UK. The whole world acknowledged me, apart from the one person I needed to. It came back to my dad, again.

It was freezing walking from Chambers street subway to the apartment, it was past midnight already but an old Chinese lady was digging through the trash for recyclables outside my building. I felt thrown-off witnessing it in that cold. I warmed myself up on the couch next to my guitar and hit the voice recorder on my phone – something was scratching its way out of me, and I needed it to just manifest itself already. I needed to acknowledge what was really below all my superficial smiles, and come to terms with the fact that I was a big girl now, deciding consciously to live my life a certain way. I needed to not only take credit, but also responsibility for that. I needed to proudly own my circumstances, because I was no ones victim anymore, but the captain of my own soul – although that didn't mean that certain choices I had to make and live with wouldn't hurt anymore – they still did, and they probably will forever, in some ways.

I wrote the song in one go as I sang it, and crawled into a fetal position when it was over, crying uncontrollably. I pushed the guitar off me, disgusted at it, feeling as though its' six not-so-loyal strings cut my heart to shreds when I thought they were going to heal me.

BELOW THE SURFACE
(Lyrics)

Boarded the 801, on my way home, from Hamilton
Just need some space to let the past two days, sink in
Thanksgiving, in Jersey, everybody, is giving thanks
I bow my head in prayer, but devil has been on attack

You seat me at the table, and my plate is stacked
I'm feeling comfortable, I don't know if y'all are all okay with that

251

Don't want to overstep, I'm holding back, I'm feeling out of place
I'm smiling but afraid you see the sadness on my face

Because I know that, they all know that
I don't have any of what they have
And I don't know where I'll go from here
And I'm knowing, that it's showing
I'm terrified inside
Because I don't know, where I'll be next year

I'm jealous but I'm grateful
Don't know how to show I'm grateful

So I hope it shows, in the inside jokes
The conversations that you have with me
That I take heart in your father's art
And your humble starts
And the room you always make for me
The conversations you all have with me

Woke up to finding my name trending in the headlines all around the globe
All I can think, my dad won't even say well done or pick up the phone, I don't
know how to brush that off
You take me diving, below the surface, round the corner at the local Knot
They won't let me sing, you yell "you're making a mistake she's fucking
famous," and we laugh it off

You swallow hard, say "tell me, at what age, did your mother pass?"
"And I'm so fucking sorry that your dad is being, such a fucking ass"
I hit back - I got nothing bad to add I think his life is sad and
My life is good, and I'm good with that, let's rather raise a glass to my mother
Let's raise a glass

But I know that, they all know that
I don't have any of what they have
And I don't know where I'll go from here
And I'm knowing, that it's showing
I'm terrified inside
Because I don't know, where I'll be next year

I'm jealous but I'm grateful
Don't know how to show I'm grateful
So I hope it shows, in the inside jokes
The conversations that you have with me

That I take heart in your father's art
And your humble starts
And the room you always make for me
The conversations you all have with me

I've been blessed with many seats at many tables
It's by choice I live my life in the company of strangers
So this one's out of frustration not out of anger
I don't mean to put you under that parental type of pressure

I feel like such an asshole
Don't know how to say I'm grateful
My emotions are unstable
And I don't want to make it a thing
So I hope it shows, in the inside jokes
The conversations that you have with me
That I take heart in your father's art
And your humble starts
And the room you always make for me
The conversations you all have with me

PART THIRTEEN

THE SUNSHINE STATE AND PRIVATE ISLANDS

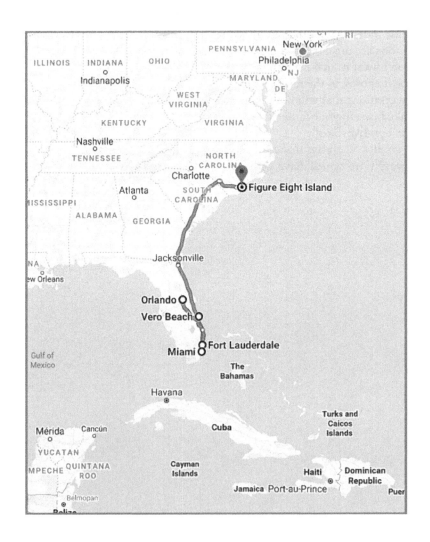

WELCOME TO THE… "FAMILY"

"The wedding is off," the very disappointed voice of my brother sounded on the other end of the line. I was still living in South Africa at the time.

"Dad won't come if you and Lee attend the wedding. So, I don't know what to do. I am calling it off." He continued.

Probably smart on my dad's part. I wasn't sure I'd be able to keep myself from giving his wife a piece of my mind given half the chance. I've fantasized about it so many times.

In all seriousness, I had repeatedly told my brother I'd keep my distance from both my dad and his wife at the wedding, and meant it. Although I was the one who was abused, although I was the one he left to fend for herself at fifteen – I was being the bigger person saying I'd be at the wedding and keep the peace for my brothers' sake – but my dad just couldn't do the same. It took my brother some time, but he finally came to the realization that my dad was the unreasonable one in the epidemic, the only one between us all who was selfish – but my brother has a way of being objective in situations, I think we are alike like that – he is seven years older than I am but celebrates his birthday the day before mine, we're both Libra's – the Scales of Justice personified.

Flash-forward a couple of years – 2019 - my brother was finally going through with the wedding, and told my dad that he is putting my sisters and I first. My dad was invited but not given any say over the guest list. He still insisted he wouldn't be there if any of us sisters were – lucky for him, but to my brother's detriment – not one of us three sisters could be there. I was stuck in New York, Lee in Durban and Leslie in Uganda – it was so hard not to be able to be there to see my brother tie the knot. He wanted me to sing their wedding song.

My brother wasn't able to attend my sister's wedding years ago either – so there was no bad blood between us siblings. We were used to having to celebrate big life events without each other around. I guess my dad looked like the hero in the story when he cut his work trip in Iraq short to attend the wedding none of us sisters showed up for.

On the morning of the big day, I sent my sister-in-law-to-be a message on Facebook. I'd only met her three times in the decade they've been together for, but I thought she was absolutely lovely and I knew that she was just the right fit for my big brother.

"Hey sis-in-law-to-b…"
(I hit delete)

"Hey hun, welcome to the fami…"
(I hit delete)

"Welcome to what god damned family?" I asked myself out loud and shook my head.

I could say those words to her but knew full well they were a lie, empty. I tried to imagine my dad saying those words to her – welcome to the family - he probably did.

It took me half an hour to find the words to say to her, half an hour to type two sincere sentences. Because the truth was there was no family to welcome her into. Each one of us is either scattered around the globe, or not worthy of the word family – so I wasn't going to pretentiously say that phrase – welcome to the family - as if it had any meaning to it.

I checked Facebook the whole weekend through for wedding photos – but they didn't show up on my newsfeed somehow. My sister finally sent them to me over text. I had to sit down. I knew it was going to be hard for me to see, but I didn't know how hard.

It cut deep, seeing my dad there next to my brother, laughing microphone in hand giving a speech to the guests – what does he know about his own son? What does he know about raising kids? I was infuriated that he was given the privilege of being there, never mind the privilege to open his goddamned mouth to say some words.

He is so old now. His hair white; not grey. I wondered how many days he had left in him and if they would run out before I ever had the chance to look him in the eye again and ask him "why."

The hardest part was, wanting to hate my dad so bad, but just being unable to. If I couldn't hate him, was I supposed to hate my brother instead? Hold his relationship with my dad against him because he still has him in his life even though he knows what my dad did to me, to all of us?

Maybe it was jealousy - seeing my dad show up for my brother but not for me? I was coming up with so many reasons, trying to hate them both.

My head and heart weren't on the same page. My brother had only been good to me, especially since my move to New York; our relationship was the strongest it had ever been. We weren't estranged anymore; we called each other every other week and sometimes talked for an hour. Still, everything inside told me to just disappear from his life, because being in it hurt too much.

I decided not to make any rash decisions, and only talked to him about my feelings months later, not attacking him, just saying how hard it was for me to deal with the fact that he has a relationship with my dad. I told him that I love him and that deep down I didn't blame him for the way anything turned out to be, that I wanted to him to have our dad in his life even if I couldn't.

He told me he would always take my side over my dads' even though he doesn't know the full extent of what went wrong between us.

I know it can't be easy for my brother to be caught in the middle, he feels some sort of responsibility to "unite the family again" someday. I told him not to put that type of pressure on himself, I said that things would probably never change and he shouldn't carry the weight of that burden around with him.

My brother wanted me to tell him what had happened between my dad and I - when I was ready to; tell him about what happened to me under my dad's watch – but I can't get myself to, because I know I would do so wanting my brother to finally hate my dad for it, and I believe that I have no right to do that, feel that way, act that way. No matter how mad I get, when I am still with myself, I always decide that I have no right to influence the way my brother experiences our dad in his life – it's not for me to take that away from him, or change the way he sees my dad. That would make me as poisonous as my father, as stone cold – but sometimes I'm afraid that I already am.

CAN YOU KEEP A SECRET?
(Poetry & Prose)

"Can you keep a secret? I was in the car and something on the radio reminded me of grandpa and I felt so sad that he doesn't want to be in my life. Why doesn't he want to be in my life?" Said my eleven-year-old nephew on the phone to me today about my dad. I told him that I am sad about it too.

I forgave my dad for abandoning me for the last ten years, but today was hard to feel so forgiving towards him, hearing my nephew go through the same emotions I went through.

I don't know how one person chooses to cause this much pain. I don't really know why this type of thing happens. But maybe it happens, so we can decide, consciously, wholeheartedly, to never be like him.

COMMON GROUND

"When you were little did you guys ever drive one of those beat-up Jetta's too?" Pieter asked as we walked along the Jersey City pier, each drinking a $6 Strarbucks cappuccino on the way to our $300 excursion we spontaneously booked after spotting jet-skis on the Hudson from my rooftop. "Yes we had one! It backfired all the time!" I laughed.

"Ours too!" he laughed back at me.

It was the first time I could have an honest conversation with someone my age in New York. Pieter didn't only share my South African roots. We both grew up poor, abused and neglected by our parents. It gave us all the more reason to enjoy the hell out of our adventures in New York together, sharing the sentiment of having escaped our unfortunate circumstances, having made something out of ourselves.

Being able to exchange stories and laugh about our messed up childhoods together was medicine.

We dried off after our jet-ski adventure and made our way back to his place in Eastchester.

I promised his husband that I wasn't looking around when they let me into their apartment to go pee. Brandon dimmed the lights and carried on apologizing for the mess. "I swear, I'm not looking!" I laughed out as I held my hands around the sides of my face as if to focus only on the steps ahead of me I needed to take to get to the bathroom.

While I was emptying my bladder I kept thinking about the half-eaten box of chock-chip cookies I saw on their couch in the living room. And how even though I swore that "I wasn't looking" - I was, in fact, looking.

After washing my hands, I walked straight past them to the box with the blue rapper. "I hope you don't mind but I can't remember the last time I had a chock-chip cookie" I explained whilst simultaneously stuffing my cheeks - figuring that, asking for forgiveness has always been easier than asking for permission – as the saying goes.

And I think I have been doing that with my life for a long time. Taking my chances and playing dumb, taking the air that I breathe for granted, but for once in my life, I really just needed to.

Because before life was better, it was a whole lot harder. And the harder the circumstances were, the easier it was to play the wild card, and I hit the jackpot a couple of times, and I've lost all of my chips a couple of times too.

I never meant to gamble with these hundred years I've been given; the truth is it's all I've ever known. Taking chances. I don't take them because I feel like having a bit of excitement in my life, a change of scenery, no. I take chances because it's all I have, it's my only ticket out of here, it's been my only option for so long and I don't even have to think about it, think about the risks involved, for the risks of what could go wrong, is as high as the risk of not taking a chance, and staying in a bad place, in anyway, and I think that would be worse.

Brandon and Pieter wouldn't let me leave their apartment until I agreed to put the half-a-box of chock chip cookies into my backpack for my train ride back home. And as I sat there on the Metro-North, stuffing them down my throat one by one, I thought of all the people who stuffed their unwanted opinions of me down my throat. Their opinions of my dating life, and career choices, and their attacks on my soul. And I thought about how they threw me out of their lives the same way I threw that empty cookie box into the trash when I was done with it. But I didn't think about it for very long. The train stopped and I made my way through Grand Central to the subway station to take the 2-Train downtown, back home.

And it's kind of strange how used to it I am, the hoards of people streaming past me, on their way somewhere like I am. And in school, I used to walk around the perimeters by myself until the bell rang to start the day. I had social anxiety as

258

a kid that was never addressed or treated or even acknowledged. It is only now, that I am much older and can cope, that I take the time to deal with the things no one had the time to help me through.

Maybe that's why I feel so at home in this city of orphans, I don't have to explain anything to anyone about why I don't have parents, because, this city does not exactly have the type of dating scene where you will ever have to worry about meeting anyone's parents in anyway.

And I think they all do. They all walk around this city with their headphones in, blocking the outside world out completely in order to cope, the same way I walked myself around those schoolyard perimeters anxiety-ridden.

My body must have clicked that I was in midtown before I even really put any thought into it, because I started singing out loud to the music in my headphones. I walked isle to isle from Grand Central to the subway trains and I sang at the top of my voice how I used to last year when I spent a lot of time in Times Square.

Because everyone is wearing headphones too, I can sing at the top of my voice in a room full of strangers and no one would hear me, look at me, or even notice that I was there, and if the odd person did notice me, it was no big deal, because this place is filled with crazies, doing what I do and worse. No one would stare at me for long; it's kind of standard here. There's at least one crazy person per train who is doing something absolutely absurd, speaking to themselves, shouting at strangers, begging for money or dancing around content and happy. And I wanted to feel that liberated tonight, that shameless, and I did. I do.

People back home tell me all the time to loosen up, to have more fun, but they have never lived here, they have never lived my life, but I have been trying to be more open.

And I've sat in conversations with born and bred New Yorkers my age here, and just known with my whole being that most of my peers here don't get me at all. Making peace with the fact that they have picture perfect memories of their childhoods, and knowing that I hardly have the guts to visit that place in my mind most nights – making peace with that, is on me, and I am getting there but, when they look at me like that, when I'm the only one in the group who doesn't have a house in the Hamptons for summer like the rest of them, that's on them. I sit there and take the condescending entitled blows, and I could open my mouth and paint the picture to them of exactly how much it took for me to make my way this far, and sleep in a warm bed, with a full tummy, clothes on my back and wifi for my phone, in this room on the 12th floor in an apartment 2 blocks away from the One World Trade Center Freedom tower. I almost wish I could help them understand how fast I've had to run up hills and through fires to have this tonight, and how it is a miracle, but they have a house in the Hamptons for the summer so my achievements pale in comparison to theirs, even though they don't know that we were never running in the same race, and not competing for the same prize.

And all these things, they don't make me feel bad, they don't make me feel like the victim, I am so grateful that all I've ever known is running, and jumping without looking, unafraid of falling because I know I'll be there to catch myself, hold my own hand. Temporary loneliness is real, sadness is real, but when I look at the last year, it's all a win in the bigger picture. I see one massive win and I am happy, overjoyed, always celebrating.

Celebrating because when everyone told me to play it safe and go for option "F" on my list of career choices, I ignored them. They said it's the way it's done, and that I wouldn't want to fail and that I should forget about my option A and B's because they were just too risky.

You know what? You know what scares me more than failing at my option A's and B's on my list? Winning at option F and being miserable as fuck in anyways, because it's not my passion. THAT is what scares me. And even though they are the ones who have never known what it means to go to bed hungry, they are the ones I feel sorry for, because while they're out hustling in their blue suits to make their parents happy, I'm the lucky one who don't have parents I have to please, parents I have to be scared of letting down. Nothing to lose if I fail at my plan A's and B's.

And I think that when you can be that real with yourself, when you can be that ignorant towards the option of failing, ignorant of what others think is best for you, when you can play dumb and take chances despite the fact that you're walking on thin ice, that's when the magic happens.

"I never thought I'd live to see this" Pieter texted. He sent me a news clip of a hospitalized man begging for help to afford treatment after a heart attack. It was his dad.

"I just want to get better so I can work and earn money to take care of my family" he cried in broken English.

"TAKE CARE OF HIS FAMILY?" I shouted angered over a phone call with Pieter.

I couldn't believe the words coming out of the mouth of the man I was told abused and neglected Pieter as a child. At sixteen, Pieter boarded a three hour bus ride to Sun City after school everyday to work and provide for his family when his parents failed to.

"TAKE CARE OF HIS FAMILY?" I shouted again.

"What are you going to do?" I asked.

He showed me the messages from his dad. He was on his deathbed and asking for forgiveness. And money.

The thing about being an abused child is that, no matter the hate in your heart, some part of you will always love your parent, and I understood that better than anyone else in Pieter's life.

It is almost unreal that us two kids with the background we share - now live close to perfect lives in New York, with amazing people around us.

But when you least expect it – sometimes just for a split second - you still miss your incompetent parents. You still miss the broken home you grew up in, as shitty as it was. And the picture perfect world you live in now, it pales in comparison for a moment, and you almost wish you could go back. And then you hate yourself for thinking that. You hate yourself for still loving them.

"I'm not gonna do anything. I'm just ignoring his messages." Pieter calmly replied. But I knew just how tormenting it must be to get an apology now. To know his dad is dying now.

I always imagined I would be in his shoes, that my dad would be the one eating humble pie on his deathbed and I'd be the one not giving him the chance to make his peace. I envied Pieter for getting to experience that unintended revenge. And then I started asking myself if it would really make me feel any better if I were in his shoes, because I stared at the expressions on his face every time we spoke about it, and he didn't look much happier after getting that apology from his dad in anyway.

UNINTENDED REVENGE
(Poetry & Prose)

And I think it's better than a one-night-stand, better than fame, better than being out-of-your-mind-drunk on a Friday night. Because when you're airborne at sixty five miles per hour and ignoring the possibility that your wrist might be fractured after hitting that wave so hard, and you're laughing from the adrenaline and yelling out "go faster!" - that's when you feel what being alive really feels like. And you feel it in your bones, and in the leg muscles you didn't know you had until your only option of staying aboard, was clenching your thighs together around the jet ski so tight that you might have peed yourself a couple of times. And there's a taste of blood in your mouth because you bit your tongue upon impact - and you know what? It tastes good. It tastes like you're fighting for your life, and that's when you see yourself clearly. When you know that something could go wrong at any given moment and you might not make it out in one piece. And you ask yourself if you are happy about what you did with your twenty-five years if you were to breathe your last breath today. And I hear that my dad was a parachute instructor in the Special Forces for years, and I think if he took the time to sit down and talk to me about what it felt like every time that he jumped, he would be surprised just how much we are alike. But for now I am a distant memory of a little girl he used to know, which he only had patience for until I was big enough to talk and make my mind up for myself, became too much work, too hard to love.

And the only time he makes time to see me, is when he switches on the TV, or reads about me in magazines. Only brave enough to peek into my world when he has the power to turn the volume down or close the book when what I have to say is no longer relevant to him. And I have peace with the fact that he prefers it that way. I think the biggest revenge is, me choosing to be happy - and THIS ALIVE - anyway.

261

AMOR FATI

(Amor Fati, Latin phrase: a love of fate, or in simpler terms, to accept and love everything that happens.)

I walked into my five star hotel room. The TV and complimentary iPad read "Welcome to Surfside, Florida Ms. Lyla Illing" on the homepage. "So this is what it feels like to be treated like the music legend that I am," I smirked for a moment – only, the royal treatment had nothing to do with my talents – I was on a workation, traveling with my host family, doing my own thing during the day and babysitting for them at night.

It was a perfect reflection of the past four years working in radio in South Africa, and then as an au pair in America. I lay on the California King bed in white sheets, opening and shutting the window wall's blinds with the remote in my hand. I lay there taking in the Miami views thinking about everything I ever dreamt of doing. I got the chance to be part of each of those things but in different ways than I anticipated I would. Through my job as a radio producer, I met every one of my South African music influences and every other media personality and celebrated person I grew up worshiping – only I was part of the team interviewing them for work purposes. I wasn't collaborating with them personally creatively – the only way I ever imagined I'd have met all of the people I got to.

Being a junior radio producer for some of South Africa's biggest household names broadened my horizons, in almost frightfully massive ways. Frightening, not because I was amongst my heroes daily, interviewing and interacting with the most talented and celebrated legends – that part came naturally to me. What frightened me was that after two years I realized I was sitting on the wrong side of the mixing desk, writing the interview questions, instead of being the one who was being interviewed.

My feelings stemmed less out of the celebrity status equation and more out of the deep realization that I was spending all of my time contributing to everyone else's careers instead of spending my time being creative in my own right.

As for my cultural-exchange-visitor life in America, I had found a lifestyle in which I had the time and resources to pursue my personal creative goals actively, but was experiencing New York and LA and every other place as just another tourist or visitor so to speak – not what I had pictured. Moving to New York being my first ever trip abroad – I was sort of thrown in the deep end and was a tourist by default because I didn't ever have the opportunity to travel before. Navigating this new life was hard, and I was hard on myself for it - could hardly enjoy every excursion I went on without guilt tripping myself for being out and about instead of knocking on record label's doors every free moment I had.

I was moving very slow in terms of connecting with the right people, hadn't been networking as much as I should have – and every concert I attended that wasn't my own, felt like a punishment for not working hard enough. Sitting in the audience at Madison Square Garden once, was being in the audience and not on stage, one time too many. I wanted to be on bigger stages than the open mic nights were getting me onto – and I wanted it now, yet, not in an impatient way, just an urgent calling.

Moving – and staying in New York was no small task, I went through some tough times emotionally, and was overwhelmed at other times not knowing how to get my priorities straight.

Although I was always aware of the fact that I had traded in my radio career for "just another day job" playing with bubble guns and dealing with toddler tears – I wasn't sad about it. I embraced it as an incredible opportunity - having my whole day for my own creative projects before working the live-in-au-pair-job in the evenings. The job came easy to me and with so little interest in going out clubbing or any other nonsense, it was easy for me to build up a good relationship with my hosts and be on call whenever they needed me. Reflecting on my life, I had only had one single year I remembered as "a good year" out of all twenty-six –and it was my year with Neil at age twenty-two. But twenty-six, it was finally another "good year" – one that topped them all. That being said, living this nomad-au pair lifestyle, I keep hearing Dido's lyrics repeating in the back of my mind… "If my life, is for rent, and I don't learn to buy – then I deserve nothing more than I get, because nothing I have is truly mine."

I'd lie if I said I didn't know my life would be of this nature, all along – I always felt it would, since the day I left my dad's home - age fifteen. I was aware of the fact that I didn't have what my peers had – stability, support, the same opportunities as a result. I was aware of those things but decided to see them in a not-so-harmful way. I rather looked at it, knowing I would have to work a lot harder, find a lot of loopholes, would have to do things differently than everyone else in order to catch up to my peers so I could stand a chance at being someone. Living that TV show -"Shameless" - type of lifestyle, it always seemed exciting in a way – I did like the challenge and being able to say; "hey everybody look at me, I'm a little different than the rest of you. Peh weh."

It's the reason I didn't think twice to start working as a waitress at sixteen so I could complete school when my dad stopped paying tuition, it's the reason I figured I'd work in radio in order to I find a way to break into the music world, it's the reason I felt no shame working as an au pair (and in some cases the help) if it meant I'd have the opportunity to experience and try to conquer America. There's always been method to the madness. I guess that sometimes I just get so ahead of myself that I forget I meant for it all to be this way – that I chose it.

I grabbed the iPad next to my bed that could probably sleep five.

"Welcome to Surfside, Florida Ms. Lyla Illing."

I clicked through the room service menu when my shuffled play-list spat out a Mike Posner song. I had been listening to his album "At Night, Alone." heavily the past few months in New York. I liked having it on repeat for my morning CitiBike cycle around the tip of the island, starting on the West side from

Rockefeller Park ending up at the helipads on the East side. I liked docking my bike there and sending Yvette podcast-length voice notes over the "chop, chop, chop" of the helicopter blade noises. But I always ended up losing network and with no phone to distract me, no Yvette to spill my guts to, I'd cry a few tears along to the Mike Posner album, helping me to go through all the motions of dealing with the depression brought on by the contrasts I was experiencing in my life.

When my move from South Africa to New York was confirmed, one of the first things I did was Google Mike's tour dates. He played a show in New York the same weekend I arrived to the states – it was too chaotic for me to make it. I was so bummed when he stopped touring shortly after that and I eventually gave up on looking up his concert dates because there were never any, coming up.

I ordered the cheapest thing off the iPad menu - the $48 Wagyu beef burger, which turned into a seventy-something-dollar-meal after taxes and service fees. I had a hard time wrapping my head around my current situation with currency. I couldn't stop thinking about how I used to do a monthly grocery shop in South Africa, barely scraping together that same $48 – so many times. The contrast didn't make me feel happy nor sad, just puzzled with questions regarding all the contrasting experiences I've lived through in my young life. I welcomed the distraction when I realized I hadn't checked Mike's concert dates in a year. I was still listening to his music but had no idea what he was up to lately, so I started a search on the Internet.

Still no concert dates, but up popped a string of YouTube videos labeled "Amor Fati Application" – Mike had started a yearly one-week mentorship program for aspiring artists, and I missed the very first program that took place earlier in 2018. I couldn't believe I didn't know about it. In 2017 I cold-emailed my song "Bodega Raffy" to an email address I found for him, in the hopes of being mentored – so I was just about kicking myself for having missed this information.

Applications for the 2019 scholarship weren't open yet – in fact, they were still four months away, but with my million-dollar-burger in one hand, and the hotel pencil in the other, I started jotting down notes, putting together my application game plan late into the morning hours, with Miami's skyscraper-lights winking at me through my hotel window-wall – my only company.

I found myself watching every 2018 scholarship application video – obsessively. Vetting each applicant, trying to suss where I stood in comparison to them – if I had done more work or less, if I had more talent or not. I guess I was just trying to see if I even stood a chance with the competition. Eventually I realized how much time I'd spent doing this, and took a break to visit Miami Bayside where I got on a speedboat – my favorite thing to do when exploring a new place.

Back in New York City just in time for Christmas celebrations, I left my bags unpacked for days as per usual, but one specific piece of paper, crumpled and tucked between my luggage - had me tossing and turning for nights until I finally gave in, switched my lights back on and pulled my Amor Fati notes out of my suitcase, brushing the beach sand off them.

I printed out information on all the coaches and the class of 2018, and started following their respective journeys on social media. Some part of me couldn't wait six months for the opportunity to start learning from these folks - if I got into the program. I wanted to start learning from them right away, and so I did, almost subconsciously so.

I emailed the five musicians who made out the class of 2018, asking to be considered as an opening act if they play in New York City. Their growth after attending Amor Fati was obvious, I fell in love with their music more than I intended to – Mike chose well. And so, I made myself part of these new artists' worlds – even if that meant just being part of the Dwilly, Myylo, Valentina fan club – I was learning from them, making notes on the venues they played, the press they spoke to, the order in which they released singles. I also related so much to Alex Banayan's book "The Third Door" and started following his journey as an author.

Even though I was observing - more than interacting with this group of people, I felt like surrounding myself with their stories had me carving out a new world for myself and the way I saw my place in it. It's like I blinked and all of a sudden my mindset had changed, I entered one of the most inspiring phases of my life in ways that kept me up till 3am night after night.

Christmas blurred into a very rainy New Years Eve. I didn't watch the Times Square ball drop with Ryan Seacrest, on TV this time, neither was I in the crowd – I was in my room behind my desk brainstorming 2018 into 2019. Sometime after the fireworks died down past midnight, I took a break from my desk to take in the moment, hug 2019 hello. All the party boats on the Hudson moved in one direction past my window - left to right – a very unusual sight to see being used to constant two way traffic on the water all year round. Their lights were dim in the foggy rain weather, for a moment I felt like the city was a ghost town, as if I was the only one in the entire world witnessing the fleet of boats float by in front of the Jersey City backdrop and disappear up the west river – something out of a movie scene. I didn't want to be anywhere else but right there, alone in my room, smiling a 4am-goodbye to the boats, to return to the pen and paper on my desk eagerly waiting for me to breathe more ideas out of them.

From the very first week of January, I made Monday my new favorite day of the week by booking recording time at Lounge Studios (aka Atlantic Records Recording Studios) once a week for the next four months. Each week started with a two-hour visit to the studio and a bit of banter with my new "best friend" – Joseph, keeper of every one of my good - as well as flat (deleted) vocal takes - the sound engineer and only familiar face I saw often during that time of my life.

I already had a bit of radio play in South Africa, a handful of original songs on my iTunes and Spotify and YouTube platforms, but wanted my Amor Fati application to be as strong as possible so decided to record (almost) every song I'd ever written, I also figured by doing that, I'd be able to tell the good ones from the bad and decide which ones to use in my application. With recording on Mondays out of the way, I used the rest of each week to categorize the songs into who they were written about and released them as EPs accordingly. I made a lyric video to get each one of the songs onto YouTube and sent them out to my friends and the media via my weekly email newsletter. This was my routine, week in and week out until I wasn't seeing any of my friends anymore, not even watching TV. I didn't mean for it to happen that way.

In February I had the apartment to myself for five days, which meant no interaction with another human being other than the under-my-breath hello to the doorman the one time I went out for fresh air. I hadn't responded to any of my friends or love-interests' messages for weeks, and didn't want to start now. Part of me started seeing my social life as a distraction so I opted for not having one. By day two, the silence echoing the picture perfect, empty place I called home - was deafening, and unexpectedly drove me into a depressed state. I wondered if it was time to reply to some texts, time for company, but I decided "no, not like this."

I felt, almost, in pain – being alone, and wanted to get to the bottom of "why" even though I had no idea how to. I kept waiting for the heaviness on my heart to disappear magically, but it didn't. I felt confused, disorientated in trying to answer the questions – "who is Lyla these days, and what is this thing that's goddamned-near killing her?"

Since I moved to New York, spending time alone was my new normal, but I always had people around in the house in the other room – who I knew was "there." So, being completely alone, with no one around to wear a mask for, with no one to have to keep my shit together around – I lost it. Not even the throwing of paint onto canvasses calmed my mind.

All my Amor Fati research saw me stumbling across Mike's podcast, I was aware of his guided meditation clips but hadn't listened to them yet. I decided to pull one up there and then – day three of being alone, somewhere around 4pm. I dragged out one of the dining room table chairs, plugged my headsets in and tried mediation with his voice as guidance.

At first, all the meditation-session felt like was more silence, and I wasn't sure how much more dead air I could handle. In radio I was trained to start counting the seconds out loud if we were off the air due to technical difficulties – the bigger the amount of seconds of silence you counted, the bigger trouble it meant you were in. Everything in me fought the quiet.

Then I heard background noises in the silence - the beeping of a construction site miles away, the whooshing of an airplane in the sky. The silence wasn't so empty anymore. The sounds drifted around me like clouds – like he said they would. I acknowledged them – I hadn't for months.

With the symphony of sounds faded in the distance, I found a place for me to acknowledge my own presence, too – I hadn't for months. I smile-cried when I realized that. It was both bitter and sweet – a tragedy that I'd been living past myself for so long, but a hopeful wish for it to happen less.

Acknowledging my own presence felt as jaw dropping as the spiritual awakening I experienced when at the tender age of ten, I saw my mom lifeless. And it felt as urgent as the spiritual awakening I experienced when I left home at fifteen after telling my step mom for the first and only time that she will never lay a hand on me again. And sitting on that dining room chair in that empty Manhattan apartment alone, there was no one belting me through the face I had to run away from, no one I had to witness breathe out their last breath of air – but I still felt some sort of tragedy before I saw the light at the end of the tunnel. I felt something die and something begin within me by the end of the meditation clip.

I have found that once you have that kind of awakening, it is in no way the end of your troubles, but more often the start of hard but worth-wile work, a daily commitment to get to know yourself again, adjust to what you thought you knew about your world and how much control you have over your circumstances.

A bit like how I felt on my twenty-sixth birthday when I accepted that I was responsible for my own reality, and felt like I chose every moment consciously – that the good and the bad, was all a result of my own choices.

I started thinking about things differently. Like my dad not being in my life – I felt that even though he was the one who threw me away; every day I chose to stay in New York and carried on with my life, was another day I decided not to fly back to South Africa, track him down until I stood in front of him and asked him the questions I had been wanting to – whether or not I'd find the answers I was looking for, whether or not him and I could find a way to make peace and be in each others lives again. It was as much my actions as it was his that resulted to us being estranged today – although no parent should ever abandon their child, I decided to look at things objectively. Not excusing his behavior, but not hating him for not putting his life on hold to try and fix things between us when I wasn't either.

Taking responsibility for every situation in my life, good or bad, made me feel in charge of it too, and that was a feeling of hopefulness I got to walk around with in my pocket.

In the questionnaire section of my application for the music scholarship, I had to answer questions like "what do you hope to learn during your time at the academy?" and "what are your career goals?" My answers didn't come down to a simple "it would be a great opportunity to be part of the program." No. I saw myself viciously clear when writing out my responses. I saw what I wanted for my future in the finest detail – which skills I wanted to acquire, and I realized where my songs belong. Because when writing out my application - I listed all the charities I performed for, for the first time. Before that moment, I didn't realize that I had made charities a priority in my music ventures until I saw how long my list was. I liked realizing that being a music volunteer was important to me. And for the first time, I said out loud "I want to have a song on Grey's Anatomy" – and writing that down in my application sparked my interest in exploring the field of film scoring.

An unusual feeling came over me when I paused before clicking to submit my application. It was March second, four months since I first learned about the academy. I looked back at how much work I had done since December, in an attempt to be one of the best applicants amongst my peers. The research and networking I'd done, the new connections I made, the thirty songs I recorded and released, and how through the process of producing all those songs, I slowly but surely learned to turn my acoustic songs into songs with stronger production, the number one thing I wanted help with if I got into the academy.

I looked at that "submit" button, shaking my head as new conclusions formed in my mind. I smiled wholeheartedly when I clicked it because I realized that the process of wanting to get into Amor Fati pushed me to grow, pushed me to walk a new path in my music ventures already. Whether or not I was going to get in, I felt like I had already won, I felt like the purpose was already served, I felt like Mike already mentored me. Although I could mentally see myself "sitting next to people I don't know around an open flame" in the mountains of Telluride, being mentored by them – I understood for the first time that in my particular journey, it wasn't about actually getting to do that, it was about wanting to. Picturing myself successful in music, a good enough musician worthy of such mentorship – changed me.

I decided that no matter the result, no matter whether or not I got in, I wanted to make peace with the fact that the process of pursuing that goal made me a better human being and musician already – and I'd like to believe that it did. After submitting the application, I managed to sleep properly for the first time since the whole thing started keeping me up in January.

Back in Miami vacationing with Yvette that April, I was truly in love with my fate when I opened an email that read the academy was cancelled for the year due to Mike's foot injury delaying the start of his walk across America leaving them with no choice but to cancel the program for 2019.

I was at peace because I knew I didn't put my soul on hold waiting for that email to say whether or not I got it, waiting for that chance to learn from the coaches – how that waiting would have been in vain, and that was a lesson in itself I didn't want to forget. I was in love with the choice I made to already start learning from them, the moment I decided I wanted to apply in December. The Amor Fati tribe was in my life for five months already, I felt like I didn't lose anything by the 2019 program having been cancelled. I was thankful for feeling that way about it too. I said to Yvette "hey, leave me alone for half an hour." I decided to celebrate the Amor Fati tribe's energy that was with me, with a meditation-session in the slap-bang-middle of South Beach.

Music from yachts in the distance and the sounds of beach balls being banged back and forth – floated like clouds around me as my higher self thanked the coaches for the things they let me learn from them already, unknowingly. And for a split second I thought, maybe I'll go walk a few miles across America with Mike, and maybe I'll get to tell him about the things he taught me after all.

LYLA WHO BELONGS TO EVERYBODY (AND HAS NO ONE)

"This is a nice place." I said as he reached for my hand from across the table in some pasta place in the East Village.

"I'm just trying to get you into bed." he laughed, and I coughed on the half-a-mouth full of gin and tonic I somehow managed to not spit out, being caught off-guard.

"I'm just trying to crack you up." He continued, and I gulped my drink down faster but it just didn't get me as drunk as I needed to be, for that to be funny, or charming.

I wondered how Brian and I made it to our fifth date with nothing else in common other than both being musicians.

We stopped at a French place for some wine after our dinner-date, and I really thought I fell for him that time. Being with him, was like floating on your back in the ocean. Calm, fine. And then every now and again a wave would throw you off and it was kind of fun to get thrown around, you'd laugh a little bit. There were moments he'd look at me and I felt a butterfly in my tummy, but only one. Riding the wave was not worth the mouthful of seawater I swallowed and the handful of sand in my bikini bottoms I had to empty out when the fun was over.

We left the bar and tried to get a cab, but it was raining and they were all taken. Eventually we got onto the subway. Seated with our arms interlocked, we were laughing about something - God knows what – when I threw my head up and my eyes interlocked with the letters on the billboard above me.

"FUCK ME." I said before I could stop myself, while staring at it. The words fell out of my mouth like it completely bypassed my though system - out loud and in the tone of someone who had just accepted defeat. "FUCK ME."

"Is everything okay?" he asked. I told him it was just cool to see a billboard with an ad of a friends' lingerie company. I couldn't exactly tell him that I was upset for seeing Willem 2.0's company ad hang above my head as if it was there with the sole purpose of dragging my soul out. Out of all the subway lines and subway cars I could possibly get into on a Friday night, it had to be the one that had my French fuckboy's branding plastered all over it. I had just started to get over his hot and cold motions with me, why did I have to be reminded? At that moment I was happy to have Brian's hand to hold – anyone's hand to hold.

This poor guy I was on a date with really wasn't winning with me – my heart was somewhere else.

I saw Willem 2.0's name pop up in my social media notifications four times in the next week, received a few steamy texts from him out of nowhere again, and you know what I thought? I thought that we might actually be the generation of lovers with the least guts in history. We can't give someone up 100%, even when we've walked away from them. And maybe following them online is a way of convincing ourselves that our hearts aren't quite THAT broken, because, we still have "access" to that person, right?

And I bet he thinks he does. Thinks that he still has access to me and I wonder if that makes him feel good. He didn't want me but he spends Sunday clicking through my profiles and stories for a play-by-play of my day. They all do. They didn't want me but they keep an eye just to make sure they are not missing anything.

Does it make them feel better? To see what I am doing now? And text me "congrats" because they (in their words) "briefly" saw my achievement online, making sure to let me know I happened to randomly slide up their screen "briefly" along with twelve other more interesting posts and now they feel the need to downplay it so that they don't come across as "too interested." Do they look at my profile and think, "yeah I made the right choice back then by being a dick, I still wouldn't want her, but let me click through it anyway."

And I used to be with a man who convinced me that exes could and should be friends, until I was his ex. Then he saw for himself that being my friend was a bad idea, because he kept on telling me that I was the exception and that it will always be me for him. So I get it, I get that it works for some people to stay on each other's social media and for some people it doesn't. And I let Neil say what he needs to say to me, because it was 3 years, it was real, it's not like he got bored and broke my heart on purpose after 3 dates. And we have a friendship, and he calls me on my birthday.

But now? Right now I have to stare at the names of six guys that I "kind of" know, I've "kind of" been intimate with over the last year, I "kind of" am pissed off at for playing me and ghosting me after I thought we were dating, after I bought a new dress I wanted to wear on our next date and he stood me up. I have to deal with the reminder of six guys who rejected me. Because it's a reminder each time they insert themselves into my notifications on social media that THEY DIDN'T LIKE ME ENOUGH to see me again. Don't you think it's a little spineless to hit the "like" button on social media now? Now that I've gotten past your rejection, now that I moved on?

Living my "I love my fate" and "I accept and love everything that happens" life wasn't working out for me so well anymore. I didn't feel in control of anything when all the love interests I'd had in the past years decided to all come at me at once – wanting access to me but not wanting me exclusively.

Brian and Willem 2.0 aside, Sam who cheated on me as I was about to leave South Africa for the states, still called me awake some days to tell me he still thought of me and missed me – all while he was still with that same girl he dumped me for. I couldn't find it in me to reject his calls, I still thought of him and missed him too after all this time.

Then a friend I made the news with, wanted to do a lot more work together. He often asked me to move to LA, spent hours on the phone with me on Saturday nights – but I only wanted to work with him if he was my boyfriend – and I was clear about that. I wasn't ready to put my energy behind someone else's career other than my own - like I did in South Africa. I couldn't always read the

270

situation but just felt like he wanted too much of me creatively, emotionally, on his terms – although he never did me wrong, what he was doing wasn't right either.

I thought I could handle all of this, have them all in my life - accept every situation for what it was. For a while I had peace with the fact that none of them were my boyfriend but that we still cared for each other and that it was okay for us to be in each other's lives, steal a secret glance and secretly feel a butterfly now and again. I tried to do what I thought I did best – pretend that I was okay with being "Lyla who never gets mad at anybody, Lyla who always says let's try again."

My make-believe front crumbled down when then the one person I love having around the most, the one person I didn't have to be afraid of losing, my best friend in New York – decided to randomly kiss me while we were out singing karaoke one night.

All of a sudden we were both confused about what we wanted from each other, our once – simple friendship turned into "terms and conditions" discussions and then the words - the final blow that knocked me down - fell from his mouth "I want you to be part of everything I do but I'd be lying if I said I was irrevocably in love with you."

I had enough.

Enough of being Lyla who belonged to everybody.

Lyla who belonged to men across the globe but had no one to hold.

Lyla who belonged to the media, or sold myself to it.

Lyla who belonged to my mentors, some of who'd like to believe I learned from them when they learned from me.

Lyla who belonged to all the strangers who raised me as their own, I forever felt I owed a debt to.

Lyla who belonged to every person who was a mom or dad to me in bad ways and in good.

I used to take pride in belonging to everybody. But then he said those words, and for just a moment - belonging to everybody was the most painful thing in the world. I had enough of being everyone's "very own Lyla" and feeling like I had nothing to show for it.

I felt delusional, could hardly type through the shaking or make out the letters on the screen through the tears. I searched up every man in my phone book's number and blocked them, deleted them – on social media too. Not every one of them deserved that. I lost some friends I'd never get back in the process. I ripped them from my life, one by one, like ripping off band-aids that had been stuck to my open wounds for too long, almost one with my skin, infected. The pain dizzied me as I pulled each one of them off of me, but when it was over, my wounds could breathe, and so could I.

ENGLISH
(Poetry & Prose)

I believe in loving many people
Sometimes, all of them at once
I don't know why they say it's a sin

I believe that I have been loved deeply
Without being explicitly told so
I don't know why not hearing it out loud, hurts though

I believe it's possible to speak without using words
So
I don't know why I'm so obsessed with English coming from his mouth
When I know I understand him without it, clearly

I believe we forget, often
The things we already know

I believe we don't always need words
But we're only human
And it's nice to hear them
Sometimes

Can you believe?
I'm so obsessed with hearing them in English from him, that when I don't - I
tell him that he is dead to me.

A SORE THROAT AND DEPRESSION

The good news is, I was unable to contain my laughter when the soccer ball
flicked up and hit the kid in the face and he fake fell into a fetal position on the
9am-dew-grass, where I was sitting cross-legged with a can of soda for breakfast
in one hand. I was taking in the morning sun, trying to figure out if I was hung
over or just happy after drinking alone the night before.

And I laughed, not because he fell, not because he got hurt, or because the
show he put on pretending that he was hurt was down right hilarious. No... I
laughed because life has hit me in the face the same way that soccer ball smacked
him, so many times. And I laughed because each time life punched me in the face
- it always happened when I least expected it to, when I thought I was having the
time of my life, the same way he was innocently running around enjoying his
soccer practice, moments before the unwelcome surprise.

And sometimes I do, I fake fall with my entire body weight onto the floor into a fetal position out of shock, and I lie there and cringe and feel sorry for myself and I don't know how to deal with it. The world stops for a second and I overreact in the pursuit of protecting myself, entertaining the absurd idea, that one punch in the face has the power of ruining me.

But I found out I was stronger than that when my wounds breathed and healed after I pulled the men from my life like old band-aids. I saw the world, and my place in it clearly again.

With my previous dick-distractions out of the way, I had my routine back, and also my dignity. I was meditating everyday. I spent my Mondays in the studio again, and whenever I missed one of the boys, I paused, acknowledged it and in my heart I wished them love and light, wished them well on their own personal journeys. I didn't hate any of them, I wasn't mad at any one of them – I just needed to be free from them.

I used my reclaimed freedom and reignited spark to take painting more seriously, I switched from acrylic to watercolor. My work started looking less like kids' drawings, so much so that I wrote and illustrated my first children's book that I went on to self-publish and sell hard copies of through Amazon.

National Crime Victims' Rights Week was coming up and WestCOP – the organization that helped me with my sexual assault recovery - invited me to perform at their annual art show again. I was rehearsing my songs when Tyrone - a friend from Durban reached out, voice noting me with a special request to write and record a wedding song for his special day. I could hardly wrap my head around the idea of someone thinking I was capable of doing any such thing, trusting me with such a big job.

"Don't people just use Ed Sheeran songs for weddings these days?" was my first thought. Maybe I was afraid to write about feelings I'd never had, or commitments I had never made. Maybe I was afraid to sing a wedding song because it reminded me of my mom singing at weddings when she was still alive. Maybe I was afraid to believe in love and marriage - to write about it while someone close to me had just signed divorce papers, and I had booted just about every man in my life out in an attempt to get as far away as possible from my own feelings.

But all my self-doubt aside, the only thing that scared me more than actually doing this, actually writing and recording this song, was the fear of looking back and regretting, NOT doing it. So, *I said yes.*

I asked all my friends on social media to comment their wedding songs I could listen to for inspiration, I studied the words, the melodies. I had to. I have never written a love song, a feel good happy song. I write when I'm sad, so writing a wedding song was complete new territory for me.

I started writing lyrics almost immediately, but every verse that spilled out of my pen onto paper sounded generic, like a lie, like something I knew nothing about and was obviously making up.

I got so frustrated trying to write the damn thing, I wanted to call Tyrone many times with a list of good Ed Sheeran song-suggestions as my sorry for saying "I can't write your wedding song."

On my way to the studio one Monday I walked past Tyler's office building in Times Square. I had a half hour to kill before my session started. The weather wasn't supposed to be that cold anymore but it was - still, I sat on a park bench and just looked at his building, shivering, wondering if I made a mistake for walking away the way I did. Our friendship didn't feel quite over but I brushed it off and went to go see the only man who had no impact on my emotions, a person I paid to spend time with me – Joseph the sound engineer. I recorded my song "27 Boxes" and a cover of Lady Gaga and Bradley Cooper's "Shallow" during which the thought of Tyler kept creeping in.

Back at the apartment I immersed myself in some quiet time, I envisioned him walking away and into the light during a meditation session. I was ready to let the memory of him go – completely.

Against all odds, my conjuring included - he found a way back into my life that very night. The conversation wasn't sunshine and roses, no part of speaking to him again was easy, but for some reason unknown to me – I wanted to try.

I agreed to dinner later that week, but when the time came to put my dress on and get in my silver carriage – I threw on a pair of sunglasses and flip-flops, walked myself to the convenience store for a bottle of Nyquil, the drowsy type. Medicine for a severe cold, but brought me temporary relief for a (not too) sore throat and depression – as tested by yours truly.

I couldn't get myself to choose between sticking to my quiet, safe, no distractions life, or seeing Tyler again, and risk losing all of that if things were to go wrong between us again. I was so afraid to lose my balance, but also afraid that I didn't have anything to offer him - I wasn't the same person I was the last time he saw me. I had no interest in giving my heart away again, at least not without putting up a fight first.

I canceled our dinner last minute, and felt like a bitch for it.

Conflicted and overwhelmed with emotion, I found the words I had been looking for, for so long, the words I'd never tell Tyler out loud - I wrote Tyrone's wedding song with them at 4pm that afternoon after which I knocked myself the fuck out with that bottle of Nyquil before the sun even thought about calling it a day – something I'm not proud of, but saved me from the voices in my head.

TYRONE'S WEDDING SONG
(Lyrics)

I want you to be happy
I want to say
I'll never get mad
But we both know that I can't promise that

I want you to be happy

I wish I could say
I'll never make you sad
But we both know that I can't promise that

So today
Hope it's enough for me to say –
Yeah today
I hope it's enough for me to say –

That I will try to be the person that you deserve
Try to always show you just what you're worth
Try now and then not to get on your nerves

And I will try
My very, very best to swerve
At every bump and every curve
To show you, you're my universe

I want you to be happy
I'm doing all I can
So I hope that you'll forgive me
If things don't always go as planned

I want you to be happy
There'll be things that I don't understand
But even if we argue, let's argue
Hand in hand

So today
Hope it's enough for me to say –
Yeah today
I hope it's enough for me to say –

That I will try to be the person that you deserve
Try to always show you just what you're worth
Try now and then not to get on your nerves

And I will try
My very, very best to swerve
At every bump and every curve
To show you, you're my universe
And always, always put you first

I never want what we have to change

And no matter what, I'll always stay
I will always let you have your way

I'll try to be the person that you deserve
Try to always show just what you're worth
Try now and then not to get on your nerves

I want you to be happy
I want you to feel loved
I want you to know that -
For me you will always be enough

APRICOT
(Poetry & Prose)

You're a scent –
The smell of apricot, hanging in the air – burning me to the stomach.
You live in the cologne hanging like a force field around the stranger passing
me by and suddenly I smell you out of thin air and I want to call you up although
it's been so long.

You're a song –
The hopeful sound coming out of a hopeless busker, singing Hallelujah for
the fourth time in the subway today.
He plays the song for no one person in particular but it's heard by the ones
who need to hear it - every time. His good deed, done.

You're the weather –
You change when you want to, and I dress accordingly.
A sky that's been grey, dusk to dawn for months on end; that I wait through.
Just to see you turn the ceiling of our globe back to a baby blue
playground for plains to disappear into, through perfect cotton wool clouds.
I like having you around, but your thunder is too loud.
Yet, I never know when you're gonna rain on me, and I'm not the type of girl
who carries an umbrella around just in case
You ruin the makeup on my face.

And I hold grudges against boys who make me cry off my mascara.

You are urgency –
And I, a kid – consuming you in the same manner in which I listen to my
favorite song. I stop enjoying myself halfway through, anticipating its end. And
then I do it again.

Yes.

As soon as we are best friends, I anticipate our end. I never know if I should write about you in past or present tense.

Hey,

You're Zac Efron to a girl who grew up on High School Musical. You're probably too old to know what I'm talking about.

You're LSD –
You see the world differently than me.
And although I would never stick out my tongue, say: "give me some too"
I wonder about the way the world and I look to you
When you are under –
The influence and if it's a work of art, some different dimension and I'd ask you to paint it but sober or not you would not know how to paint me – not even by numbers. You just don't know me that well, not even after all this time, and that makes me wonder.

You are temperature –
Scorching my skin open on my thigh when the iron slipped as I pressed the dress
I was going to wear for you and then you never called. How could you be so cold?
Even when you're lukewarm- somehow I always get burnt.
You once told me that people don't change, and that I never learn.
But I will always have hope, hope that you will be a better you – that's the type of woman that I am. And I hope to be a better one, too.
And maybe my optimism and argument that everything matters - is my downfall.
But the day that I die, I'd rather know I found meaning in everything rather than in nothing at all.

You're a language –
One that I don't understand.
Though I'd understand you better if you'd just hold my hand, Manhattan man.

You're a question, an unsolved sum –
And I'm not quite sure if we're done or if we have just begun.

But if it's really over
What else is left for me to do?
Know that it was never my intention
To make only art out of you

"I LOVE YOU AND YOU'RE MY BEST FRIEND"

"How long did you two date before getting married?" I asked after bragging about my song that will be played for my friend's first dance.

"Our first few dates were a mess, his friends drank me under the table. I was like… this isn't going to work! One of our first dates we had bad wine and I had too much of it, I got sick and messed up the hotel room!" she laughed.

"I love you and you're my best friend," he interrupted her.

She stopped mid conversation, looked him in the eye and said: "I love you and you're my best friend too."

I felt like a fly on the wall as they sat there, completely in their own world for a second smiling away at each other like teenagers. I found some sort of comfort in their exchange of words and glances, like maybe I haven't found that yet but at least I know it exists.

I lay in bed that night and all I could think was "he stayed."

"She messed up the hotel room and he stayed."

I had a few getting-sick-in-hotel-room stories of my own, none of which I shared with them that night.

For a year I hated myself for getting sick in Willem's hotel room the last time I saw him. Having to live with knowing that - that would be the way he remembered me, killed me. I wished so many things – that maybe I didn't party on an empty stomach, or that maybe I'd acted more like a lady. I blamed myself so hard for his absence that followed that unfortunate series of events.

But for the first time I thought that just maybe his absence had less to do with me getting sick in his hotel room and more to do with the fact that I did move across the globe, and maybe we just weren't meant to be. There is a galaxy full of possible reasons – yet, somehow, I decided to narrow it down to just that one thing that went wrong, and pin the whole heartbreak on it. My mind's way of trying to make sense of it, justify why he didn't stay in my life.

I think we do that sometimes. Make our own personal list of all the things we think we ever did wrong that caused all those people to march right out of our lives.

Maybe if I spoke up more.
Maybe if I spoke up less.
Maybe if I didn't wear that dress.
Maybe if I was skinnier.
Maybe if I was more fun.
Maybe if I spent more time getting tanned in the sun.
Maybe if I gave him more space.
Maybe if I looked the other way.
Maybe if I didn't get into a fight with him that day.

Maybe then he would have stayed?

I kept tossing and turning that night replaying her story in my head.
Then I smiled.
"Maybe, it doesn't work that way."

FULL MOON ON FIGURE 8 ISLAND (WHO TAUGHT ME TO THINK THAT WAY?)
(Poetry & Prose)

I think about our planet earth a lot
The people who've walked it
And the people who won't
And the fact that I have forgotten more days spent on this globe
Than ones I will ever be able to recall
It took me twenty-six years to start to think about our planet earth a lot
I hope she will forgive my ignorance
She is all I've ever known
And no one ever taught me to question it all
Her wonder, and why I'm even allowed here
What a tragedy - she continues to exist in all her glory every time I lock myself away in my skyscraper-room – for whatever reasons that I do, bad or good.

She continues to exist in all her glory - and I am not around to see her do.

What a tragedy – all her sunrises, all her full moons I have missed – for whatever reasons that I missed them – bad or good.

What a tragedy – for it to be humanly impossible to be part of it all, all the time, God, I want to.

When I die, make me come back an owl so I can witness the night in its deepest darkness. And then when I die, make me come back a humpback whale so I can witness the deep blue parts of you, not even technology can get to. And then when I die, make me come back a wildebeest, so I have no other option than to call all of Southern Africa my home, be woken up by the sun every morning, witness vengeful rainfall, dance under angry clouds lit up by lightning. And then when I die, make me come back a star so I can be called a friend by the moon, who I will shine next to.

I do, I think about the moon a lot, and how it is positioned just close enough, and just far enough away, to be part of our reality.

The way it's small enough for me to hold in my hand – from down here.

I wonder about the things that have to fall in place in order for it to shine, and about

The way I have subconsciously made peace with the fact that I will likely never touch it with my fingertips, walk on it myself.

Who taught me to accept that, to think this way?

And were they right for doing so?

I think about the sun a lot

If I have looked it in they eye for a total of sixty seconds over the span of my life – that's a lot –she makes my eyes water when I try.

I do try.

I think about the way I have subconsciously taken her warmth and the energy she provides for granted

And even though I have told countless lovers otherwise,

I know tonight, that really the sun is the only one in the world I couldn't survive

Without

All the times I've given people power over me – played right into their hand - in vain. All this time, I encouraged their delusions – when they told me I needed them or else I'd die. I entertained it when the only thing I - realistically speaking – would die with out, is the sun.

But I know they would hate me for saying so, maybe that's why I haven't before.

I think about the Seven Seas a lot, and its never-ending dance with our moon.

The only one the waves listen to.

The only one who knows how to make an ocean, wide and wild, abide by a strong set of rules.

And when the moon pulls the ocean towards itself, when the moon makes the sea rise and fall twice a day -

What made me think I was exempt from its forces?

Why have I subconsciously taken part in speculating that he doesn't make the water between my flesh and bones rise and fall, too? Put me in different moods?

Who taught me to think that way?

And were they right for doing so?

Because I want it to be true

I want to believe that the moon knows me too

Like it knows the ocean – though, I know I am just a drop,

I think about our planet earth a lot

And know that as much as I don't want for it to be this way – I've forgotten more days spent on this globe, than ones I will ever recall

So let this be the night I will forever remember as the night I begged the moon to change something inside me, once and for all.

DON'T ROCK STARS DIE AT 27?

I ran out of the movie theater with my sunglasses on despite it being 10pm, and settled on a park bench where I continued to cry further.

Months before when I heard about Rocketman coming out, I thought it was weird that they'd make a movie celebrating Elton John's life – while he was still alive and kicking and around to watch the thing himself.

This type of movie sells better once the person it's about has passed on, I thought to myself. It was the radio producer in me speaking, and I was disgusted with myself for it. Having worked in the media and creative industries, I knew all about authors and filmmakers having their books written, their documentaries packaged and ready, waiting to be released as soon as a certain person dies – the authors or filmmakers waiting in anticipation when the person is ill, knowing they'd breathe their last breath of air out soon.

And as said celebrated person leaves this earth, their soul still dwindling in the air, barely arrived at the afterlife - the book hits the shelf. The documentary is out. And somebody makes a lot of money.

It happened with Nelson Mandela, and Springbok legend Joost van der Westhuizen (who entrusted our radio show with his last ever interview.) We had our tributes ready for when the news of his passing broke, too.

And I watched the Avicii documentary, I couldn't help feeling that while Tim was alive it was filmed in such a manner that it had to be obvious to the producers that he was going to commit suicide soon – almost as if that was the ending they drove him to give them.

For as long as I knew what the 27 Club meant, I wondered if I was born with a membership pass for it too.

Because that's the way the story goes, isn't it? That's the pre-calculated route, the already-decided-on storyline laid out for us by history, the media, and the musical prodigies before us. An unspoken law that tells us our art is worth more, we are missed more, celebrated more once we are gone.

And I think Mike Posner saved his own life the day he decided to embark on his walk across America, put tour life on hold to put his own mental health and happiness first. That is what I take away from it, a wish to break the pattern engineered by our heroes who died young. "My heroes all died young, they hung themselves with fame, and these lunatics molded me" he sang.

I didn't have the opportunity to see Chester Bennington live in concert either – he took his own life a week before the Central Park concert I was going to go and see Linkin Park perform at. A year later we celebrated his life at his band

281

mate Mike Shinoda's concert on Pier 17, NYC.

This storyline just repeats and repeats and repeats itself around me, no matter in which direction I look.

But Elton John escaped the whole thing – yes, early on he drank himself into the hospital and made drugs his best friend for a while, but he is alive and sober to produce and watch and witness the film that celebrates his life. And I cried when I realized that.

Elton was already heading for his sixties when I was a little girl just old enough to be familiarized with his work. I didn't get to hear the story of the life he lived at ten, twenty, thirty. No one was interested in talking about that part. He was just Elton to me, the guy with glasses who sang the Lion King song I liked and the Princess Di one too. By the time I was all grown up I didn't put any thought into Elton's life either.

So I sat there in the movie house, turning my neck around giving death stares to people chattering away in the distance every now and again. I sat there watching his story – and felt bombarded with another common theme amongst creatives – a not so picture perfect childhood. Perhaps one of the triggers most responsible for creatives taking their own lives, I feel. They say that fame kills celebrated people, but I think the hurt in their personal lives do.

Of course I could relate to his story – in some small way at least - his dad abandoning him, and not giving him so much as a pat on the back or an "I'm proud of you" after all he had achieved.

When I finished crying out my own pains about my father, I got up from the bench and walked myself home with a new dilemma on my mind.

If Bernie wrote the lyrics, and Elton wrote the melodies - who was I actually celebrating then? Words are everything to me, so understandably, I felt conflicted for a while. And what were the chances that those exact two people found their way to each other in a world so big? What if they never found each other? What if Bernie's words never had the chance to come alive through Elton? What if Elton had nothing to sing about if Bernie didn't post him those lyric sheets?

Based on the above, I believe in miracles – that's all the proof I've ever needed.

And I like to think about each stranger who entered my life as proof of miracles as well. How did they know to enter my life at just the right time? And when each one of them entered my life, so much went right. If it wasn't for the kindness of strangers I met along the way after I was orphaned – I might not have stayed in school. I might have gotten lost in the system. I might not have stayed out of trouble. I might not have learned to stand on my own two feet. I might not have become a radio producer. I might not have traveled to America and pursued my wildest music dreams. My mom and dad didn't make these things possible - it's the people I met after they left, that did. The countless friends who took me in for months when I had nowhere to go at age fifteen. Each family who decided to give me love, a place to belong, feed and clothe me instead of calling welfare to take care of it. My driving instructor Darin, who sponsored my drivers-license-lessons and was there to hug me congratulations when I passed my test. Without his help – without a drivers-license - I wouldn't have qualified to come abroad as an au pair at that time. Those are the kind of miracles I've lived through in my young life, so perfectly timed. My parents failed so rigorously. God, they let me down, but there was always some person coming into my life, temporarily being the parent I needed, and getting me through.

And at twenty-six I feel I've lived so many different lives, experienced more than my share - so don't rock stars die at twenty-seven? I think the harder thing would be to stay alive. I think the braver thing to do is keep on breathing.

Because I can't deny that I walk around with a death wish in my pocket sometimes – seeing my mom die was difficult, but having to mourn my dad while he is still alive, that is something that hurts me everyday, something no amount of luxury can take away.

But the second chance at life I was blessed with by every stranger that helped me on my feet - that is something I try to keep myself alive for, and honor every day. No matter how much I question life, no matter how flustered and tormented the contrasts I've lived through left me feeling, I feel I have no right to let that drive me into the ground. I feel I have a responsibility toward every person who gave me their presence, their time, their energy, so I could be the person I am today – a responsibility to make my life into a work of art. A responsibility to be happy. A responsibility to make sure their efforts were not in vain. A responsibility to be Lyla who belongs to everybody. And that is as much a burden as it is a privilege.

A responsibility to not *have to* rely on the kindness of strangers, but to learn what it is to stand on my own two feet. I will never know what truly resulted to the fact that my mom was down and out, and left me with only a piano to my name when she passed on. And I will never know my dad's reasoning behind abandoning me, forcing me to rely on other people when he was financially capable of taking care of me. But it's my responsibility to break that cycle.

And as hard as it is for me to say, I'd like to argue that I would have been less successful if my mom lived on and I was left to live my life in small-town Hluhluwe, God knows if I ever would have gotten out. And I would have been less successful if I carried on living with my dad and his abusive wife, I can't imagine I would even have been half the woman that I am today.

So, I've never felt like anyone owes me anything, I am content with the cards life dealt me. I celebrate them in their pain and glory.

I never put any thought into the question "what if things were different?" Because I don't believe I would have stood any better of a chance at achieving my dreams if I grew up with a mom and a dad anyway. They wouldn't have been able to give me the life I have today – and knowing that, helps me to find some comfort in their absence.

There will always be a fraction of sadness in my greatest moments of joy, and a fraction of joy in my greatest moments of sadness. I've stopped trying to make them balance each other out. I choose to live with both. What I value is that the little girl inside of me can smile because a few of my wishes came true, and in some ways I got further than I ever allowed myself to dream I would. Of course there is still so much I want to create, learn, be – but if I never achieved another single shard of success in my career I would still die a happy woman, because I have lived each day consciously choosing that my circumstances would never define me and in that I have settled the score of my own life, am content with how far I've come – so whatever lies ahead, it is all borrowed time to me. Time to be my free self with. I have peace.

There is no deadline for when I will "stop trying to make it in music." Accomplishing my creative goals is an urgent calling, but not a rushed process, to me. Deciding to strive to be a great musician comes with great responsibility, a massive amount of work and discipline too, not to mention miracles and luck. Being a great artist is not something I expect to just achieve overnight, and by overnight I mean in the next ten years. I can't force a chart topping single out of my guitar strings, and no part of me wants to – the right songs will come when it is their time to. For me it is a lifelong game, and I want to play it my way.

I have busked in a subway where not even one commuter put down a dollar for hours, and I have performed in a stadium, sang the national anthem of my country on international television. I try to find joy in both extremes, and in all the rest in between. I want to experience everything.

I find myself oddly grateful for the mediocre, not-always-easy life I have outside of my creative ventures and quest for success. I like that I am written about in magazines, and then not thought about for weeks. I like to go and hang out with my street performer buddies in Central Park, after vacationing on a private island with millionaires. I like to eat a cheap packet of 2-Minute-Noodles after a week's long $30 meals. It makes me feel like I'm not missing out on anything. It makes me feel undefined.

Having that outlook on life is a mind mangle at times. The small things seem big and the big things seem small. Sometimes I lose perspective. Fifteen-year-old me would have freaked out for the opportunity to play just one single show in New York.

Twenty-six-year-old-me gets into the prestigious Musicians On Call Volunteer Program, makes the New York City team, is really happy, but carries on with her day working towards the next goal – no stopping for a solo sixty-second dance party behind my bedroom door to celebrate first.

I don't know if that's a good or bad thing – maybe a bit of both.

I don't like to refer to our world as "today's throw-away society" … I'd like to believe there's a lot more to the so-called trend and saying, but, living in a time where everybody is one click, one video, one share away from their fifteen minutes of fame – working in the music, media, showbiz industries as we know it has changed, and is ever changing from this point on. With the Internet leveling the playground, almost anyone has access to the opportunity to work in these industries and to be self-made. I celebrate it but also can't help but see some ways in which it simplifies and cheapens the experience of art.

If I was a reporter who had been given the opportunity to interview Elton John thirty years ago, people were going to wait for my show to air with great anticipation and probably talk about it for weeks. If I was a reporter in that same situation today, people would or wouldn't click on the interview, and if they did watch it, would have forgotten about it the hour after.

I'm not trying to say: "those were the good old days." I think the only way forward is to adjust accordingly to how things work today, and I am still trying to figure out how to do that, where my place is, and what my priorities and career goals are now that I have had a taste of what it feels like to work in today's music, media and showbiz industries. I think some parts of these industries don't bring as much value to consumers or creators today as they did a couple of years ago – based on the fact that everyone has access now in anyway. When I was twenty-one and interning for the radio station 5FM, all I wanted was to be an entertainment reporter – but that's not true for me in my journey anymore. My outlook and priorities changed, and I think they still will, many times. After a lot of exploring and much consideration on which way to head in with my career next, I opened a door that lead me into the world of film scoring – a different medium to tell stories through. One that is almost in the background - doesn't scream for the spotlight. I like that, and am currently working on my first project for the NYC Web Series Film Fest.

Making music in the day and age where "anyone can be famous" ... or is for fifteen minutes, I know full well – and have peace with the fact – that my voice and the words I have to say won't always be heard, might get lost amongst the rest of the noise. But to quote a poem I once stumbled upon – I choose to honor "the gift to write and express, whether or not it gets read."

I don't live in an era where talent scouts are actively sniffing music acts out at open mics like you see in the movies – not even in New York. Agents or publishers won't even look at you unless you are semi-famous already. And sometimes it costs more to get a song onto the radio than the royalties you will earn from it. Starting out in the music industry is one tough act, but it is my firm belief that a good song will always be heard. And I hope to grow into a good enough songwriter whose songs will stand out above the rest of the noise one day, but that's not what drives me.

When I write a song, I get to show someone what they look like through my eyes, what they feel like in my mind, what they sound like when my fingertips hits an instrument.

Recorded in four minutes and thirteen seconds, I get to capture and tell the story that replayed in my head for hours on end night after night, to the point that it was unhealthy, and obsessive. And I finally get to show it out loud, the only way I know how. I show them how I experienced them, and then in return, I get to experience the anxiety, of not knowing if they might turn on a different station or song and ignore my voice, my advances, ignore the way I told the story of them through my pen and paper and guitar. I don't know.

But at some point, maybe only a year later, I finally start to sleep a little better at night. At some point, I find an ounce of peace in the possibility, that just, maybe, without me ever knowing, they'll play it out loud on repeat, long after I'm gone and have moved on, and think about how I made them feel too, and smile or cry a tear for me when they remember that time in our lives.

And I think that's why I do it. I think that's why I write.

PART FOURTEEN

DESTINATION: UNKNOWN

THINGS I WANT TO DO BEFORE I DIE

☑ SING IN A STADIUM

☑ TREND IN THE NEWS WORLDWIDE

☑ SING AND WORK FOR CHARITIES

☑ BUSK IN THE NYC SUBWAY

🧩 HAVE A SONG ON GREY'S ANATOMY

🧩 WRITE FOR ED SHEERAN

🧩 GIVE MIKE POSNER THIS BOOK

🧩 VISIT MY SISTER IN UGANDA

🧩 GIVE A TED TALK

🧩 HIKE THE GRAND CANYON

🧩 KISS MORE GIRLS

🧩 BE BRAVE ENOUGH TO GROW OLD?

🧩 GROW OLD IN AMERICA?

🧩 SEE MY DAD AGAIN.

1. "The Room On The 12th Floor" 2. Yankees Stadium 3.Brooklyn 4.Statue of Liberty

1. Atlantic Records Recording Studios
2. National Crime Victims' Rights Week Concert
3. Café Wha? 4. Times Square 5. With David Kau 6. Brooklyn Bridge

1. Brooklyn 2. America's Got Talent
3. Recording The National Anthem 4. Amish Country 5. First Time In NYC &
Wearing My Swaziland Lihhiya 6. Busking In Front Of The White House

1. Alone In Las Vegas 2. The Glittering Gold Las Vegas dress
3. Washington, D.C. 4. Grand Central 5. Vlogging In Times Square
In My Sharks Jersey 6. With Springbok Prop, Beast

SEARCH FOR LYLA'S MUSIC ON
YouTube
iTunes
Spotify

MORE BOOKS BY LYLA (AVAILABLE ON AMAZON)
The H-Man: Children's book written and illustrated by Lyla Illing
Private Poetry: Let your imagination teleport you to New York City and the
long list of unexpected places, where Private Poetry author, Lyla Illing penned
her first collection of poems.

TAKE PART IN LYLA'S CREATIVE VENTURES
Become a Patron: https://www.patreon.com/join/lylailling
Donate on Paypal: paypal.me/lylailling1
Donate on Venmo: @Lyla-Illing

CHARITIES LYLA HAS PERFORMED FOR
Musicians On Call (NYC team) - bringing live and recorded music to the
bedsides of patients in healthcare facilities (2019 – present)
WestCOP – National Crime Victims' Rights Week (Art Show 2018, 2019)
Ubuntu Pathways (Wall Street Rooftop Heritage Day Fundraiser, 2018)
Amish Heritage Foundation (2018)
The Set NYC – Ending Child Trafficking (2017)
Plushy Fest Jacaranda Children's Home (2016)
SPCA Roodepoort (2015, 2016)

GET SOCIAL WITH LYLA
Instagram: @lylailling
Facebook: https://www.facebook.com/lyla.illing
Twitter: @lylailling
LinkedIn: https://www.linkedin.com/in/lylailling/

For Lyla's latest news and tour dates, please visit her website
www.lyla-illing.com

LISTEN TO TO LYLA'S INTERVIEWS

Apple Podcasts: The New York Minute

EP1 Being an actor in NYC – Lyla interviews Remi Moses (in a bathroom!)

EP2 Being a bartender in NYC – Lyla interviews Siobhan Forgarty

EP3 Being Gay in NYC – Lyla interviews Diego Saxy

EP4 Being a PR professional and foodie in NYC – Lyla interviews Joyce Jones (in LA)

EP5 Being South African in NYC – Lyla interviews expats (in Times Square)

EP6 Being a "bubble busker" and homeless in NYC – Lyla interviews Kishan (in Central Park)

EP7 Being an actor in Hollywood – Lyla interviews Edwin Gagiano (in a car!)

EP8 You Are Not Alone, NYC – Lyla interviews humanitarian Mary-Anne Write

EP9 The New York Times, Lagos photographer – Lyla interviews Oladapo Ogunjobi

EP10 Being a CEO at 19 – Lyla interviews Steven Jonathan (from Germany)

EP11 Being a photographer in NYC – Lyla interviews Justine Hery (from France)

Made in the USA
Middletown, DE
27 November 2020

25363031R00169